PUBLIC POLICY
IN
SOVIET PRIVATE INTERNATIONAL LAW

ACADEMISCH PROEFSCHRIFT

TER VERKRIJGING VAN
DE GRAAD VAN DOCTOR IN DE RECHTSGELEERDHEID
AAN DE UNIVERSITEIT VAN AMSTERDAM,
OP GEZAG VAN DE RECTOR MAGNIFICUS MR. A. D. BELINFANTE,
HOOGLERAAR IN DE FACULTEIT DER RECHTSGELEERDHEID,
IN HET OPENBAAR TE VERDEDIGEN IN DE AULA DER UNIVERSITEIT
(TIJDELIJK IN DE LUTHERSE KERK, INGANG SINGEL 411, HOEK SPUI)
OP VRIJDAG 13 DECEMBER 1968 TE 2.30 UUR

DOOR

ANDRÉ GARNEFSKY
Geboren te Markovo (Bulgarije)

THE HAGUE
MARTINUS NIJHOFF
1968

PROMOTOR: PROF. MR. L. I. DE WINTER

ISBN 978-94-015-2252-6 ISBN 978-94-015-3492-5 (eBook)
DOI 10.1007/978-94-015-3492-5

To My Wife and the Memory of My Parents

PREFACE

This study is based on original Russian sources, due attention being paid to some authoritative views advanced by foreign lawyers.

Leaving aside the essentials of the work in the hope that they will speak for themselves, I should like to make some preliminary remarks regarding the linguistic and other formal aspects.

First of all it should be noted that many of the Soviet laws have already been translated into English either in the USSR itself or in Western countries. This fact is fully reflected in the bibliographical survey at the end of this study. Some laws have been translated both in the Soviet Union and abroad, as for instance the Fundamentals of Soviet Civil Legislation. In such a case I have used the translation made in the USSR even though linguistically it may be inferior to the translation made in the West. The author has translated only those legal provisions of which no English translation was available.

For transliteration, I have used the system of the Library of Congress of the USA without its diacritical marks.

Further, a word should be said about the references in the notes. They are very brief and consist of the surnames of the authors concerned and if necessary an additional element, e. g. the year of publication, or a part of the title. For the full names and titles the reader is referred to the bibliographical list. Extensive annotation with regard to legal documents has also been avoided. It was considered that a special bibliographical list would provide sufficient details about the titles and the origin of these documents. The same applies to the court decisions, whose sources are mentioned only in the bibliography. It is important to note, in this connection, that there are no extensive collections or compilations of Soviet court decisions relating to private international law. The decisions which have been used in this study are quoted either from the Bulletins of the Supreme Courts of the USSR and the RSFSR and other official periodicals or, in the last resort, from legal treatises published in the Soviet Union or abroad.

Finally, I should like to mention some names intimately connected with the realization of this study.

My research work was carried out under the supervision and

guidance of Professor L. I. de Winter. For his inestimable help as a man of science, for his encouragement and noble tolerance my deepest appreciation.

I am also very grateful indeed to Professor Z. Szirmai for his critical perusal of my manuscript and for the many valuable suggestions he has made.

For some essential improvements in the original concept of the general part of this study I am greatly indebted to Professor J. E. J. Th. Deelen.

Very warm thanks go to my good friend A. G. Macrae, M. A., for the many substantial corrections to my English, and to Mr. M. L. Saunders, LL. B., for the final revision of the manuscript.

Grateful acknowledgement is also due to Professor S. van der Woude and J. R. Defraipont, Senior Scientific Officer, for the indispensable facilities they granted to me as an employee of the Amsterdam University library, as well as to all colleagues for their kind assistance and interest in this work.

The sacrifices which my wife willingly made are innumerable. For her assistance, encouragement and patience and, above all, for the extremely pleasant conditions at home, I am eternally grateful.

TABLE OF CONTENTS

INTRODUCTION

SOME GENERAL FEATURES OF SOVIET PRIVATE INTERNATIONAL LAW

The assertion of Marx and Engels that the law, like every other form of civilization and culture, is only a phenomenon of a derivative superstructural character, determined by the economic basis of a given society, has been found sufficient by the Soviet authorities to explain their legal system, which is considered as a practical implementation of Marxist ideology. "From the socialist economic relationships, from the economic basis of the socialist society arises not only civil law, but also every other branch of Soviet law", explains a modern Soviet legal writer (1). As to the economic basis of the USSR, it is defined by Article 4 of the Soviet Constitution of 1936:

"The economic foundation of the USSR is the socialist system of economy and the socialist ownership of the instruments and means of production, firmly established as a result of the liquidation of the capitalist system of economy, the abolition of private ownership of the instruments and means of production and the elimination of the exploitation of man by man".

So-called "socialist property" manifests itself either in the form of State property or as co-operative property (Article 5 of the Constitution). The latter, however, is under total State control and being of a transitory character it aims eventually at a merger with the former. The qualification of socialist property as the "basis" of Soviet society does not apply to the property permitted to private persons, which is limited to commodities for consumption only (2) and is intended to serve the strictly personal needs of the owner.

When dealing in detail, however, with the scope of private international law, i.e. with the question of what rules belong to this branch of law, opinions are divided. For instance, Lunts disagrees with Pereterskii, who maintains that substantive law rules, such as the rules of foreign trade, governing relation-

(1) Ioffe, p. 14 (An author taken at random as there is no difference of opinion on this point among Soviet legal writers). See also: Osnovy teorii gos. i pr., p. 365.

(2) Some minor exceptions to this principle are made in favour of peasants and craftsmen. The means of production, however, which these persons can own are of insignificant value and may not be used for the exploitation of employed labour (Article 9 of the Constitution).

ships with foreign elements should be included.
According to Lunts, private international law predominantly consists of conflict rules. He admits, however, that some of the Soviet laws and decrees regarding foreign trade, although of a substantive nature, implicitly contain conflict rules prescribing the application of Soviet law, for instance, the laws relating to the procedure for signing foreign trade transactions. These laws and decrees have, according to him, extraterritorial effect. Thus they too should find a proper place in the treatises on private international law. In principle, however, substantive rules directly regulating legal relations with international elements do not belong to the domain of private international law unless they are introduced as unified substantive civil law by appropriate international agreements (1).

Soviet writers are quite unanimous in their opinion as to the function which the conflict rules have to perform. All of them consider that the primary function of the conflict rules is to define the limits of application of a foreign law in the USSR, delimiting in this way the sphere of operation of the Soviet and foreign legal systems. In this connection they oppose conflict rules to substantive civil law, whose function they see as the direct regulation of civil law relations, whereas a conflict rule by itself does not tell us what rights and obligations arise between parties. Where they speak of a regulatory function of the conflict rules, they regard it as an indirect regulation through the medium of the substantive local or foreign law to which the conflict rule refers or, as Orlova puts it: "The conflict rules must be considered in conjunction with those substantive rules to which they refer, because a conflict rule as such cannot be applied. Only in connection with those substantive laws to which it refers, does the conflict rule make a norm of behaviour, not only for the courts as State agencies but also for the parties of the legal relation complicated with international elements" (2).
The purpose pursued by Soviet private international law changes with Soviet foreign policy, because, as Lunts says, "The legal acts of a State in the field of private international law

(1) Lunts, I (1959), pp. 25-26; see also: Voprosy, pp. 11-13; Lunts, 1955, p. 90; Pereterskii, 1946, pp. 17-30; Pereterskii, Krylov, 1959, pp. 10-11.
(2) Orlova, 1960, p. 11; On this question as well as on the function of conflict rules see also: Lunts, 1949, pp. 17, 78, 87-90; Lunts, 1959, p. 137; Pereterskii, Krylov, 1940, pp. 7-8, 37; Pereterskii, Krylov, 1959, pp. 10-11; Pereterskii, 1946, pp. 8-9; Krylov, 1930, pp. 11, 22; Stalev, p. 41.

are to be regarded as an expression of its foreign policy" (1). While for instance a writer in 1934 said that private international law pays the role of form and instrument in the struggle between the communist system and the system of capitalist societies (2), fifteen years later private international law purported to serve not only the struggle but also the co-operation between the two systems (3). The present most immediate purpose of the Soviet foreign policy- consolidation of the conquests resulting from the Second World War- has also determined the purpose of private international law. Thus, summarizing present day opinions, Boguslavskii declared: "Soviet legal literature always proceeds from the fact the USSR and the other socialist countries use the institutions of private international law to promote peaceful business-like co-operation among all countries, regardless of their social and economic system, on the basis of equality and respect for their sovereignty" (4).

There is no unanimity among Soviet writers on the widely disputed question as to whether private international law has to be treated as domestic, national law or as a branch of public international law. The dominating opinion as presented by Lunts (5) and Pereterskii (6) regards private international law as national law, while some dissenting writers, such as Krylov, Grabar and Ladyzhenskii consider it as a branch of public international law. According to the latter, so-called "internationalist" point of view, private international law is international law governing interstate relations concerning topics of civil law. "Behind each firm, behind each individual in international intercourse stands a government and each dispute, also in the domain of civil law and even in family litigation, as for instance divorce, can as a result grow into a conflict between States". Furthermore, according to Krylov, the basic sources of private international law are international conventions containing rules of conflict of laws so that "in in-

(1) Lunts, 1959, p. 33; Lunts, 1964, pp. 630-631. In the last-mentioned study based on the Fundamentals of Soviet Civil Legislation and of Civil Procedure of 1961 the author observes that all private international law problems dealt with in the said instruments are solved "conformément aux maximes de la politique extérieure de l'Union Soviétique". See also Pereterskii, 1946, pp. 17-30; Drucker, pp. 384-389.

(2) Raevich, pp. 14-35.

(3) Lunts, 1949, pp. 3, 16.

(4) See the foreword to the chapter on private international law in: Literatura, pp. 235-236. See also: Lunts, 1959, p. 33; Lunts, Les règles de conflit..., 1964, pp. 630-631. Pereterskii, 1946, pp. 17-30. This opinion has been taken over by some authors of the other East European countries. For the Western lawyers see Drucker, pp. 148-150.

(5) Lunts, 1959, pp. 9-15; Szászy, Budapest, 1964, pp. 44-45.

(6) Pereterskii, 1946, pp. 17-30; Krylov, 1947, p. 30.

ternational treaty law must be seen the basic content of private international law" (1).

Soviet "nationalists" on the other hand plead for a clear distinction between private international law and international or interstate law. According to them, private international law is not a law between States, but is international only in the sense that it regulates legal relations arising out of international intercourse. Both branches of law, however, have the same points of departure and rest upon the same principles without which international relations would be impossible. The common principles according to these lawyers are derived from the sovereign rights of State or from the purpose which both laws are intended to serve. In the first category the communist writers place inter alia the absolute immunity of jurisdiction as claimed by the communist tates, the recognition of the communist economic system and in particular nationalization, State property with respect to means of production and the State monopoly of foreign commerce. As to the second category of common principles, we shall limit ourselves to the restatement of the general communist thesis that private international law as well as public international law are instruments of the foreign policy of the State and serve its purposes (2).

The national character of Soviet private international law is accentuated by the fact that its conflict rules are inspired by political chauvinism. Legislators and lawyers have always proceeded from the premise that communist substantive law is superior to any non-communist law. That is also one of the principal reasons why Soviet private international law is concerned with the application of Soviet law rather than with the admission and solution of international legal conflicts. This particularism of Soviet private international law manifests itself in every branch of law and is also reflected to a great extent in some of the general principles, such as *renvoi*, classification and autonomy of the parties. While reserving the particular legal questions for a later stage of this study, a word should be said here about the Soviet doctrine relating to the last-mentioned general principles.

The basic arguments in favour of *renvoi* (3) adduced by spe-

(1) Krylov, 1930, pp.18-21; Krylov, 1947, p.30. The same attitude see: Ladyzhenskii Vestnik Moskovskogo Universiteta 1948, no.5; also Grabar, p.463.

(2) See supra, Note 1 p.11; see also Szászy, Budapest 1964, p.47.

(3) The admission of renvoi by Soviet law is inferred from some special legal instruments, such as the Soviet law on cheques of 1929 (Article 36) and several international agreements (Geneva Convention on Bills of Exchange and Promissory Notes of 1930, Soviet-French commercial Agreement of 1951, etc.)

cialists of Soviet private international law more than thirty years ago, and never changed since then, are noteworthy. It was argued that in as far as the acceptance of *renvoi* extends the limits of application of Soviet substantive law there is no ground for objection to this concept. In other words, the principal consideration for acceptance of *renvoi* in Soviet courts was (and still is) the limitation of the number of cases where foreign "bourgeois" law must be applied. The same consideration has prompted Krylov and Peretерskii in their early writings to propound non-acceptance of transmission by Soviet courts (1).

The paramount importance of this argument has been emphasized by the very fact of its constant reappearance in the very latest literature.

"The application", writes Pereterskii, "of a bourgeois law in the USSR is an exception to the system of application of Soviet law. If a Soviet conflict rule points to a bourgeois law, we are obliged to apply it precisely and loyally. But where the foreign law refuses to regulate the question at issue, there is no ground for extending the sphere of its application" (2).

The same attitude, although expressed in a different way, has also been taken by Lunts (3). In his opinion, the principal consideration to determine the acceptance or rejection of *renvoi* is that of expediency (4). Although such legal considerations as "bringing into harmony the conflict rules of two States" may appear from time to time in Soviet literature (5), they are still of secondary importance.

In their studies devoted to the problem of classification Soviet specialists in private international law use either Bartin's term "qualification" (kvalifikatsiia) or Kahn's "Latente Kollisionen" (Skrytye kollizii). As to the legal significance of this concept, most authors do not go further than to mention the problem or to criticize judicial practice in the West (6). The first attempt to present the Soviet view on this problem was made by Lunts (7). His starting point is that "the choice between classification according to *lex fori* or *lex causae* is determined in all cases by those purposes which a State pursues in establishing and applying its conflict rules". (8).

(1) Pereterskii, 1924, pp.40–41; Krylov, 1930, pp.53–54; Makarov, 1933, pp. 122–123; Makarov, 1931, pp.514–516.

(2) Pereterskii, Krylov, 1959, p.50.

(3) Lunts, 1949, p.129; Lunts, 1959, pp.251, 253.

(4) Lunts, 1959, p.255.

(5) Koretskii, pp.136–137; Lunts, p.251.

(6) Krylov, 1930, pp.44–46; Pereterskii, Krylov, 1940, pp.42–43; Koretskii, 1948, p.146.

(7) Lunts, 1959, pp.195–215; Lunts, 1947, pp.18–28.

(8) Lunts, 1959, pp.200–201.

Lunts divides the problem into two aspects. Firstly, how must foreign courts classify Soviet legal rules when considering a case with foreign elements? Secondly, how must Soviet courts classify foreign legal rules when considering a case with foreign elements?

To the first question he gives the following answer: "Soviet legislation establishes new institutions and new legal concepts, which are unknown and cannot be known to the legal systems of bourgeois countries. That is the reason why all attempts of the bourgeois courts to apply to Soviet law the classification of their own law are dictated only by an endeavour to distort the essence of Soviet law, to confer on it foreign contents and to avoid its application. When a conflict rule of a bourgeois law orders a court to apply the Soviet law, that court ought to apply the law just as it would be applied by the Soviet authorities" (1).

This view is shared by the Czechoslovakian scholar Bystricky, who also maintains that the 'socialist' legal institutions cannot be classified according to 'capitalist' law. When a conflict rule of a Western country refers to a socialist legal system therefore, it is indispensable to comply with the classifications made by the latter system (2).

As to the second question, Lunts considers it more expedient for "Soviet foreign policy" if the Soviet courts are left free to choose the criterion of classification according to the case to be decided. Whether a legal rule is to be classified according to *lex fori* or *lex causae* cannot be decided in advance "once and for all". The choice between classification according to *lex fori* or *lex causae* is a question of interpretation of a conflict rule referring to a foreign law, and forms part of the problem of the admissibility of the foreign law on Soviet territory (3).

In interpreting each conflict rule the court must decide what criterion must be applied in classifying a foreign legal provision: *lex fori, lex causae* or another criterion.

To illustrate the matter an example can be given with respect to the concept of "private property".

For claims of Soviet citizens on property rights to means of production abroad, Soviet and foreign courts alike are expected to classify the term "private property" according to Western law systems, as this category of property has been abolished in the USSR. In this spirit "Circular letter" no. 329 of 23rd October 1925 issued by the Soviet Commissariat of Foreign

(1) Lunts, 1949, p.100; Lunts,1947, pp.26-28; Koretskii, 1948, p.146.
(2) Bystricky, pp.7-38; 196-199.
(3) Lunts,1949, p.101; Lunts I (1959), p.212.

Affairs was formulated. It reads: "A Soviet consul may assist a Soviet citizen in the exercise of ownership of land in the country where the consul is stationed, although the right of private ownership of land has been abolished in the Soviet Union" (1).

Conversely, when the realization of property rights on Soviet territory is at issue the legal concept of property must be interpreted in the sense determined by Soviet law -means of production, including land, cannot be owned by private persons.

Although recent Soviet legislation has favoured the *lex fori* classification in one particular case (2), this cannot be taken as an indication of a change in the Soviet attitude to the problem under consideration (3). Flexibility, the strongest weapon of the Soviet legal system, requires that the judge use his discretion to choose classification criteria guided by the interests of the Soviet State.

Strong indications of particularism in Soviet private international law can also be found in the domain of the autonomy of the parties. At present the matter is governed by Article 126 of the Fundamentals of Civil Legislation (4). According to this legal provision, the parties may freely choose the law which will govern their contract, provided that it is a foreign trade contract. The choice of law is admissible only with regard to the substance of a contract, the form being imperatively governed by Soviet law (Article 125, paragraph 2) (5). The *lex voluntatis* principle as interpreted by the Soviet doctrine has the following scope of operation:

1. The choice of law by the parties is admissible only with respect to questions which pertain to the substance of obligations. Questions outside this sphere cannot be regulated by *lex voluntatis*. Outside the scope of the parties' autonomy are placed the administrative regulations relating to export and import, foreign exchange regulations and the rules governing the form of foreign

(1) Gsovski, I (1948), pp.299-300.

(2) See Article 126 of the Soviet Fundamentals of Civil Legislation, which provides: "The rights and duties of the parties to a foreign trade transaction shall be determined pursuant to the laws of the place where it is concluded, unless otherwise provided by agreement of the parties".

"The place of conclusion of the transaction shall be determined pursuant to Soviet law".

(3) See Lunts, 1961, p.272, where he analyzes Article 102 of the draft Fundamentals, which corresponds to the definitive Article 126 quoted in the preceding note. See also Lunts, 1964, p.639.

(4) See note 2

(5) This rule is rather a legislative confirmation of court practice. See: Ramzaitsev, 1957, p.55; Pereterskii, Krylov, 1959, p.127; Genkin, p.20; Lunts, 1961, p.261; Lunts, 1962 (in: Novoe) pp.101 et seq.; Lunts, 1964, pp. 634-641; Ladyzhenskii, 1961, pp.25-26; Avsov, Egorev, Keilin, p.102; Makovskii, pp. 82-96; Shmigel'skii, Iasinovskii, pp.220-221.

trade transaction to which a Soviet organization is a party.
2. The admissibility of foreign law in Soviet courts with respect to contracts presupposes the participation of a foreign firm in the contract. In cases where both parties are Soviet legal entities theyare not permitted to choose a foreign law to govern their contract. This is explained by the fact that in the majority of such cases the mutual rights and obligations are based on and imperatively determined by the State economic plan or other Soviet legislative or administrative acts. In other words, the will of the State expressed through laws, plans and other governmental acts, entirely replaces the will of the parties.

It must further be added that, although on the surface Soviet solutions of the problems of parties' autonomy are in many respects reminiscent of those advocated or operative in countries with a free economy, there is a fundamental difference between the two systems as far as the nature and function of this legal device are concerned. In the orthodox sense of the term, the autonomy of the parties is the international aspect of the freedom of contracting enjoyed by private persons. It purports not only to facilitate and foster international intercourse, but also to promote the individual's freedom. From this point of view there is no autonomy of the parties in the USSR as foreign commercial transactions where free choice of law is admitted are carried on only by the State monopolistic organizations.

The autonomy of the parties under Soviet law is only conditional in character. In actual fact it is not a question of autonomy of the parties *stricto sensu*, but of the administrative discretion left to the economic officials of the State for the purpose of expediency.

LEGAL SOURCES

Before 1st May 1962, the date on which the Fundamentals of Civil Legislation and the Fundamentals of Civil Procedure of the USSR and the Union Republics came into force, the rules on Soviet private international law were not only dispersed, but also very few. By means of analogy, many provisions laid down in special laws and decrees were declared applicable to cases outside the sphere of operation of these laws. (1). Moreover, where there was a gap in private international law, the courts were to be guided by the general policy of the Sovjet Government (2).

(1) Lunts, I (1959), p.53; Pereterskii, Krylov, 1959, p.30.
(2) Krylov, 1930, p.68; Lunts, I (1959), p.51.

These two guiding principles must also be adhered to by Soviet courts in the future when statutes do not provide direct solutions, as the new legal provisions of private international law are far from being exhaustive.

The new legal provisions (conflict rules or substantive provisions governing cases of international law) as laid down in the Fundamentals of Civil Legislation and Fundamentals of Civil Procedure, have not brought about essential changes in the existing system. Consequently, as the majority of old principles have been preserved, the classification of the sources of private international law, as set out by Soviet legal writers before 1961, retains its validity.

The Constitution of the USSR and those of the various Union Republics are considered as a source of primary importance as they contain inter alia basic rules regarding the admissibility of foreign law on Soviet territory (1).

An article very often referred to by Soviet authors is Article 123 of the Constitution of the USSR, which provides:
"Equality of rights of citizens of the USSR, irrespective of their nationality or race, in all spheres of economic, governmental, cultural, political and other public activity, is indefeasible law. Any direct or indirect restriction of the rights of, or, conversely, the establishment of any direct or indirect privileges for citizens on account of their race or nationality as well as any advocacy of racial or national exclusiveness or hatred and contempt, is punishable be law".

This constitutional provision, according to Lunts (2) restricts, for instance, the applicability of the conflict rule contained in Article 137 of the Code on Marriage, Family and Guardianship of the RSFSR and corresponding articles of the Codes of other Republics, which prescribe the application of *lex loci actus* regarding the validity of marriages contracted abroad by foreigners. Accordingly, foreign laws which forbid marriages on the ground of racial of religious differences are inapplicable on Soviet territory. A constitutional provision of the greatest importance is Article 4 of the USSR Constitution, which proclaims "the abolition of private ownership of the instruments and means of production". No private person, irrespective of whether he is a Soviet citizen or a foreigner, can realize or exercise property rights to such assets on Soviet territory. This rule is absolutely binding, pertaining as it does to the fundamentals of the Soviet system.

(1) On this basic source of private international law as well as on the classification of the sources in general see: Lunts, I (1959), pp. 49-55; Peretcrskii, Krylov, 1959, p. 30, 36; Levitin, p. 226.
(2) Lunts, I (1959), p. 234.

Before the recent attempt at codification, one had to seek out the rest of the Soviet conflict rules in the various USSR laws and decrees as well as in the legislation of the several Union Republics. The most important sources in this category were:
a. The Introductory law to the Civil Code of the RSFSR, and in particular Article 8 of this law, which regulated the legal capacity of foreigners;
b. The RSFSR Code Civil Procedure. Its Article 7, providing that the courts shall take into consideration the *lex loci contractus* when dealing with contracts made abroad, has been the object of constant discussions and controversial interpretation as to whether the courts always had to take the *lex loci* into consideration, or whether the place of contracting was only one point of contract which the court had to take into consideration along with many others. Article 7 dealt not only with the form of a contract, but also with its substance. Article 8 of the Code governed another important question of private international law, viz. the ascertaining of the contents of a foreign law.
c. The Merchant Shipping Code of the USSR, Articles 4 and 5, the former determining the scope of application of the Code, the latter laying down the principle of autonomy of the parties.
d. The Statute on Cheques (Articles 34-36 relating to obligations incurred by issuing a cheque) is the only source from which the principle of *renvoi* has been derived.
Whilst the last two legislative measures will continue to govern the special matters dealt with therein, the legal provisions mentioned under "a" and "b" have been repealed.

At present the majority of rules pertaining to private international law are incorporated in the following fundamental laws. "The Fundamentals of Civil Legislation of the USSR and Union Republics" (Part VIII, Articles 122-129) and the "Fundamentals of Civil Procedure of the USSR and the Union Republics" (Part VI, Articles 59-64), both promulgated on 8th December 1961 and published in "Vedomosti Verkhovnogo Soveta SSSR", no. 50 of 15th December 1961; Principles of Legislation of the USSR and Union Republics concerning Marriage and Family, of 27th June 1968 (Part V, Sections 30-36), published in "Izvestiia", 28th June 1968.

The Fundamentals of Civil Legislation deal with the following questions:

the civil law capacity of foreign citizens (Article 122);
the civil law capacity of stateless persons (Article 123);
foreign commercial transactions on Soviet territory (Article 124);
the law applicable to the form of a contract (Article 125);
the law applicable to the substance of foreign commercial

transactions (Article 126);
the law applicable to succession (Article 127);
restriction of the application of foreign law (Article 128);
international treaties and agreements (Article 129);
Further, a special Article is devoted to the question of the application of the civil legislation of one Union Republic in another Union Republic, i.e., interrepublican law (Article 18). Questions usually referred to International Law of Civil Procedure are dealt with in Part VI of the Fundamentals of Civil Procedure. This part covers rules regarding the civil procedural rights of foreign firms, foreign citizens and stateless persons (Articles 159, 160), actions against foreign States and immunities which they and their representatives enjoy (Article 61), legal aid and the enforcement of foreign judgements and awards (Articles 162, 163) and the interrelation of treaties and internal procedural laws (Article 64).

Before entry into force of the Principles of Legislation of the USSR and Union Republics concerning Marriage and Family (1st October 1968), the main conflict rules relating to this matter were to be found in the Codes of the various Republics on Marriage, Family and Guardianship and in the Consular Statute of the USSR. Such rules included, for instance, Articles 136 and 137 of the RSFSR Code on Marriage, Family and Guardianship and Article 57 of the Consular Statute of the USSR (all regarding marriage), Article 141 of the RSFSR Code (on divorce), Article 51 of the same Code and Article 45 of the Consular Statute (on adoption), Article 85 of the RSFSR Code and Article 45 of the Statute (on guardianship).

At present the conflict rules relating to the issues just mentioned are contained in the Principles of Legislation of the USSR and Union Republics concerning Marriage and Family. The corresponding Sections are the following: Section 30 (on the citizenship of the child), Section 31 (on the conclusion of marriages on Soviet territory), Section 32 (on the conclusion of marriages abroad), Section 33 (on divorce), Section 34 (on adoption), Section 35 (on the applicability of Soviet family legislation to persons without citizenship) and Section 36 (on the public policy clause of reservation and the interrelation between treaties and Soviet family legislation) (1).

International treaties concluded by the USSR with other countries occupy a particular place among the sources of Soviet

(1) The English translation of the Principles of Family Legislation used in this paper is based on the translation of Z.Szirmai being published in: "Themis", 1968: 3 et seq. The changes and additions in the definit law are translated by G.P.v.d. Berg and are expected to be published in "Themis" in the Spring of 1969.

private international law. They facilitate the economic relations between the USSR and the countries with a free economy, giving to them an element of certainty. With regard to the role which treaties play in Soviet private international alw in particular and in international intercourse in general, Stoupnitzky wrote in 1927: "On peut donner une définition assez exacte du rôle que joue le droit conventionnel en disant que c'est cette source qui joue dans le système international privé soviétique, doué d'un caractère très particulariste, un rôle de facteur du progrès en rapprochant le droit international Soviétique privé des autres systèmes nationaux" (1).

This role of Soviet treaties has been increased by the fact that the principle of priority of treaty law over international law has been laid down in the Fundamentals of Civil Legislation, Fundamentals of Civil Procedure and the Principles (or Fundamentals) of Family Legislation (2).

The incorporation of this almost universally accepted rule in Soviet law was necessary because its operation on Soviet territory was not recognized without an appropriate legislative measure. As Ladyzhenskii explains: "The priority of an International treaty over internal law is granted by Soviet law alone and not pursuant to some principle unaccepted by the USSR that international law is superior to national law" (3).

International customs are also to be mentioned among the sources of Soviet private international law. They are not *ipso facto* a source of law, however. In order to be made fit for this purpose, they have to be accepted by the USSR either by practical application or by special diplomatic acts.

Finally, as sources of Soviet private international law we have to mention the civil codes and the codes of civil procedure of the various Soviet republics in so far as they restate the conflict rules laid down in the Fundamentals and contain imperative substantive rules applicable also to cases of private international law.

(1) Stoupnitzky, p.425; see also Lunts, 1961, p.275.

(2) Section 129 of the Fundamentals of Civil Legislation provides: "Where an international treaty or international agreement to which the USSR is party establishes rules other than those contained in Soviet civil legislation, the rules of the international treaty or international agreement shall apply.

The same rule shall apply in the territory of a Union Republic, if an international treaty or an international agreement to which the Union Republic is party establishes rules other than those provided by the civil legislation of the Union Republic".

The corresponding provisions of the other fundamental laws are of similar significance.

(3) See Ladyzhenskii, 1961, pp.25-26.

GENERAL PART

1. SOVIET CRITICISM OF WESTERN PUBLIC POLICY

Preliminary Remarks. Soviet legal writers approach the public policy problem as they approach any topic of private international law, in a distinctly dualistic manner. While Western public policy is the object of constant criticism, the public policy manifested in Soviet legislation is either overlooked or promptly justified by pointing to some important social functions it is intended to fulfil.

There is no legal study in the USSR in which a serious effort has been made to give an objective picture of the Western public policy systems. Very often Soviet lawyers pick up some dubious decisions (1) from practice or extreme, isolated critical remarks (2) from legal writings and present them as characteristic of the countries concerned. Furthermore they abstain from tracing the development of certain legal concepts and their interpretation and, by keeping silence about such developments or by presenting some of them just as confirmation of their own attitude (3) they try to create, at least among Soviet readers, the impression that Soviet doctrine is responsible for them. This approach is, in fact, in conformity with the officially sponsored general assertion that the Soviet legal system has nothing to do with burgeois theories and legislation (4).

(1) See infra: English and American systems.

(2) See e.g. Levitin, p. 212.

(3) Even in the most recent studies relating to ordre public this approach is followed. Lunts and Levitin, e.g., accept the German solution that, when a foreign law is rejected as contrary to the public policy of the forum, the lex fori should not necessarily be applicable. While Lunts gives no further explanation of the background to his attitude, Levitin follows a quite different approach. First he explains in general terms that according to the capitalist legal systems the rejected foreign law (for reasons of public policy) is replaced by lex fori. Declaring that such an attitude is unacceptable for the Soviet legal system, he proposes a solution identical with the German one and concludes laconically: "Sometimes the judges of the capitalist countries also adhere to such a practice". As an example Levitin gives here the classic German decision relating to Swiss prescription. See Lunts, I (1959), pp. 236-237; Levitin, pp. 227-228. See more particularities infra: Soviet legal writers on their own system.

(4) In the initial years of the Soviet State there were some indications that the communist government was willing to recognize, though indirectly, a legal community with the other civilized countries, invoking in some official documents "the general principles of international law". The legal significance of this expression was refuted by the Soviet lawyers at an early stage, however, and since then no opportunity has been missed to emphasize the fundamental difference between the two legal systems - the communist and the capitalist. (On the initial period see: Pereterskii, 1924, pp. 7, 17, 26 et seq; Goikhbarg, p. 9. For the negative at-

From general observations in Soviet treatises one can deduce the following highly distorted idea of the raison d'être of the rules of *ordre public* in the West. They are created to frustrate the application of foreign law, and this frustration is a purpose in itself. Accordingly it is not a need for the defence of the economic, political and moral foundation of a society that has necessitated the creation of such rules, but merely a policy of non-application of foreign laws (1). If a Soviet lawyer occasionally talks about Western public policy as a measure of defence, the object of that defence is understood to be not society's basic values, but the interests and values of "the governing capitalist class". In the eyes of Soviet writers the concept of public policy in the West appears as a monstrous "elastic criterion", vague and indefinite used irresponsibly by the judges in rendering arbitrary decisions "which correspond to the interests of the dominating class". And all that takes place in conformity with the "general tendency of bourgeois law in the period of imperalism" (2).

Very often in Soviet legal writings we find the paradoxical conclusion that public policy in the West once played a progressive role when it was used against slavery and racial discrimination, but that it has now lost its progressive character altogether and became a reactionary instrument because of its use against the laws of "the countries of peace and socialism" (3) and because as Koretskii put it: "In the form of ordre public the bourgeois clique guards its own order, which ensures it a capitalist exploitation (directing its laws against the masses, against the working people)" (4).

Following the firmly established tradition of denying any legal community between a communist and a free society, modern Soviet writers, although avoiding too frequent a use of the earlier general formulas, do not fail when dealing with some particular issues of private international law to attack the notions more or less common to the Western legal authorities. "Bonae mores", "fun-

titude of Soviet lawyers with regard to Western legal systems see Feldbrugge, pp. 38-39; Verdam, pp. 229-244.

(1) See Levitin, p. 208.

(2) Pereterskii, Krylov, 1940, pp. 48-49; idem 1959, pp. 57-58; Koretskii, p. 103; Tumanov, pp. 234-235; otherwise Goikhbarg, pp. 44-45.

(3) Koretskii, 1948, p. 102; Lunts 1949, p. 116; Tumanov, p. 231; Levitin goes still further in his criticism, maintaining that even in the earlier periods of development public policy has not always played a progressive role in the West. (levitin, pp. 223-224).

(4) Koretskii, p. 102.

damental principles of justice", or "principles of natural justice" are never accepted as a basis for explaining the function of public policy because as Levitin puts it: "they are as ambiguous and idefinite as the notion of public policy itself" (1).

The criterion mostly used by Soviet authors to determine whether an appeal to public policy is progressive and justifiable is the way in which the system works with regard to communist laws, especially the laws of nationalization. Courts' decisions and authors' statements acknowledging the extraterritorial effect of such laws are declared good, progressive and in accordance with international law. Every invocation of public policy to frustrate the application of these laws is branded as contrary to international law. In other words, the unreserved recognition of the so-called "Socialist economic system" with whatever legal consequences there may be is elevated to a main essential and prerequisite for the existence of private international law (2).

After these general remarks, it may be useful to say a word about Soviet criticism of some particular systems.

The French System. Although the founders of Soviet private international law, when formulating their conflict rules, without doubt, proceeded from the premise that for the admissibility of a non-communist law minimum of similarity with the Soviet law is required, and admitting the absence of such a similarity, they excluded *a priori* the application of any foreign law in most vital cases, Soviet lawyers have reacted violenty against the same approach when used by Western courts and authors. Typical in this respect is the criticism of Lunts (3):

"Of all bourgeois theories on ordre public, the most reactionary is at present the 'theory' of Niboyet (4); he maintains that the application of the foreign law to which a French conflict rule refers has as a precondition some minimum of similarity between the foreign law and the French legal system......... This 'theory' ...has a pronounced antisoviet character; it is directed towards a denial of the legal effect of the Soviet law.... But to base the notion of *ordre public* solely on a difference between the local civil law and the foreign one means denying

(1) Levitin, p. 210. See also Tumanov, pp. 233-234. For this author the meaning of such concepts are clear enough, but inconsistent with the interests of the Soviet State. With great reluctance and indignation he talks about e.g. Niederer, who declares as contrary to natural justice the laws which encroach upon private property and especially the communist nationalization decrees.

(2) Lunts, 1949, p. 109; Lunts, I (1959), pp. 232-233; Koretskii, pp. 22-103.

(3) Lunts, 1949, p. 108; Lunts, I (1959), pp. 219-220.

(4) Niboyet, III (1944), pp. 488 et seq.

private international law altogether since the problem of conflicts arises only in cases of such a difference".

It is difficult fo find a well-founded reason for a Soviet lawyer to scorn this aspect to the theory of Niboyet. The possibility, however, that Soviet economic interests might be effected if foreign lawyers put such a theory into practice, probably motivated the whole attitude of Lunts. In fact he does not cite the excessive public policy examples of Niboyet (1), but only that relating to the communist expropriations without compensation, which is a comparatively moderate example. Moreover the assertion of Lunts that Niboyet bases the public policy concept solely on a difference between the local and foreign laws is not strictly correct, as the following statement of Niboyet demonstrates: "Chaque pays doit, en effect, posséder un droit adapté a ses besions, et c'est dans la diversité que réside la véritable civilisation. Le droit international privé part de cette diversité, et il se propose seulement d'établir une sorte de collaboration possible entre les législations, les autorités et les juridictions" (2).

With minor exceptions the general remarks with regard to all Western systems that public policy is vague and indefinite, reappear over and over again in the criticism of individual systems and in particular of the system under consideration. According to Soviet opinion the French legal writings consciously avoid a definition of the concept of public policy in order to justify the "arbitrariness" in the court practice (3). The vagueness in its turn was regarded by Lunts as a logical result of a "vicious" conception of the changeability of public policy (4). Later on, probably changing his opinion, Lunts paid due hommage to the almost universally acknowledged idea of relativity omitting in his more recent publication (1959) the previous statement on this issue.

It is further worth mentioning that according to Levitin, the distinction between "ordre public national" and "ordre public international" introduced by Brocher and accepted by many French scholars has been an important obstacle to the development and better understanding of the French notion of *ordre*

(1) "Pactes sur successions futures" as admitted in Switzerland, but considered contrary to French public policy; the French provision according to which children adopted outside France cannot claim succession rights in France against children born in marriage, etc. See: Niboyet, III (1944), pp. 511, 512.

(2) Niboyet, III (1944), p. 497.

(3) Lunts, I (1959), p. 221; Levitin, p. 213.

(4) Lunts, 1949, p. 109. Otherwise Krylov. He points out that "many theorists correctly mention the changeability of the public policy notion". See Krylov, 1930, p. 57.

public (1).

"In reality", says Levitin, "no special international *ordre public* distinct from the internal one exists. There is only a national *ordre public* which operates either in the sphere of the municipal civil law (Article 6, French Civil Code), or in the domain of private international law (Article 3, French Civil Code)" (2).

French court practice has also been judged more ore less according to its attitude toward the Soviet nationalization decrees (3). Perceiving that French courts have invoked *ordre public* against such decrees and following the official line of Soviet criticism Pereterskii wrote: ".... this notion has been used as a weapon in the political struggle against Soviet interests". The classic example in this respect for all Russian treatises is the so-called "Ropit Case" (1928), where the French *Cours de Cassation* refused to recognize the extraterritorial effect of such decrees with respect to ships owned by Russian refugees in France. The decision was based on the usual ground that compulsory expropriation without compensation was contrary to French *ordre public*.

The German system. The Soviet-German agreement of 1922, by virtue of which Germany recognized the nationalization of its nationals' property situated in the USSR, deprived Soviet lawyers of a favourite ground of criticism. This agreement has been interpreted by Russian lawyers as a practical implementation of the German view that the difference in the contents of the *lex fori* and a foreign law does not necessarily lead to the invocation of public policy; it is the application of foreign law which may offend German public policy. That is one side of the coin, which has not only been accepted but has even been made an integral element of the Soviet theory on public policy (4). Further to that, however, Soviet writers refused to go, and the corollary that in some cases a similarity between German and foreign legal provisions would not be an obstacle to declaring the foreign legal provisions as contrary to German public policy has been branded as abominable. Such was also the fate of the following classic formulation of this idea:

"Public policy is one-sided and self-motivated. There is neither

(1) A quite different opinion has been expressed in this connection by some Western legal writers. Neumayer, e.g., says that "cette distinction rend de grands services au développement du conflict des lois". (Neumayer, p. 54).

(2) Levitin, p. 213; a different attitude was taken by Krylov, who in 1930 declared that the distinction made by Brocher was "absolutely correct" (Krylov, 1930, p. 56).

(3) Pereterskii, Krylov, 1940, pp. 49-50; idem 1959, pp. 58-59; Lunts, 1949, p. 109; idem, 1959, p. 220

(4) See infra: Soviet legal writers on their own system.

inconsistency nor hypocrisy in the fact that a court will not carry out foreign measures injurious to the forum although the forum has enacted, or may in the future enact, similar measures injurious to others. No moral or ethical structure is involved in the public policy concept; all that is involved is that where public policies collide, the court will apply the policy of the forum rather than any other" (1).

Lunts views this thesis as "a moral impoverishment". According to him "such a view of *ordre public* turns the law into lawlessness and replaces it in the particular case by considerations of interest, characteristic of the crisis of bourgeois legality in the epoch of imperialism" (2). This criticism is either born of a deep misunderstanding or is a natural result of the remarkable dualism in attitude, already mentioned, which Soviet lawyers persistently adopt when considering the Soviet and Western legal systems. We can only comment that Soviet practice is one of the most striking confirmations of the doctrine that in public policy concepts no moral considerations are involved. It is perhaps superfluous to repeat that the interests of the Soviet State are the dominating factor in many of the conflict of law solutions proposed in Soviet literature (3). Let us take the following example. According to Soviet law the means of production are the exclusive property of the State. This is a fundamental principle of the system, an integral part of its *ordre public*. If there were real moral considerations in declaring for instance that private land is contrary to the fundamentals of the Soviet system, one would expect Soviet citizens to be barred from exercising such "immoral" rights even when they were in countries with free economic systems. The Soviet authorities, however, have not gone so far. On the contrary, they have not only permitted their citizens to enjoy such rights abroad, but have even bitterly complained when a foreign country has made restrictions in that respect (4).

The English system. The principal elements of English public policy against which the Soviet criticism has been launched are the term itself, the sphere of operation and the legal effect with regard to Soviet expropriations. In his extensive study on the English-American system of private international law, Koretskii

(1) Nussbaum, 1939, p. 489.

(2) Lunts, 1949, p. 111; Lunts I (1959), p. 223.

(3) See the introduction.

(4) See infra.

(1) sees the term "public policy" in a quite different light than for instance such a prominent lawyer as Martin Wolff has done (2). "Policy of law and 'ordre public' must not be confused" - says Koretskii -. "English lawyers, however, dissolve 'ordre public' into 'policy of law'". The "policy" element, according to the writer, gives to the notion under consideration the elasticity which the English bourgeoisie needs, to bring about the changes dictated by the interests of capital. Apart from the substantive inconsistency of this statement, it is difficult to reconcile it with the dominating idea in Soviet literature that private international law is an instrument of Soviet foreign policy.

The sphere of operation of English public policy has also been object of constant discussion. Some writers have restricted their criticism to a restatement of Western arguments, though in a specific communist formulation. Lunts, for instance, observes that English judges very often use other legal techniques, (for instance qualification according to *lex fori*) instead of public policy when they wish to avoid application of a foreign law; notwithstanding this fact they pretend that an excessive invocation of public policy is contrary to the spirit of common law. "Herein", says Lunts, "must be seen the traditional hypocrisy of the British bourgeoisie" (3). Koretskii, in his turn, tries to trace the "viciousness" in the development of English public policy and concludes that in earlier periods characterized by the occupation of new territories and the unlimited expansion of English capital, the courts evidenced a more liberal attitude towards the application of foreign law and seldom invoked public policy; in recent times of decolonization and protectionism a wider reference to public policy has been made as this is dictated by the interests of "the most conservative circles of the English bourgeoisie" (4).

In the opinion of Soviet commentators British courts have pursued a half-way policy with regard to Soviet nationalization, beginning with a correct decision in the case, of Luther A. M. v.

(1) Koretskii, pp. 29 et seq.
(2) "The continental conception of ordre public" says Wolff, "as excluding the application of foreign law reappears in England under the name of public policy". Or again: "Where there are both English and French authentic texts of a State Treaty the 'ordre public' and 'public policy' are used as equivalents" (Wolff, p. 176).
(3) Lunts, 1949, p. 112; Lunts I (1959), p. 224. Cf. however Graveson, p. 572.
(4) Koretskii, p. 30.

Sagor & Co. (1) (1921), but later on according to this precedent a restrictive interpretation: this decision was concerned only with one aspect of the nationalization viz. its effect on property situated in the nationalizing State.

According to Soviet writers, this decision played a positive role at the time because the court had refused to declare the communist nationalization as contrary to English public policy, and so doing, it had recognized the communist property system. The same decision, however, has been attacked for the reason that the recognition of the Soviet government was advanced as the principal ground for the validity of the decree. This disapproval is prompted not so much by legal considerations as by a consideration of affected economic interests. Whilst the English court accepted recognition as the basis for application of Soviet law, other countries not yet having recognized the Soviet government have decided that the acts of a non-recognized government were not applicable (2).

The American system. The Soviet approach to the public policy system of the USA does not differ substantially from that outlined in the commentaries relating to other Western systems, although the specific political structure of the USA has given a somewhat different colour to the discussion. These discussions are based, as ever, on the attitude of the courts towards the Soviet nationalizations. Most of the studies begin with a violent criticism of an earlier American decision in which the legal effect of the Soviet decrees on property situated in the USA was denied altogether either on the ground of non-recognition of the

(1) The principal points of the case of Luther v. Sagor were the following:
The Soviet Commissariat of foreign affairs had sold to the British firm Sagor & Co. a quantity of veneer which formerly belonged to the nationalized company A.M. Luther. The veneer was stored on Soviet territory when the nationalization took place. The former owner brought an action for recovery of the goods when they arrived in Great Britain, supporting his claim with the argument that the communist nationalization decrees being of a confiscatory character were contrary to British principles of justice and morality. The English Court of Appeal rejected the claim on the ground that the decree involved, being an act of recognized governement, must be respected. In connection with this case a central place in Soviet literature is accorded to the following, not very sound, argument of Scrutton: "It appears a serious breach of international comity if a State is recognized as a sovereign independent State, to postulate that its legislation is contrary to essential principles of justice and morality; such an aiegation might well with a susceptible foreign government become a casus belli and should in my view, be the action of the Sovereign through his ministers, and not of the judge". For the complete text of the decision see: Luther, A.M. v. Sagor & Co., 1921, 3 K.B., 532.

(2) On English practice relating to public policy see: Koretskii, p. 59-62; Lunts, 1949, pp. 112-114; Lunts I (1959), pp. 224-225; Levitin, p. 219.

Soviet government by the United States, or by classifying these decrees as penal, or from time to time as contrary to American public policy. Such decisions are rejected as reactionary, contrary to international law and as encroaching upon the rights of a foreign sovereign.

There came a turning point in the American court practice with the conclusion of the notorious Litvinov Assignment, by virtue of which the USSR ceded to the USA "all its claims as to the accounts in American banks belonging to private Russian enterprises nationalized by the Soviet government". The Litvinov Assignment formed the basis for one of the most celebrated decisions, from the point of view of the Soviet Authorities, rendered by the Supreme Court of the USA in the so-called "Pink case" (1). In this case the Government of the United States brought an action against the New York branch of the First Russian Insurance Co., claiming the assets of the branch remaining after the payment of all its domestic creditors. The claim was upheld and one of the defendent's arguments that Soviet nationalizations without compensation were contrary to the public policy of the State of New York and therefore without effect in that State, was rejected in accordance with the Act of State doctrine.

Instead of considering this case in the light of the Act of State doctrine, which was involved in this case and which the Supreme Court of the USA applies on occasion "however offensive to the public policy of this country and its constituent States an expropriation of this kind may be......" (2), Koretskii considered the above decision together with the Assignment as an expression of Federal public policy directed against the public policy of individual States.

This erroneous conclusion has also influenced the attitude of Koretskii with regard to American writings. He divides American authors into two groups: reactionary and progressive. "The reactionary forces have supported the public policy of the individual States whereas progressive ones, - the public policy of the USA. At present the most reactionary forces of the USA in the struggle against the Soviet State maintain that the *ordre public* of the individual States is of decisive importance. The progressive forces, supporting the policy of the USA, directed toward the development of good relations with the USSR, attached greater

(1) USA V. Pink, Superintendant of Insurance, Febr., 2, 1942; Am. Journal of International Law, Vol. 36, p. 309 et seq. See also Editorial Comments of "Am. J. of Int. Law", vol. 36, 1946, p. 275; pp. 277-278.

(2) See the motives of the U.S. Supreme Court in Banco Nacional de Cuba v. Sabbatino. Am. Journal of Internat. Law, LVIII (1964), p. 796.

importance to the ordre public of the USA.... The cause of the nation or the cause of the most reactionary circles of monopolist capital..... a dilemma, which of course had to be settled by recognizing that only the government of the USA had the right to determine whether the application of a foreign law is contrary to the public policy of the country" (1).

By dividing American public policy into reactionary and progressive according to the criterion mentioned, Koretskii can hardly pride himself on the consistency of his conclusions, as this thesis is in direct contradiction to other statements in his study. Together with Lunts and Levitin (2) he admitted that when slavery was still permitted and legal in the Southern States it was considered by the Northern States as contrary to their public policy and that therefore the latter then played a progressive role.

On several occasions it has been pointed out that the Soviet approach is a dualistic and casuistic one. Only in this light can one explain the fact that while in Soviet literature complaints and criticism of American public policy are found when it operates against Soviet confiscations, there is also approval of the same public policy when invoked against the national-socialist legislation affecting the rights of the Jewish population (3).

2. SOVIET LEGAL WRITERS ON THEIR OWN SYSTEM

Preliminary Remarks. In spite of the vigorous hostility of Soviet writers towards "bourgeois" public policy and of their attempts to give this notion a Marxist interpretation, Soviet legal literature has always borne strong traces of the influence of Western scholars. It is no exaggeration to say that public policy in the Soviet doctrine is and has always been a reflexion of the developments taking place in the West. This way of legal thinking had been established by the very founders of Soviet private international law, Pereterskii, Krylov, Goikhbarg, etc., who either failed to create or consciously abstained from building up a general theory of public policy of their own (4). All of them limited them-

(1) Koretskii, p. 38.

(2) Lunts 1949, p. 115; Lunts I (1959), p. 226; Levitin pp. 223-224.

(3) Koretskii, pp. 56-57.

(4) That is admitted also in the communist literature. See e.g. Lunts, 1949, p. 120; Szászy, Budapest, 1964, p. 168. Reczei, p. 112.

selves to adopting an attitude with regard to the dominating ideas of that time, of Brocher, Pillet, Bahr, Kahn and others, and to applying them to the Soviet legal system.

The pioneer work of Pereterskii, "Ocherki mezhdunarodnogo chastnogo prava", Moscow 1924, is an interesting illustration of this thesis. Pereterskii opposes "territorial" ordre public to the "national" or "internal" one (cf. Brocher, 1888 and Valery, 1914). "Ordre public territorial" according to him, enbraces all the laws of a country which are to be applied imperatively on its territory to citizens and foreigners alike to the exclusion of any foreign law. Under "ordre public national" (or "interne") on the other hand, Pereterskii ranks the laws unconditionally applicable to the nationals irrespective of whether they are within or outside their country (1).

Krylov, in his turn, called the distinction made by Brocher "perfectly correct" (2), while Goikhbarg (3) adhered to Pillet's ideas of classification of laws according to their social purpose. In Goikhbarg's opinion this theory is workable in relations not only between countries with similar systems, but also between countries whose laws differ fundamentally in their social purposes. Goikhbarg subjects his conclusion, however, to the reservation that in a sphere in which different political and economic systems are involved, each country will insist on the binding force of its laws within its territory, so that a greater consession has to be made to the territoriality of laws than would be the case if the theory of Pillet were strictly applied.

An original concept introduced in the Soviet literature on public policy, more sociological and political than juridical in character, can be traced in Pereterskii's work of 1924: "Ordre public... is a class notion. It is the complex (totality) of rules necessary for the preservation of the class structure of a given society" (4). This

(1) "Ordre public national" according to Pereterskii is incorporated e.g. in circular letter no. 42 of the RSFSR. People's Commissariat for Foreign Affairs of 12th April, 1922. This instrument provides that: "Legal relations pertaining to property which is located outside of the territory of the RSFSR and connected with it, cannot be judged outside of the confines of the RSFSR under the Russian laws, and they are subject to the effect of the local legislation, regardless of the nationality of the persons involved in such legal relations, even if they are Russian citizens.... However, the limits within which the protection of such rights may be extended shall also be determined by general bases of the concept of law of the Soviet law. No protection may be extended, therefore to claims and acts which though legitimate under the law of the country of a person's residence, are contrary to the opinions established in the RSFSR as to the limits of what is permissible. This is subject to appraisal in each individual case. (See: Pereterskii, 1924, pp. 28-29. 34-36 et seq. Russian text of the latter citation see idem p. 128. Transl. in English see: Gsovski, I (1948), pp. 300-301. Conf, also Krylov, 1930, p. 56, note 1.

(2) Krylov, 1930, p. 56.

(3) Goikhbarg, p. 20-21.

(4) Pereterskii 1924, p. 30; see also Krylov, 1930, p. 57.

typically Marxist interpretation has become an indispensable postulate in Soviet legal writings. Its practical significance, however, is no more than that of a colourful mark of distinction in a sphere dominated by foreign conceptions.

These general observations remain valid with regard to the present-day publications. Neither the great experience and coordinated efforts of the old specialists Peretersk ii and Krylov, nor the prominency of such a modern authority as Lunts, has brought about any fundamental changes in the approach followed in the formative period of Soviet law. Soviet writers have devoted more effort and more space in their publication to critical commentaries on foreign doctrines than to their own legal system. The studies concerned with Soviet public policy in the proper sense of the term, reveal only a communist interpretation and implementation of principles and solutions propounded abroad. It must be admitted, however, that the Soviet general theory on public policy is still in the making and that, for the time being, its foreign ingredients cannot be dispensed with altogether (1).

(1) In connection with these general remarks it is of interest to mention two East-European attempts at a comparison between Communist and "bourgeois" public policy systems. The first and rather original thesis originates from the Bulgarian scholar Ivan Altanov. Considering the prohibitive and permissive function of public policy, Altanov observes that bourgeois systems use public policy predominantly in its prohibitive function and only very seldom in its permissive function. In the Soviet system on the other hand, it is the permissive function which plays a more important role. (Altanov, p. 23-24). Szászy made a broader comparison, but limited himself to summarizing the opinions of the communist writers, instead of giving his personal views.

a. The first difference according to Szászy concerns the definition of the concept of public policy. The majority of authors in the People's Democracies "see, as do the Germans, the essence of the principle of public policy..... in the reservation clause, in the dismissal of foreign law propter normam externam. ... The concept of public policy is of a purely defensive character and its purpose is to protect from the aspect of general interests the domestic order and political programme of the State. Protection in this sense does not mean the defence of the individual interests and subjective rights but that of the State as a political unit".

b. "The opinions adopted in people's democratic countries...stress in a much more energetic manner the exceptional character of the use of public policy than is the case in Western literature...".

c. "The third principal disagreement between people's democratic and Western opinions on public policy consists in the fact that the first sees the positive effect of the principle of public policy exclusively and always in the application of the rule of the lex fori and never considers the foreign public policy, whereas in Western countries an increasing number of authors support the view that, if foreign law is precluded, the rules of the foreign State or of a third State should be applied and that in certain cases, foreign public policy should also be considered...." (Szászy, Budapest, 1964, pp. 175-177). Cf. also Szászy, the Hague, 1964, p. 245.

As will be seen below, the last conclusion of Szászy does not cover the prevailing opinions of Soviet legal writers.

Exceptional character of Soviet public policy. Soviet specialists in private international law realized at a very early stage that the international confidence in the whole legal system of a country depends to a great extent on its public policy. This conviction and the desire to present their private international law in as liberal a light as possible have prompted most of the Soviet writers to adhere to the dominating theory of public policy, which claims only the minimum of imperative legal provisions (1). There is almost an insistance, one might say, that the public policy clause is intended to restrict a conflict rule referring to a foreign law (2). Bearing in mind the principal motives guiding Soviet authors when accepting or rejecting legal ideas and solutions, one can understand why the exceptional, abnormal character of public policy has been so vociferously emphasized in Soviet literature. It is only Pereterskii who, probably under the influence of Pillet, formed an exception by declaring in his early publication that "with a Marxist class understanding of the law, the notion of ordre public has for us nothing shocking" (3). Otherwise, Soviet lawyers often assert with pride that Soviet courts very seldom have recourse to public policy, so putting into practice the idea of the exceptional character of public policy, in contradistinction to the "bourgeois systems", where this idea is without practical significance (4). Lunts has given a quite clear formulation of this attitude: "Where there is a conflict between our law and the law of a capitalist country, it is between legal rules based on fundamentally different economic systems and originating in an essentially different political and legal ideology. Our conflict of laws, however, starts from a recognition of the fact of coexistence of the two economic systems; it is, as already mentioned, the legal expression of our readiness for peaceful collaboration with all countries, irrespective of their economic and social order. It follows from this that the application of the public policy clause, limiting the effect of a conflict rule in this country, may only be an exception requiring serious motivation in every concrete case. This motivation, however, may not be a mere indication of the fundamental difference between the conflicting Soviet and bourgeois laws, as

(1) For the characteristic features of this theory see infra.

(2) Pereterskii, 1924, pp. 27-28; Goikhbarg, p. 44; Krylov, 1930, p. 55 et seq.; Koretskii, p. 23; Lunts 1949, p. 106; Lunts, I (1959), p. 217; Recently Lunts expressed a quite different opinion in his lectures at the Summer Session of the Hague Academy of International Law, (1965); about this new attitude see below.

(3) Pereterskii, 1924, p. 29.

(4) Levitin, pp. 209-210.

such an indication would exclude the possibility of recognizing the effect of almost every bourgeois law. Under the condition of coexistence of the two property systems, a similar use of the public policy clause will amount to a negation of any private international law" (1).

The assertion that the Soviet public policy clause has a really exceptional character reaches its culmination whenever the legal relations within the communist block are considered. In this respect it is maintained that the nature of such relations based on the same economic and political foundations and inspired by so-called "socialist internationalism" exclude any necessity to invoke the public policy clause (2).

What is relevant for determining whether a foreign law is contrary to Soviet public policy? Initially there was a tendency to look at the contents of the foreign law in order to decide whether it had to be applied or not. This was done for instance by Pereterskii in his work of 1924. According to him, there were qualitative requirements which the applicable foreign law had to satisfy. A foreign law failing to meet these requirements had to be discarded. In other words, "the foreign legal rule is not applied if it is contrary to the public policy of the forum" (3). This opinion did not receive much support and at present it seems even to have been abandoned by the author who first propounded it. It was Krylov who for the first time drew the attention of the Soviet authorities to the sound principle laid down in art. 30 of the Introductory law to the German Civil Code, according to which it was not the foreign law but its application that had to be repugnant to German public policy for it to be discarded. Krylov saw this rule as a prerequisite for the existence of international intercourse (4). From more recent publications, one can deduce that this opinion has become a dom-

(1) Lunts I (1959), pp. 235-236.

(2) Lunts I (1959), p. 238; Levitin, p. 229; Averin, p. 146. This opinion is shared by the lawyers of other communist countries. See e.g. Ionasco, Nestor, pp. 199-200; Jezdić, pp. 189-201. From the Western lawyers see: Hazard, 1963, pp. 133 et seq.; Verdam, pp. 229, 243.

(3) Pereterskii, 1924, pp. 27-28. Similar interpretation has been given by Réczei. He maintains that: "a) der sowjetische Standpunkt bei der Anwendung der Vorbehaltklausel den Inhalt des ausländischen Gesetzes berücksichtigt, b) das ausländische Gesetz nicht nur in dem Falle ausser acht gelassen wird, wenn es einem sowjetischen Gesetz widerspricht, sondern auch dann, wenn es gegen eine, im Gesetz zwar nicht ausgedrückte, doch als eine Grundlage dienende politische Zielsetzung oder gegen die Grundlagen des Sowjetischen Systems verstösst". (Réczei, p. 113).

(4) Krylov, 1930, p. 59.

inating one in the USSR. According to Lunts, the prior condition for the invocation of the public policy clause is that the application of a foreign law must be incompatible with the Soviet system. It is immaterial whether the foreign law as a law is considered good or bad from the Soviet point of view. The question to which the Soviet judge must provide an answer is this: will the application of the foreign law bring about results contrary to the Soviet legal order? "It is not a question" - says Lunts - "of the contradiction of laws, but of cases where the application of a foreign law would produce results inadmissable from the point of view of Soviet legal conceptions" (1). Or as Pereterskii in a more recent publication put it: "the foreign law is not to be applied in the USSR if its application appears incompatible with the fundamentals of the political and economic system of the USSR" (2). In short, Soviet authors have, in this respect, unreservedly adhered to the school of Von Savigny.

The Legal consequences of repugnant acts and situations.
It seems at present that Soviet authors have definitely accepted another almost universally acknowledged rule relating to public policy, according to which legal consequences of repugnant foreign acts and situations can be recognized unless they themselves are contrary to public policy of the forum. This rule made its appearance in Soviet literature on private international law with the following statement of Pereterskii:"Von Bahr correctlyobserves that a State cannot disregard the consequences deriving from a foreign institution not recognized by the former, if those consequences are not in direct contradiction with the local law" (3). In more recent publications Soviet writers accept this rule without making references to its theoritical background, a fact which is to some extent an indication that the rule is firmly integrated in Soviet teaching (4). In Soviet literature the classic example in this matter of poligamous marriages and their legal consequences has become a favourite one (5).

Effects of the rejection of a foreign law. With regard to the effects of the rejection of a foreign law due to public policy considerations, Soviet doctrine has exhibited, historically speaking,

(1) Lunts, I (1959), pp. 235-236; Lunts, 1964, pp. 633-634.
(2) Pereterskii, Krylov, 1959, p. 56; see also: Tumanov, pp. 230=231; Levitin, pp. 209-210; Averin, p. 136.
(3) Pereterskii, 1924, p. 29; see also Krylov, 1930, pp. 57-58.
(4) Lunts, I (1959), p. 235; Levitin, p. 227.
(5) See e.g. Pereterskii, 1924, p. 29; Krylov 1930, p. 57; Lunts I (1959), p. 235.

a striking shift from the French to the German position. Until recently, it was, one might say, unanimously maintained that when a foreign law was declared inapplicable as offending Soviet public policy, the substantive law of the forum had to take its place. Pereterskii for instance considered that a basic function of public policy was to "discard the foreign law and to replace it by the local one" (1). A similar opinion is to be found in the writings of Krylov (2) and even those of Lunts as far as his work of 1949 is concerned (3). More recent publications on the subject reveal a tendency to favour the solution according to which *lex fori* is not necessarily applicable when a repugnant foreign legal provision is discarded. Lunts (4) has accepted the latter opinion, although with the general reservation that "in the great majority of cases of application of the public policy clause, the discarding of a foreign law leads to the application of Soviet law", while Levitin considers it as the only opinion which is in harmony with the Soviet legal system (5).

According to Lunts, the gap which is opened by refusing to apply a foreign law can be filled up by the application of another law with which the legal facts are most closely connected. "The question of the validity of a marriage concluded in Paris between nationals of Texas (white and negro) must be decided in the USSR not according to the law of Texas (discriminating against negroes) but according to the French one which does not know such discrimination, i.e. not according to the personal law (whose application is excluded by public policy motives) but according to *lex loci celebrationis"* (6). The second suggestion introduced in Soviet doctrine by Levitin relates to the filling up of a gap by legal provisions taken from the system to which the rejected provisions belong. When the foreign law contains a rule contrary to Soviet public policy but can be made acceptable to the Soviet court by referring to other legal provisions from the same legal system, the case must be decided according to that foreign law. If, however, such a solution appears to be impossible, according to Levitin, the Soviet substantive law has to be applied (7).

(1) Pereterskii, 1924, p. 31.
(2) Krylov, 1930, pp. 56-57.
(3) Lunts, 1949, p. 124.
(4) Lunts, 1959, p. 236-237.
(5) Levitin, p. 227-228.
(6) Lunts I (1959), pp. 236-237.
(7) Levitin, pp. 228-229.

The contents of public policy (changeability and precision). It is difficult to trace the present attitude of Soviet legal writers with regard to the dominating idea in Western literature that public policy is a concept subject to development and changes and that actuality is one of its essential characteristics. In the early postrevolutionary writings it was taken for granted that "to the extent that a society's structure changes, its public policy also changes" (1). The authors of today have not yet expressed a clear opinion on this question. As has already been mentioned, Lunts touched on it indirectly in his treatise of 1949. Criticizing the French system (2) he branded the conception of changeability of public policy as vicious, but this view did not reappear in the edition of 1959. If we might venture a deduction from his failure to treat this matter a second time, we may expect that the old opinion will regain authority in the Soviet literature.

With regard to the relativity of public policy as to place, there is no difference of opinion among Soviet authors. All are agreed that the contents of this notion differ from State to State. In particular, it is emphasized over and over again that there is a fundamental difference between the public policy of the communist and non-communist legal systems.

In conclusion it should be mentioned that according to East-European writers the idea of the relativity of public policy is generally accepted in all communist countries. In the words of Szászy: "The opinion prevalent in people's democratic literature ... admits that the actual content of the concept of public policy is relative, that its substance cannot be defined with general validity because the content of the public policy of a State can be determined only on the ground of legislative and political ideas of the State concerned" (3). This assertion, however, finds support in Soviet literature only in respect to relativity as to place. It has already been pointed out that one of the main subjects of Soviet criticism is the wide-spread opinion in the West that the contents of the public policy notion cannot be defined and that precision is even undesirable, as it must remain open to change and development. It seems that Soviet teaching, as presented in the most recent works on private international law is in favour of a clear and precise formulation of the public policy concept. Moreover, modern Soviet authors maintain that

(1) Pereterskii, 1924, p. 30; of the same opinion: Krylov, 1930, p. 57; Goikhbarg, pp. 45-46.

(2) Lunts, 1949, p. 109; see also this paper, supra: Soviet criticism on Western systems.

(3) Szászy, Budapest, 1964, p. 176.

public policy in the USSR, in contrast to the Western systems, does in fact bring about the desired precision. According to them, it is implied in the fundamental principles of the Soviet political and economic system as laid down in the Constitution. They even insist that only these fundamental principles may be invoked as *ordre public* and that nothing outside the Constitution can be brought within this concept (1). The precision understood in this way, explains, according to Levitin, the fact that Soviet public policy is not a subject of controversy in literature and that it is seldom invoked in judicial decisions (2).

3. GENERAL REMARKS ON THE CURRENT DOCTRINES ON PUBLIC POLICY AND THE APPROACH TO BE FOLLOWED

Current doctrines. Proceeding from the major lines of legal thinking, we may assume that the essential points around which the theoretical controversies on public policy have revolved are its *scope* of operation (3) and the *function* it is intended to perform. We have to admit also that however important the first-mentioned controversial point may seem to be, it is the function of public policy which has constituted the demarcation line between the various theories in this domain. It makes a great difference whether we maintain that the immediate function of public policy is to bar the application of a foreign legal provision otherwise applicable or whether we say that public policy purports to make some legal provisions of the forum absolutely binding. These two kinds of functions have been considered by the majority of legal writers separately, with the result that either the former or the latter was elevated to an essential qualitative element of the public policy concept. Moreover, there are also lawyers who see public policy as a legal device performing both functions. Accordingly, we are confronted at present with three groups of theories each of which approaches the problem in a different way.

The first group of legal writers considers public policy as a defensive device intended to frustrate the application of a foreign legal provision normally applicable if this provision or its application happens to be intolerably incompatible with some fun-

(1) Pereterskii, Krylov, 1940, p. 47; Lunts I (1959), pp. 55-56; Levitin, pp. 224-226.
(2) Levitin 1960. p. 224. The Soviet assertion regarding the precision and the legislative concretisation of public policy is deemed to have an equal validity for all East-European communist legal systems. See e.g. Ionasco, Nestor, pp. 198-200; Szászy, 1964, p. 176.
(3) See p. 46, note 2.

damental moral, economic or political principle of the forum State. The founder of this school of thought was Von Savigny (1). His starting point was a community of law existing between the civilized nations which was the basis of private international law. This community of law required, according to Von Savigny, that the courts should apply foreign laws when the cases under consideration were intimately connected with them. This was the principle which should normally be applied. There were, however, some exceptional, abnormal cases outside the legal community between nations where the application of the competent foreign law was inadmissible. This could happen either when a forum's law was of a strictly positive, imperative nature or when a foreign legal institution was not recognized in the forum State. The abnormal cases would, in the opinion of Von Savigny, gradually diminish with the legal development of nations.

These original but very generally conceived ideas were further developed and transformed into a dominating public policy theory only through the valuable contributions of Von Bar, Zitelmann, Kahn and others. Especially attractive to the internationally-minded lawyers was Von Bar's view that the non-application of a competent foreign law may not be motivated solely by the circumstance that it is repugnant to the forum's laws or legal conceptions. "Es kann sich immer nur darum handeln, ob diejenige *Wirkung* des fraglichen Rechtsatzes oder Rechtsverhältnisses, welche im Bereich unserer Rechtsordnung zu Tage tritt, in Widerspruch steht mit absolut gebietenden Rechtssätzen unserer Rechtsordnung oder mit bei uns herrschenden sittlichen Grundsätzen" (2). Thus what could be open to objection was not the foreign law as such but its realization, its direct application on the forum's territory. This strongly mitigating element in the

(1) Von Savigny, 1849, § 349; Engl. transl: Von Savigny, 1869, § 349.
The general principle of private international law together with its exceptions are most characteristically presented in the following brief statement of Von Savigny:
"Unsere Untersuchung hat bisher dahin geführt, dass auch bei der Entscheidung über solche Rechtsverhältnisse, welche mit verschiedenen unabhängigen Staaten in Berührung kommen, der Richter dasjenige örtliche Recht anzuwenden hat, dem das streitige Rechtsverhältnis angehört ohne Unterschied ob dieses örtliche Recht das einheimische Recht dieses Richters, oder das Recht eines fremden Staates sein mag.
Dieser Grundsatz aber musz nunmehr beschränkt werden mit Rücksicht auf manche Arten von Gesetzen, deren besondere Natur einer so freien Behandlung der Rechtsgemeinschaft unter verschiedenen Staaten widerstrebt. Bei solchen Gesetzen wird der Richter das einheimische Recht ausschliessender anzuwenden haben, als es jener Grundsatz gestattet, das fremde Recht dagegen unangewendet lassen müssen, auch wo jener Grundsatz die Anwendung rechtfertigen würde".
(2) Von Bar, pp. 128-129.

teaching of Von Savigny appears over and over again in the writings on public policy.

The essential elements of this theory in its modern form are to be found in the following thesis of Niboyet: "L'exception d'ordre public est l'appelation donnée au moyen dont dispose le juge pour barrer le passage au droit étranger dans certain cas.... On ne peut concevoir l'intervention de ce remède que si le droit étranger est compétent, c'est-à-dire normalement applicable. L'intervention de l'ordre public prend nécessairement un caractère exceptionnel, exhorbitant en quelque sorte, abnormal, si du moins elle est nécessaire" (1). Or to use a highly illustrative aphorism inspiring recent publications "public policy in its restricted conflict sense, can properly be used as a shield but not as a sword" (2).

This is in essence the puristic interpretation of the public policy concept as a clause of réservation (clause de réserve, Vorbehaltsklausel, etc.). There are, however, many lawyers from this school who propound a more extensive interpretation of this concept by recognizing that certain internal legal provisions have an absolutely binding force. A word will be said below about this important line of thought.

A second group of lawyers, following an approach diametrically opposed to that just described, maintain that every legal system contains a special category of "lois d'ordre public" or legal provisions which are absolutely binding.

This approach is closely associated with the name of Mancini, the founder of the so-called Franco-Italian (Roman or Mancinian) school of thought. Mancini propounded an aprioristic solution of conflicts of laws on the basis of the nationality principle, with the imperative applicability of the public laws and the laws of public policy *(droit public et lois d'ordre public)* of the forum as a corrective. According to the nationality principle, individuals when abroad remain subject to their national laws in-so-far as these laws are designed to protect their private interests. Such are e.g. the laws relating to persons, family, inheritance, etc. The principle of nationality ceases to operate in the domain governed by the public laws and laws of public policy of the forum State, to which nationals and aliens alike must be subject. Accord-

(1) Niboyet, III (1944), p. 490.
(2) Reese, p. 395. See also: De Winter, 1964, p. 332.

ing to Mancini, the laws of public policy express the basic moral and economic conceptions of a State. They can be contravened neither by foreign official acts and judgements nor by private claims and agreements (1).

The development of this theory, furthered by Brocher, Weiss and Despagnet, and reaching its culmination in the works of Pillet, has been directed towards a clear concretisation of the laws of a public policy character operating in the domain of private international law. This ultimate goal motivated the distinction made by Brocher, Weiss and others between "lois d'ordre public interne" and "lois d'ordre public international" (2). It also prompted Pillet to classify the laws into "lois de protection individuelle dont le but commande qu'elles soient extraterritoriales" and "lois de garantie sociale ou d'ordre public qui manqueraient leur object si elles n'étaient pas strictement territoriales" (3).

All adherents of the Mancinian school, however different their particular systems may be, have as a common starting point the assumption that there are legal provions of public policy nature which must be applied absolutely. All of them would have agreed with Despagnet that the provisions in question are "les règles.... dont l'observation.... est considérée comme indispensable pour le maintien de la bonne organisation sociale, politique, économique et morale" (4). Furthermore there are no essential differences of opinion with regard to the manner in which these legal provisions operate: they are self-sufficient and act by virtue of their own content, independently of conflict rules or foreign laws to which they would refer. These functional characteristics of the public policy rules are defined in a recent textbook of Netherlands private international law as follows:

"A public policy rule is always of an independent character and operates by virtue of its own contents, while in some cases it also forms an exception to a particular conflict rule" (5).

As has already been mentioned, not all the adherents of the school of Von Savigny insist on the exceptional character of public policy, i.e. not all of them refuse to consider the imperative

(1) Mancini, 1874, pp. 296 et seq.

(2) Brocher, pp. 106 et seq.; Weiss, pp. 392 et seq. For more details see below.

(3) Pillet, 1923, p. 110; See also Pillet, 1929, pp. 407-515.

(4) Dispagnet, p. 13.

(5) Kosters, Dubbink, p. 339.

rules of the forum in this context. Whilst preserving their classic point of departure, according to which the public policy clause presupposes the operation of a conflict rule referring to a foreign law, many writers admit that under each legal system there are imperatively binding legal provisions which also have to be taken into consideration in international cases. Usually placed in this category are substantive legal provisions of private law influenced by governmental measures of a public law character or fulfilling an important social-economic function. Amongst the numerous examples to be found in writings and court practice, the following are noteworthy: foreign exchange regulations, export-import restrictions, labour protection measures, nationalization decrees, anti-trust legislation, etc.

At the very point when it is generally admitted that there are legal provisions internationally binding by virtue of their own contents or by virtue of the will of the legislature, a fervent controversy arises as to the character and the role which should be attributed to them. Some lawyers consider that these provisions fulfill a so-called "positive function" of public policy which, as Raape (1) explains, ensures the absolute application of *lex fori* in conflict of law cases. In this respect German lawyers speak of "die zwingende Durchführung des eigenen Gesetzes" (2) or of "Durchsetzungsdrang des eigenes Rechts" (3). In particular, it is sometimes maintained that this function can also be fulfilled by a conflict rule whenever it gives competence to a local law notwithstanding the prevailing foreign elements of the case in issue; here in the opinion of Maury "il s'agit... d'une compétence fondée non sur la nature du rapport, mais, sur l'ordre public international" (4). This aspect of the public policy problem is more extensively dealt with by Kahn-Freund (5). In his opinion there are rules of a public policy nature split off from the main body of the principle of *ordre public* and made, by means of leg-

(1) Raape, p. 93.

(2) Wolff, 1954, pp. 62 et seq.

(3) Dölle, pp. 403, 406-407.

(4) Maury, 1952, pp. 72, 73. Even Battiffol recognizes that under some conditions a conflict rule can be of a public policy nature. Characteristic in this respect is his following remark: "Les règles de conflict de lois sont ainsi certainement d'ordre public en tant qu'elles donnent compétence à la loi francaise au moins en matière impérative" (Battiffol, 1967, p. 400).

(5) Kahn-Freund, pp. 45-48. A similar attitude has also been taken by Nussbaum. According to this author, the question is of "some independent rules which in reality are outgrowth of the public policy concept, such as the rules on the non-actionability of certain groups of foreign rights" (Nussbaum, 1943, p. 113).

islative or judicial cristallization, into separate norms "requiring the judge to apply his own law irrespective of the general principles of the conflict of laws and without regard to the effect the application of foreign law would have had in the concrete case" (1).

A diametrically opposed opinion is propounded by De Winter and Neumayer. De Winter denies altogether the public policy character of imperative legal provisions, whilst Neumayer still classifies them as *lois d'ordre public international* - both scholars aspiring to the recognition of a "rattachement spécial" to the imperative provisions of all countries involved, whenever a case with international elements is to be dealt with. With this "rattachement spécial" it is intended "de mettre une nouvelle règle de conflit à la place de la fonction positive de l'ordre public (2). In the same connection Nussbaum (3) wrote about "spacially conditioned internal rules" which override a conflict rule to the contrary, while Francescakis (4) preferred to call them "règles d'application immédiate".
It seems that this thesis had also had its repercussion in Soviet legal writings. Considering the question of the inadmissibility of the free choice of law where this choice is contrary to Soviet

(1) From the long list of lawyers admitting the public policy character of some substantive legal provisions see e.g. the following: Lerebours-Pigeonnière, pp. 255-270; Paulsen, Sovern, p. 1008; Lagarde, pp. 93-94; 129-130; 144, 236-237.
From Netherlands literature the following might be mentioned: Hijmans, pp. 209-237; Van Brakel, pp. 86-87 et seq.; Deelen, pp. 172-173.
(2) Neumayer, p. 77; De Winter, 1940, pp. 260-261; Idem, 1947, pp. 149-165; Idem, 1964, pp. 354-356.
(3) Nussbaum, 1943, pp. 71-73.
(4) Francescakis, 1958, pp. 13-15; 35; see also Francescakis, 1966, pp. 1-18. Francescakis proceeds from the premise that in each legal system there are two kinds of imperative rules: rules of a public policy character and others, which, although not classed under this category are of such great importance that their non-observance would be detrimental to the very organization of the forum State. The author proposes that the term "lois d'application immédiate" be used to indicate both kinds of imperative rules because of their essentially common features: they constitute a reflection of the organization of the State and, as such, they claim an absolute and immediate application (excluding the intervention of any conflict rule). Illustrating his opinion with French law, Francescakis writes: "Il y a donc quelque chose de foncièrement commun dans la solution, écrite, de l'article 3, alinéa 1er du Code Civil, et la solution jurisprudencielle, qui s'appuye sur la notion de lois d'ordre public. D'où l'idée de réunir ces deux solutions sous l'étiquette commune de 'lois d'application immédiate', l'adjective 'immédiate' étant chargé de suggérer que le raisonnement ne passa pas par l'intermédiaire du procédé du conflit de lois tel que la doctrine contemporaine l'envisage" (Francescakis, 1966, p. 4).
It must be observed further, that the puristic adherents to the school of Von Savigny have already considered the notion "lois d'application immédiate" in quite a different light. In their opinion

public policy, Lunts declared, in one of his recent publications that "le choix n'est possible, qu'autant, qui'il ne heurte pas les fondements du régime soviétique" and that "il les heurterai, s'il avait pour but de tourner des règles prohibitives étrangères ou s'il entravait le cours normal des échanges internationaux"(1).

Finally a word should be said about the third approach, which appears to be a synthesis of the preceding two. Its starting point is the assumption that the two conceptions of public policy as propounded by the schools of Mancini and Savigny do not exclude each other altogether. They are both necessary and only through their logical combination can a satisfactory comprehension of the public policy phenomenon be attained. Thus, according to Frankenstein, there are two kinds of public policy: ***absolute*** and ***relative***. To the former belong the legal rules which are absolutely binding under all circumstances. On the other hand, each system has a relative public policy which acts through a general clause of reservation with regard to the conflict rules referring to a foreign law. By virtue of this "ordre public relative" the competent foreign law is not applied, whenever its application would be considered intolerable from the point of view of the political, moral or social conceptions of the forum country (2).
This approach, with some modifications in terminology and detail, has been convincingly propounded by Louis Lucas and Goldschmidt (3). It is also followed by the distinguished Hungarian professor, Stephen Szászy, whose lucid analysis of the public policy concept justifies an extensive quotation.

the imperative laws brought under this category are divorced altogether from the concept of public policy. Thus for instance Graulich writes: "Puisque la règle d'application immédiate soumet le rapport au droit du for en l'assimilant à un rapport interne, il ne peut évidemment être question de renvoi ni d'ordre public; il en est toutefois de même chaque fois que la régle de conflit aboutit à dégager la compétance de la loi du for" (Graulich, p. 635).

(1) Lunts, 1964, p. 638.
(2) Frankenstein, 1930, pp. 321 et seq. The basic idea of this thesis can be found, according to Frankenstein, in the distinction made by Von Savigny between cases where forum laws claim an absolute application and those where foreign legal institutions are considered inacceptable (Frankenstein, 1926, p. 193). Similar interpretation of Von Savigny's teaching is made by Niemeyer: p. 64. The Dutch scholar Kollewijn, however, maintains that it is the Roman school of thought in which this idea, or as the writer calls it this "pearl of great value" originates. (Kollewijn, p. 45, note 1. For more details on this subject see ibid. pp. 29-32; 53-54; 59-60; 81; 132-133).
(3) Louis-Lucas, pp. 393-442. Goldschmidt, pp. 223-244. With regard to the terminology, it is quite interesting to observe that Louis-Lucas introduced the terms "La règle d'ordre public" as opposed to l'exception d'ordre public", while Goldschmidt distinguishes between "La clause de réserve", "les regles directes rigides" and "les règles d'exportation" relating to the latter.

"The principle of public policy asserts itself in reality in all countries on three bases: (a) *propter norman externam*, (*b*) *propter normam domesticam*, (c) *propter normam inter gentes praeceptam*.
(a) The principle of public policy asserts itself *propter normam externam* in the form of a reservation (Vorbehaltsklausel), which is but an emergency clause (Notstandklausel) and under which the application of those rules of foreign law is precluded, whose application in the given case, i.e. whose positive effect, would be at variance with basic moral, ideological, social, economic and cultural concepts of the forum, its ideas concerning equity and justice, the fundamental institutions of its legal system, or the basic principles of its social and economic life.
(b) The principle of public policy asserts itself *propter normam domesticam* by reason of the unconditional application of municipal rules which require - on the strength of their content - absolute application (e.g. statutes concerning foreign exchange). In the form of public policy previously mentioned, emphasis is to be laid on the foreign rules of law and in the second form on municipal rules which are to be applied unconditionally. In the first instance the point of departure is the analysis of the foreign rule of law, and in the second that of the rule of municipal law. In the first instance preclusion of the application of foreign law is effected *directly*, in the second *indirectly*, through the unconditional application of municipal law."

The category mentioned by Szászy under (c), which concerns the scope rather than the function of public policy, asserts itself "when the application of foreign rules of law would run counter to the binding rules of the law of nations, to the international obligations of the State concerned, to the requirement - generally acknowledged in the international legal community - of fairness (ordre public universel, vraiment international)" (1).
Finally, it should be noticed that the approach under consideration also seems to be gaining adherents among Soviet lawyers. This was revealed by Lunts in one of his lectures at the Summer Session of the Hague Academy of International law (1965). Lunts mentioned that in addition to public policy as a reservation clause expressed in Article 128 of the Civil Law Fundamentals there are, in the Soviet legal system, also "lois d'ordre public". "The difference" explained Lunts, "is very important: Art. 128 presupposes cases where the foreign rule of law is of such a character that its application would have results which are considered

(1) Szászy, The Hague, 1964, pp. 238-239.

intolerable. The "lois d'ordre public" are 'national' norms of such importance that no foreign law, irrespective of its character, may stand in the way of their application" (1).

The approach of the last group of legal writers will be used as a starting point for the present study. It is also to be recommended as it appears to have proposed a satisfactory solution with respect to the other controversial problem mentioned above, viz. the problem concerning the scope of public policy (2).
It is the system of Louis Lucas in particular which enables us to view this problem in all its dimensions. According to this author, public policy, from the point of view of its scope of operation, can be either general or special. Public policy is general if it extends to foreigners and nationals alike; it is special if it is applicable only to one of these two categories of persons, so that it can be a special public policy relating to foreigners or a special public policy relating to nationals only.
"Cette classification tripartite", writes Louis Lucas, "bien loin d'être surprenante, n'est que naturelle. Elle est l'image des trois aspects que peut prendre la nécessité sociale. Elle est la revélation des trois formes que peut revêtir la souveraineté au contact des prétentions individuelles... Tantôt la loi pose un principe premier, une règle fondamentale, qui, par définition même, doivent être respectés par tout le monde sans exception. C'est le cas des lois d'organisation et de protection sociale: lois constitutionelles, lois pénales, lois de police, etc. Tantôt la loi s'adresse avérément aux seuls nationaux. Elle ne va que du législateur à ceux qui sont soumis par le lien intime

(1) Lunts, 1965, pp. 15-16.

(2) Here we are concerned with only one aspect of the scope of public policy. It relates to the categories of persons with respect to which public policy purports to operate. The scope so understood is of great importance for the so-called "positive function" of public policy. It must be distinguished from the scope of the public policy clause as determined by external conditions. To it belongs e.g. the German theory of "Inlandsbeziehung" or "Binnenbeziehung", according to which the operation of public policy persupposes the existence of a point of contact in the case at issue with the forum territory, so that public policy may not be invoked whenever such a point of contact does not exist. The doctrine admits, however, that there are some exceptions to this principle. See: Kahn, pp. 180-190. Raape, p. 93, especially note 92a; Lagarde, pp. 55 et seq.). Another current theory is that of the so-called "effet attenué de l'ordre public", a term which points to its French origin. According to some scholars, a distinction must be made between the acquisition of rights in the forum country and the effect of the rights acquired abroad. Public policy has its full scope of operation only with regard to the former, while with regard to the latter its manifestation is limited only to gravely prejudicial cases; in other words with regard to rights acquired abroad public policy has an 'effet attenué". (See: Battiffol, 1967, pp. 415-416; Lagarde, pp. 13-55; For a comparative study on German and French theories see Maury, 1954, pp. 16-23.

de la nationalité. Telles sont les lois qui fixent l'état et la capacité générale des personnes... Tantôt, enfin, la lois ne concerne et ne peut concerner que les étrangers. Toute la réglementation de la condition qui leur est faite en France aux points de vue de la pénétration, du séjour, de l'expulsion, etc.... est marquée de ce caractère....." (1).

This threefold manifestation of public policy will be constantly recalled when the Soviet legal system is analysed. In other words, this conception together with the conclusions as to the double function of public policy form the theoretical basis of this study.

The problem relating to the scope of public policy, being controversial, merits a brief survey of the most important opinions which differ from those above.

According to the prevailing opinion, public policy is a unitary concept. It is one and the same, irrespective of the persons involved: it relates to all on the forum territory. This attitude is found both in some writings of the Mancinian school and in studies which are otherwise considered as being based on the teaching of Von Savigny. In this respect, there is no difference in principle whether we contend like Pillet that public policy is the application of certain legal rules indispensable for the preservation of the State (2) or whether we say that it is the application of a foreign legal rule which must be repugnant in order to invoke the concept of public policy (3). From both points of view it is possible to come to the conclusion that public policy is a legal device operating in private international law with an equal force towards foreigners and nationals and that therefore it is one and undivided.

A second group of legal writers follow an approach which is, in one way or another, dualistic. According to them, the scope of public policy is two-sided. And here, depending on the point of view from which this problem is considered, opinions are divided. Some writers distinguish between internal public policy and international public policy (*ordre public intern* and *ordre public international*) an approach which is usually associated with the name of Brocher and his classic interpretation of Article 3 and Article 6 of the French civil code. According to Brocher

(1) Louis-Lucas, pp. 414 et seq. In this connection cf. also Valery, pp. 197 et seq.
(2) Pillet, 1929, pp. 449 et seq.
(3) See e.g. Niboyet, 1928, p. 548.

and his followers, internal public policy operates only in the domain of municipal law, whilst international public policy extends to the sphere of private international law. Later on, these two categories of public policy were interpreted in a quite different manner, viz. that internal public policy relates to nationals while the international public policy relates to foreigners. Despagnet uses this distinction in the sense that the internal public policy purports to protect the individual interests of the nationals and international public policy - the collective interests of the State. This writer considers further that public policy also manifests its dual character in another sense of the word, viz, as being absolute and relative. Absolute public policy is more or less common to all civilized countries while relative public policy is peculiar to a definite State. In this connection Szászy, as already mentioned, talks of an "ordre public universel" vraiment international", as opposed to national public policy which asserts itself either *propter norman externam or propter normam domesticam* (1).

The approach to be followed. In the light of this and using the indicated doctrine as a basis for this study, the following additional observations might be made.

Public policy is a complex of ideological imperatives which determine in advance the general limits of applicability of foreign laws in conflict of law cases. These imperatives express the political, economic and moral principles deemed essential for the existence of a society by the dominating political forces at a definite time and place. Seen in this perspective public policy manifests itself either as *legislative public policy* or as *judicial public policy*, depending on the authorities to which it is directed and by which it is effected.

Legislative public policy, then, is the complex of ideological imperatives directly binding on the legislature and incorporated in the law as written or unwritten legal rules. They are the exclusive concern of the law-making authorities and do not leave any room whatsever for a choice of law, either by courts or by individuals. The legislature effects this kind of public policy either by unilateral conflict rules (general or special) or by substantive legal provisions. Both legal norms apply directly and exclude any judicial analysis and evaluation of foreign law, however closely the case may be connected with that law. The classic example of this kind of public policy is presented in

(1) For more details about the existing doctrines see the comparative study on public policy by Knapp; see also Louis-Lucas, pp. 406 et seq.

the various statutes relating to title to land. The motive for their being absolutely binding in countries with a free economic system is, as Weiss put it, "d'assurer l'égalité des terres et de rendre impossible le rétablissement du régime féodal dans les pays où ce régime a cessé d'exister (1). This century-old motive has been modified in the communist countries, where it tends to operate in reverse: it is the State's land monopoly which must be defended (USSR) or realized (people's democracies) against the free private property systems. The legal rules relating to the inadmissibility of divorce, as e.g. in the case of Italian law (2), fall into the same category. With regard to these rules, Edoardo Vitta has recently given the following explanation: "... sous l'influence de la conception catholique de l'indissolubilité de mariage, ils [les juges Italiens] ont fini par admettre que spécialement dans ce domaine, la législation Italienne représente un secteur du droit indisponible". (3). An universal manifestation of legislative public policy is to be seen in the ever increasing number of mandatory regulations relating to foreign exchange, export and import, labour protection, etc.

Treaty recognition of the public policy character of this kind of legal provisions can be seen e.g. in the Uniform Law Relating to Private International Law, signed by the Benelux Countries in 1951. Art. 26 of this Draft Agreement runs as follows:
"Il est fait exception à l'application des dispositions de la présente loi, lorsque cette application porte atteinte à l'ordre public, soit que celui-ci s'oppose à l'application d'une disposition de la loi étrangère, soit qu'il impose l'application d'une disposition de la loi néerlandaise/Belge/Luxembourgeoise" (4).

Judicial public policy on the other hand is the same complex of ideological imperatives directed to the authorities in charge of the administration of justice, by virtue of which a foreign legal provision normally applicable must be rejected if its application would be detrimental to some fundamental values of the forum State. Judicial public policy is incorporated in some legislations as a conflict rule and assumes the function of a general clause of reservation ("clause de réserve", "Vorbehaltsklausel") to other conflict rules which prescribe the application of foreign laws. For illustration the related German and Soviet

(1) Weiss, p. 394.

(2) Codice civile, art. 149: "Il matrimonio non si scioglie che con la morte di uno de coniugi...".

(3) Vitta, p. 277.

(4) For a brief commentrary on this article see: De Winter, 1952, no. 4238-4239.

legal provisions can be quoted, the latter, seemingly, strongly influenced by the former. "Die Anwendung eines ausländischen Gesetzes ist ausgeschlossen, wenn die Anwendung gegen die guten Sitten oder gegen den Zweck eines deutschen Gesetzes verstossen würde" (Art. 30 of the German Introductory Act to Civil Legislation, E.G.B.G.B.).

"A foreign law shall not be applied where its application contradicts the fundamental principles of the Soviet system". (Article 128 of the Fundamentals of Civil Legislation of the USSR and Union Republics).

Judicial public policy is derived from and supplementary to the legislative public policy; it fills any gaps that may be left by the legislature when effecting a legislative public policy. There are no essential constitutive differences between legislative and judicial public policy. Both of them are the expression of the same political, social and economic ideas the observance of which is considered to be of vital importance for society: both devices are conceived so as to frustrate the application of foreign legal provisions. The differences concern some functional characteristics of the two kinds of public policy. In contrast to legislative public policy, whose functioning is not dependent on any applicability of a foreign law, judicial public policy is logically preceded in its operation by the applicability of such a law. While in the case of judicial public policy the judge is authorized to proceed from the contents of a concrete foreign legal provision and to decide upon its exclusion, in the case of legislative public policy he must look exclusively at his own law, and he never considers the claim of a foreign law to application.

To elucidate our distinction between legislative and judicial public policy a word should be said about the notions "exceptional" and "abnormal" in the public policy concept.

The term "exceptional" is usually used with two different meanings. Sometimes it is intended to indicate that public policy must be invoked as seldom as possible, i.e. only in exceptional cases. This is an idea *de lege ferenda* and without great significance for positive law, which is our primary preoccupation in this study. The other meaning is used as a functional characteristic of the public policy concept: public policy forms an exception to a conflict rule referring to a foreign law. We have to consider the second meaning and define its significance for the approach we have chosen. First of all it should be observed that the notion "exceptional" cannot be used as a criterion for distinguishing between legislative and judicial public policies. It is true that if we compared them solely on the basis of positive law, some differences would be found in the degree to which the two kinds of public policy function as exceptions to some conflict rules. Whilst we can take it for granted that judicial public policy always brings about some exceptions to a classic conflict rule, we cannot do this with regard to legislative public policy; this public policy constitutes an exception only in certain cases, whilst in others it functions independently of any conflict rule or it manifests itself in a conflict rule requiring the application of the *lex fori.* Theoretically speaking, however, even the last-mentioned category of legislative public policy, which at first sight does not constitute an exception if considered in conjunction with some basic principles of private international law, may ultimately be classed under the public policy concept as an exceptional phenomenon. In any case a legislative public policy rule may always be treated as being "withdrawn from the community of law between the nations" as suggested by Von Savigny. The point may be illustrated by the following examples. If a general conflict rule according to which inheritance is governed by the law of the last permanent residence of the decendent, is followed by a special rule according to which inheritance to immovables situated in the forum State is governed exclusively by the local law, the special rule pertains to the legislative public policy of the forum and forms at the same time an exception to the general conflict rule in this matter. The legislative public policy is also reflected in the one-sided conflict rule according to which marriage and family relations are always governed by the local law. There is no doubt that such a rule constitutes an excessive exception to the principle of the international legal community requiring nations not to exclude each other's laws from application in cases with foreign elements.

Similar reasoning is also pertinent with regard to the notions "normal" and "abnormal" in the public policy concept. Whenever the judicial public policy leads to the application of the forum law notwithstanding a conflict rule to the contrary, it gives an abnormal competence to the local law. If, however, by virtue of the same public policy, a concrete foreign legal provision is set aside only to be replaced by another provision from the same foreign law, or even from the law of another country connected with the case in issue, we still remain in the sphere of the normal legal competence. Legislative public policy, in its turn, can also manifest itself in a normal or abnormal competence. The rule according to which immovables are submitted to the *lex rei sitae*, as mentioned above, was prompted by public policy considerations. It provides a normal competence because the foreign *lex rei sitae* is also respected whenever the *situs* of an immovable happens to be abroad. On the other hand, legislative public policy makes the local law abnormally competent in all cases in which the legislator has provided that some conflict of law issues will, under certain circumstances or even always, be governed by the local law notwithstanding the fact that there is a normal classic conflict rule also recognizing the competence of foreign law, depending on the points of contact. From the notions "normal" and "abnormal" one thing seems to be beyond doubt. Whenever the local law is applied by virtue of an abnormal competence, i. e. in spite of a conflict rule to the contrary, we are dealing with a matter of public policy. But the "abnormal competence" cannot be considered as a precondition for classing a certain legal provision as a matter of public policy, nor can it be a criterion for distinguishing between legislative and judicial public policy.

The only thing that matters in the distinction between these two kinds of public policy is whether the court, or another authority, in dealing with a conflict of law issue is permitted to consult a foreign law and to evaluate the effect of its application in the forum territory. If they are authorised to do so and having made use of this power reject a concrete foreign legal provision as susceptible of bringing about results detrimental to the forum country, we can speak of a case where judicial public policy has been put into operation. If, however, the court has to follow a legal imperative to the effect that municipal law alone should be applied to a particular private international law issue, without consulting any foreign law, we are concerned with legislative public policy.

It should be noted that this new terminology would be superfluous if we could use without reservation some of the existing and more familiar expressions such as "absolute and relative" public policy, "positive and negative", "règles d'ordre public" and "exceptions d'ordre public", etc. These terms are too ambiguous to be used without further explanation. Besides, each of them gives rise to objections. With regard to the distinction, mentioned earlier, between absolute and relative public policy, is must be admitted that it has been used by the various legal writers with quite a different significance. Let us take for example the teachings of Despagnet and Frankenstein, where this distinction forms the basis of two essentially different theories of public policy. According to Despagnet each legislation contains two kinds of public policy rules: absolute and relative. Absolute public policy rules (such as the prohibition of polygamous and incestuous marriages) are common to all civilized countries and their observance is absolutely necessary for the maintenance of good order and the functioning of the State. Relative public policy on the other hand differs from country to country and depends on the circumstances obtaining in a particular State. (Rules of this nature according to Despagnet include e.g. the prohibition of marriages between black and white, which is prompted by the fear of an undesirable racial influence.) (1). Frankenstein also based his theory on the same distinction but, as already indicated, with a completely different signifance. In his opinion, absolute public policy relates to legal rules which are absolutely binding under all circumstances, whilst relative public policy serves as a corrective or as an exception to the conflict rules referring to foreign laws (2).

As to the distinction between positive and negative public policy, it must be admitted that this is sometimes misleading as it is difficult to understand without express qualifications whether the function or the effect of the public policy is being dealt with. That is to say in the first case-whether public policy is used as a defensive weapon and forms an exception to a conflict rule (negative function), or whether it is employed as an offensive weapon through the media of imperative rules which apply by virtue of their own content (positive function); in the second case-whether public policy is directed towards the creation and granting of rights which are not admitted under the competent foreign law (positive affect) or conversely, whether on the ground of public policy the legal rights acquired under a foreign law are denied any effect by the forum (negative affect). In this connection it is interesting to note what e.g. Nussbaum understands by a negative or limitative function of public policy. He distinguishes between two kinds of negative public policy functions: "a) public policy limits freedom of contracts, invalidating for instance yellow-doc contracts or agreements in restraint of trade. Comparable to the contract use is the use of public policy in invalidating testamentary provisions because, for instance, of the presence of illicit conditions. b) Public policy furthermore limits the application of foreign law (and the recognition of foreign judgments)". It is clear that only the second function or as Nussbaum calls it the "conflict" function of public policy corresponds to the negative function as understood by most European lawyers making use of the distinction between "positive" and "negative". The first function mentioned by Nussbaum as "negative" can be, in principle, a positive one (3).

(1) Despagnet, pp. 217 et seq.

(2) Frankenstein, 1930, pp. 322 et seq.

(3) See Nussbaum, 1940, pp. 1027-1028; Idem 1943, p. 111.

In my opinion the distinction of Louis-Lucas between "règles d'ordre public" and "exceptions d'ordre public" is also open to objection because some "exceptions" are as much "règles" as the "règles" themselves and vice versa.

SPECIAL PART

I. SOVIET LEGISLATIVE PUBLIC POLICY

Preliminaries. As pointed out above, Soviet legal writers have limited themselves to an explanation of their judicial public policy and they are perfectly right in maintaining that public policy, so conceived, is very seldom invoked in Soviet courts. This assertion, however, has no justification at all as far as Soviet legislative public policy is concerned. This public policy, imperatively solving many of the legal conflicts in favour of Soviet law does not constitute an exceptional phenomenon, but a rule with a considerable scope of operation and practical significance. As Makarov once put it "les lois soviétiques s'appliquent généralement à cause de leur propre teneur et non à cause de la teneur des lois étrangères dont le champ d'application d'après les dispositions du droit international privé soviétique est bien étroit". (1) Makarov set out this feature of Soviet law against the background of the teaching of Frankenstein and his distinction between absolute and relative public policy, and came to the conclusion that the Soviet legal system, unlike the Western systems, in which a relative public policy is generally used, is rather dominated by an absolute public policy. This conclusion, although never accepted by Soviet lawyers (2), is arrived at by many Western commentators. It also prompted the American lawyer Pisar to declare that "choice of foreign law is, as it were, the exception and the public policy of the forum is the basis of Private International Law as applied in Soviet courts". (3) The situation has not changed even after the

(1) Makarov, 1933, pp. 134-135 et seq. See also Makarov, 1931, p. 511.

(2) There were even Soviet writers inclined to exclude the public policy concept altogether rather than to admit that the latter was the basis of all their laws. A suggestion of similar effect was made for instance by Raevich in a study before the last war. Raevich promptly admitted that the scope of application of foreign laws in the USSR was much narrower than was the case in the "bourgeois" States. Therefore, Soviet courts seldom need to have recourse to the public policy clause in order to frustrate the application of a repugnant foreign law. This concept, according to him, can be dispensed with altogether without any prejudice to the principles of the Soviet system. He explains this by the fact that Soviet judges may refuse the application of a foreign law on one of the following two grounds:
1. Soviet substantive rules are of a predominantly imperative character.
2. If in exceptional cases foreign law is admitted by a Soviet conflict rule, the latter must be disregarded where it is contrary to "revolutionary expediency". (Raevic, 1934, pp. 67-68.)

(3) Pisar, pp. 621-622.

most recent legislative reforms in the USSR relating to civil law and civil procedure. Interpreting Soviet public policy in the light of the new legislation, Grzybowski was right in pointing out that "the Soviet public order clause, in addition to the blanket formula of Article 128, consists of a built-in system of protective measures designed to assure the ideological cohesion of the Soviet legal order, and to shield the monopolies of the Soviet State from the intervention of foreign rules. Some of these measures, " continued Grzybowski, "take the from of specific reservations of the public order type. Others, although ostensibly designed in the form of a general principle of the legal order, and conceived in the form of the grant of status, also restrict the application of the foreign law, inasmuch as they affect the regime of private rights and the status of foreigners" (1).
Soviet public policy originates in the Marxist ideology as professed by the Communist Party of the USSR. It is the Communist Party which determines in advance the political, moral and economic principles of Soviet society, because, as Article 126 of the Soviet Constitution provides, the Party "is the vanguard of the working people in their struggle to build a communist society and is the leading core of all organizations of the working people, both public and State". The preamble of the "Fundamentals of Civil Legislation of the USSR and the Union Republics" (1961) is quite clear on this point: "It is the task of Soviet civil legislation actively to promote the solution of the task of communist construction". In a recent commentary devoted to some aspects of private international law, Fleishits explained that said "Fundamentals", designed to serve as the foundation of all Soviet civil law during the period of the full-scale building of communism, are based on the demands of the Programme of the Communist Party of the Soviet Union and, like all Soviet law, promote communist construction" (2). The apprehension of an intolerable infringement of the fundamental communist principles through the application of foreign laws, has brought about the creation of rigid limits to the activity of law-making authorities which, where not indentified with the Communist Party itself, are under the supreme supervision of the latter. These limits amount to a total or partial prohibition of the application of foreign laws whenever there would be a latent or an actual possibility of affecting some of the basic economic, moral or political principles of the Soviet system.

(1) Grzybowski, pp. 155-156.
(2) See: Fleishits, pp. 398, 405.

The *economic principles* of the USSR wich are clearly defined by Soviet laws (constitutional or civil) are e.g. the exclusive right of the State to own land, waters, minerals, forests and the basic means of production; the State monopoly of foreign trade and foreign exchange, etc. Of the *moral principles* purporting to guide individual conduct we might mention: the duty to assist in the building up of a communist society; the duty to work and the complementary duty to live only from means acquired by personal work and to abstain from using other men's labour except through the intermediary of the State; equality between men and women as to rights and duties; equal treatment of individuals, irrespective of their race and origin, etc. The basic *political principle* of the USSR is the dictatorship of the Communist Party, whether this principle is officially admitted or not. The sovereignty which the Soviet State enjoys for self-preservation and the furtherance of its aspirations has also been invoked in private international law cases, especially in the notorious nationalizations without compensation and in its claim to absolute immunity from jurisdiction. Furthermore, it is an unwritten postulate for the legislature and courts alike that Soviet private international law cannot run contrary to the foreign policy of the USSR. It would be contrary to Soviet foreign policy, for example, to tolerate commercial or money relations detrimental to a friendly nation or to the ultimate goal of world communism.

All these principles and the legal provisions based on them will be dicussed in the following pages.

1. CAPACITY REGULATIONS AND THE POSITION OF FOREIGNERS IN THE USSR

A legal provision of great significance, imperatively binding on citizens and foreigners alike, is laid down in Article 8 of the Fundamentals of Civil Legislation of the USSR and relates to legal capacity. Historically speaking this article reproduces to a large extent the rules contained in Articles 4 and 7 of the RFSFR civil code of 1922; it can thus be assumed that the interpretation given to these articles in Soviet writing and by the judiciary also has a bearing on the new legal provision.
Article 8 of the Fundamentals reads as follows:

"The capacity of having civil rights and duties (civil legal capacity) equally belongs to all citizens of the USSR. The legal capacity of a citizen begins with his birth and ceases with his death.

The full capacity of a citizen to acquire by his acts civil rights and to create for himself civil duties (civil legal ability) arises at majority, i.e. upon the attainment of the age of eighteen years. The limited ability of minors, and also the cases and manner of imposition of restrictions on the legal ability of adults, shall be determined by the legislation of the Union Republics.

No one may be restricted in legal capacity or legal ability, except in cases and in the manner established by Law. Legal transactions seeking to limit legal capacity or legal ability shall be void."

For the purpose of private international law in general and our subject matter in particular, this basic legal provision must be considered in connection with Article 122 of the same Fundamentals (see infra), laying down the principle of the equality of rights of Soviet citizens and foreigners. Articles 122 and 123 of the Soviet Constitution (1936) proclaiming the equality of men and women "in all spheres of economic government, cultural, political and other public activity", and the equality of all citizens "irrespective of their nationality or race", must also be taken into consideration. The above rules have an absolutely binding force on Soviet territory with regard to foreigners and citizens alike.
In this connection, two aspects are of particular interest: the scope of operation of the age-of-majority rule and the general significance of the equality clause.

All foreigners and citizens alike are submitted on Soviet territory to the rule that majority is attained at eighteen years. (1) At this age an individual enjoys full capacity (civil legal ability) to acquire rights and undertake obligations of a civil-law character as understood by the Fundamentals. (2) The rules relating to the limited legal ability of minors and to the restrictions which under some circumstances may be imposed on an adult's legal ability, are endowed with the same binding force. The details of this are governed by the civil codes of the individual republics. For example, the RSFSR Civil Code (1964) lays down the general rule that until the age of 15 citizens are regarded as not having legal ability, while persons aged between

(1) Pereterskii, Krylov, 1940, pp. 70, 73. Idem 1959, pp. 78, 81; Boguslavskii, Rubanov 1959, pp. 60-61; Boguslavskii, Rubanov, 1962, pp. 60-61; II (1963), p. 33.

(2) According to Article 2 of the Fundamentals, family, labour and land relations are not considered as civil law relations. They are therefore governed by special laws.

15 and 18 years possess limited legal ability. The former cannot enter into legal transactions, which, where necessary, are concluded by their parents or guardians; the latter, having reached the age of 15, may enter into such transactions with the consent of their parents or curators. These being only general rules, some exceptions are provided by this codes, which permit minors to conclude some transactions or undertake obligations of limited scope, strictly delimited by the law. (RSFSR Civil Code, 1964, Articles 13-16).
The mandatory character of these legal provisions makes any interference of the *lex patriae* impossible whilst it is considered by many legislations to be decisive in this matter. It is quite difficult to understand the real motives for declaring Soviet law to be exclusive in this domain. In any case it seems improbable that moral or sociological considerations have played any role in the drafting of these rules. From the moral point of view an imperative legal provision relating to the age of majority would have been justified only if it had been intended to protect weaker citizens due to their youth. That is not the case with Soviet law. The law excludes from application not only foreign laws which provide for majority at an age of less than 18 years, but also those providing for it at later ages. The social conditions under which a foregner has developed his mental and physical ability have furthermore not been taken into consideration by the Soviet legislature. Otherwise it would have favoured either the *lex patriae* or at least the *lex domicilli*, understood as the law of the place of permanent residence.

The nationality principle is applied only to Soviet citizens abroad (1) whilst in all other cases, viz. where Soviet territory is involved, the territorial principle dominates. This combination of the nationality and territoriality principles guarantees the supremacy of Soviet law with regard to all persons permanently or even temporarily connected with Soviet society. Here we are witnessing an abnormally extended competence of Soviet law by virtue of a legislative public policy (2). The reasons for establishing such rules were either political or related to the protection of Soviet national interests. Whilst granting political rights to comparitively young people (18 years old) in the hope

(1) Pereterskii, Krylov, 1959, p. 81: Lunts, II (1963). p. 33.
(2) Such anomalous extension of a legal competence in this domain is to be found in some South-American countries e.g. Chile (Civil Code, Article 14 and 15), Colombia (Civil Code, Articles 18 and 19), Ecuador (Civil Code, Articles 13 and 14) and El Salvador (Civil Code, Articles 14 and 15), See also Rabel, I, p. 127-128.

of winning their sympathy, a communist government could not consider them as minors in the domain of civil law; moreover, the interests of Soviet citizens were most efficiently protected by making the local rules on majority binding on citizens and foreigners alike (1).

The principle of equality between men and women with respect to their active legal capacity as mentioned above, is applied with an equally binding force to foreigners. The Soviet authorities abide strictly by this principle even when its observance may amount to a denial of legal assistance and justice. The following case from Soviet writing may be illustrative:
"On one occasion a man applied to a Moscow notary public, stating that his wife, a Belgian subject, had inherited a house in Belgium which she wished to make a gift of to her brother resident in Belgium. To legalise the transfer, the Belgian notary public required the husband's notarially certified consent. Very properly, the Soviet notary refused to certify the statement, since that would be a restriction of a married woman's capacity at law and therefore in contravention of the constitution of the USSR" (2).

The question whether the rights of the party in whose favour the notary claimed to have acted were protected or detrimentally affected has not been posed by Soviet legal commentators. No doubt the Belgian wife would have preferred in this particular case to have had the consent of her husband required by Belgian law instead of the declaration that she is as capable as her husband. The general ideological imperative requiring the respect of the equality between men and women was so dominating in the case that it had to be complied with even although it was contrary to the requirements of justice. On the other hand, the Soviet legislature has not gone futher in this respect than to impose the obligation upon the executive and judicial authorities not to legalize or assist in the legalization of acts which would form

(1) Capacity rules primarily concerned with the national interests of the forum country or with its commercial security are to be found also in some Western European countries. Characteristic in this respect is the French doctrine of "intérêt national", based on the so called Lizardi case, and according to which a foreign minor cannot rely on his minority (under his lex patriae as against a French merchant if the latter has acted "sans légèreté, sans imprudence et avec bonne foi", (Lizardi v. Chaize a.o., 16-I-1861. Dalloz: Jurisprudence générale. Paris 1861, I, pp. 193-195: see also Batiffol, 1938, pp. 330-331).
Rules with a comparable effect are to be found also in Germany, Switzerland, Italy and Greece (cf. Kahn-Freund, p. 47).
(2) Boguslavskii, Rubanov, 1959, p. 37: Ibid. 1962 p. 34. See also Lunts II (1963), pp. 33-34.

an expression of non-equality between men and women as to their legal capacity. The law does not as yet impose an obligation on the spouses to abstain from limiting each other's rights in their family relations. Even in a Soviet sociological study it is promptly admitted that the authority of the Soviet man is still dominating. "The husband, for example, often does not interfere in the daily household expenditures but insist on having the final say on big purchases", writes Kharchev. The same author, basing his opinion on preceding ethnological studies, acknowledged that "in most of present-day collective farm families in Lithuania, for example, the husband still retains a hold on the family purse. The head of a collective farm household has no real right to spend family money on his personal needs. But in reality this rule is rarely adhered to since in most cases the husband is not obliged to account to either his wife or his children for what he does" (1).

The basic rules relating to the contents of legal capacity are laid down in Article 9 of the Fundamentals of Civil Legislation: "Citizens may, in conformity with the law, have property in personal ownership; use dwelling premises and other property; inherit and bequeath property; choose their occupation and place of residence; have the rights of the author of a work of sience, literature and art, discovery, invention and technical improvement, and also have other property and non-property personal rights" (2).

In the light of Article 122 of the Fundamentals this provision also describes in general terms the contents of the legal capacity of aliens. Moreover, not only the scope of civil rights as provided by this article but also the contents of each particular right mentioned in it are expected to be the same for citizens and aliens in so far as the latter are not subject to some more restrictive special rules (see below).

Article 9, determining the general scope of civil capacity, affects the rights of foreigners and citizens in two ways: positively and negatively. The positive effect is implied in the enumeration of rights granted to individuals by law and protected by the courts. The enumeration is not exhaustive, but it gives a general idea as to the kind of civil rights one can enjoy. The negative effect of this Article is that the holders of these rights have to exercise them within the limits and under the conditions prescribed by Soviet law, or in the wording of Article 9 "in conformity with the law". The condition "in conformity with the

(1) Kharchev, pp. 27: 28-29.
(2) See also Article 10 of the RSFSR Civil Code of 1964.

law" at first sight contains nothing unusual and may be found in Western legislations as well. It is nevertheless an imperative prerequisite implying restrictions which are either totally unknown in a legislation of a free economic system or known only to a very limited extent, but which in the USSR are of such a magnitude and character that they modify the whole complex of powers inherent in the rights concerned. In view of the fact that no inherent rights of individuals are recognized, but only rights granted by Soviet law, foreigners cannot invoke in the USSR their *lex patriae* under which they would enjoy more extensive rights. In their interpretation of Article 122 of the Fundamentals of Civil Legislation Soviet lawyers leave no room for doubt that foreigners cannot under any circumstances have more extensive rights in the USSR than Soviet citizens (1).

All restrictions, expressed or implied, relating to property, contractual rights and, the closely related right of free choice of occupation are equally binding on citizens and foreigners. Detailed treatment will be given to all these questions in the following chapters. At this point, however, a few general observations may be made.

The most characteristic feature of the Soviet economy is the monopolistic position of the State as the owner of basic instruments and means of production (land, natural sources and wealth, factories, transport, communications, banks, etc.) and as the only legitimate merchant of significance (2). In this monopolistic domain no private property or activity is admitted. The law tolerates and protects only the so-called personal property which Article 25 of the Fundamentals defines as "property intended to satisfy the material and cultural requirements of citizens" (income and savings derived from labour, a dwelling-house or part thereof and supplementary husbandry, household objects and furnishings, and articles of personal use and convenience) (3). These objects which are capable of being held in private ownership are permitted only for personal use and comfort, i.e. the owner is prohibited from deriving income from them. As the Article 25 provides: "the personal property of citizens may not be used to derive unearned income". The derivation of in-

(1) See Boguslavskii, Rubanov, 1962. pp. 55-56: Lunts, II (1963) pp. 19, 33. Szászy, Budapest 1964, p. 193.

(2) Article 9 of the constitution permits "the small private economy of individual peasants and handicraftsmen based on their own labour and precluding the exploitation of the labour of others".

(3) See: Article 10 of the Soviet Constitution of 1936, Article 25 of the Fundamentals and Articles 105, 106 of RSFSR Civil Code, 1964.

come from personal property is contrary to the purpose inherent in the property right, thus contravening the general condition under which all Soviet civil rights are granted: "civil rights shall be protected by law, except as they are exercised in contradiction to their purpose in socialist society in the period of communist construction". (Article 5 of the Fundamentals of Civil Legislation).
Since this legal provision restates the principle contained in Article 1 of the 1922 RSFSR Civil Code, we have to assume with Soviet authors that the preceding court practice in this matter is also of equal validity under the new law.

In a commentary on the Fundamentals of Soviet Civil Legislation written by S. N. Bratus, E. A. Fleishits and R. O. Khalfina, we read the following statement: "The Supreme Court of the U. S. S. R. within whose competence it is to generalize judicial practices and give instructions to the lower courts, pointed out in 1940 that if the lessee of dwelling premises in a state-owned building made a practice of subletting a separate room with the object of deriving unearned income, that room could be taken away from the lessee by the court in an action brought by the procurator or the housing agency in charge of the dwelling house." (1) There is no doubt that this restriction applies to foreigners. If a foreigner has acquired two rooms and decides to let one of them to a sublessee he could not rely on more favourable treatment by Soviet authorities than Soviet citizens are accorded in the same position. The fate of citizens and aliens alike will be the same if, for instance, they hire out a personally owned automobile or sell any items whatever for profit. Such contracts are invalid *ab initio* and are sanctioned with administrative and/or punitive measures.

A curious example from Soviet practice in this respect is provided by the case of Mervyn Matthews, the 31-year old English research student who was expelled from Russia on the eve of his intended marriage with his Russian fiancée Ludmilla Bibikova. Matthews applied to be married at the end of April 1964 and the wedding was fixed for the 9th of June of the same year. On the 25th of may they were told they could not be married. This was followed by his expulsion from the USSR. Offi-

(1) See: Soviet Civil Legislation and Procedure. Official texts and commentaries. Moscow (1963), pp. 15-16: see also paragraph 9 of the Ruling of the Plenary Session of the Supreme Court of the USSR of 12th December 1940. For more details about Soviet housing law see below under "The Law of Property".

cially he had been expelled for "indulging in economic speculation and conducting anti-soviet propaganda". Matthews dimissed both charges as quite unfounded. He admitted, however, to having sold a second-hand sweater to a Russian for £4.- the proper market price. He was unable to understand that in so doing he had violated the Soviet speculation law. The real motive for all Soviet actions against him and his fiancée had according to Matthews been purely political: "the authorities do not like marriages with foreigners, especially people who study the Soviet Union professionally". (1) Historically speaking this contention is not unfounded, bearing in mind the Edict of the 15th of February 1947, which prohibited marriages between Soviet citizens and aliens. (2) Although that edict was abrogated by a Decree of the Supreme Soviet of the USSR of the 26th of November 1953, the political motives which prompted its promulgation have never disappeared. We have to admit, however, that the officially stated reasons relating to a transaction made at a profit, may also be genuine. For similar transactions, or in more general terms, for living from incomes not acquired through labour, Soviet citizens, and without doubt foreigners residing permanently in the USSR, are threatened with more severe sanctions. On the ground of the so-called anti-parasite laws inacted in the Union Republics in the years 1957-1961, these persons could be tried at public meetings of fellow-residents or in courts and punished with exile with forced labour for a period of two to five years. (3)

These are in essence the general rules embodying Soviet legislative public policy with respect to the individual's capacity. In addition there are in this domain some special legal provisions relating to foreigners only, which, as they are imperatively binding, must be treated accordingly in this study. As has been already mentioned, the basic provision governing foreigners' rights and duties in the USSR is contained in Article 122 of the Fundamentals of Civil Legislation. This provision, which has to be used as a starting point for discussing all problems regarding foreigners, provides: "Aliens shall enjoy in the USSR civil law capacity equally with Soviet citizens. Exemptions may

(1) see for a brief report on this case in Daily Telegraph, 22nd of June 1964, p. 1. Vedomosti Verkhovnogo Soveta SSSR, 1947, no. 10. For commentaries see: Lunts 1949, p. 302, and Gsovski, I p. 361. See also infra under Family Law.

(2) Vedomosti Verkhovnogo Soveta SSSR, 1947, no. 10. For commentaries see: Lunts 1949, p. 302, and Gsovski, I, p. 361. See also infra under Family Law.

(3) See e.g. Lipson, pp. 72-92.

be established by the law of the USSR". (1)
Exemptions from the basic rule proclaiming equality between Soviet citizens and foreigners were enacted on several occasions long before the Fundamentals were published. Many of them are still in force. To this category belong e.g. the legal provisions relating to some occupations from which non-citizens are barred. The legal imperatives in this category have been motivated, according to a Soviet lawyer, by paramount economic interests and the requirements of national security (2)

With regard to special restrictions on the foreigner's choice of occupation, it is noteworthy that Article 6 of the Mining Statute of 1927 excludes foreigners from mining activities except for cases in which special permission has been granted by the Soviet Government. According to the Statute on the Protection of Fish Stocks and the Control of Fisheries in the USSR of September 1928, foreign citizens and foreign legal persons are forbidden to engage in the fishing industry in Soviet waters, including rivers, lakes, internal seas and the territorial maritime belt of 12 sea miles. Foreigners may be granted fishing rights only by special international agreements. Similar limitations are also imposed by the Merchant Shipping Code of 1929 and the Code of Air Navigation of 1961. According to Section 53 of the Merchant Shipping Code, Soviet citizenship is required for being a member of a crew. Some exceptions to this rule are provided by the Code, but they do not apply to masters of the ship, first mates and radiotelegraphist; for these functions Soviet citizenship is required under all circumstances. Soviet citizenship is also required by Section 19 of the Air Navigation Code for working as a member of the crew of a civil aircraft.

In addition, it should be mentioned that Soviet public policy concerning the position of aliens is also reflected in a number of measures governing their entry, residence and exit. In particular these measures govern the requirements as to passport and entry visas, customs and currency regulations, the limitations as to the kind of articles which may be taken into the USSR, the rule that the only point at which the USSR may be

(1) According to Article 123 of the Fundamentals of Civil Legislation, the same rule applied also to stateless persons. This additional provision, which in the official translation of Article 122 seems superfluous, is a necessary supplementary rule in the original Russian text: while Article 122 speaks of "Foreign citizens" (inostrannye grazhdane), Article 123 refers ro "persons without citizenship" (litsa bez grazhdanstva).
(2) Boguslavskii, Rubanov, 1962, p. 57.

entered is that indicated on the visa (1) and all the police measures authorising a stay in the USSR (residence permits or endorsements made in the foreigner's passport, depending on the length of residence) or controlling the movements of foreigners (who are barred altogether from some localities) etc. (2).

(1) Infringements of the regulations relating to the entry into or the exit from the USSR are punishable by deprivation of liberty for a period of one to three years. (See: Law on the criminal responsibility for crimes against the state of December 1958, Article 20).
(2) For more details see: Boguslavskii, Rubanov, 1962, pp. 44 et seq. See also the Decree of the Presidium of the Supreme Soviet of the USSR dated July 1966, according to which for a persistent infringement of the regulations concerning stay and movement in the USSR, foreigners and stateless persons shall be punished with deprivation of liberty or forced labour for one year or with a fine of 50 Roubles (Vedomosti SSSR, 1966, no. 30).

State monopoly of foreign commerce. Soviet legislative public policy relating to foreign commerce is implemented in the general system of State monopoly in this domain and in the rules emanating from this system. The Soviet State monopoly of foreign commerce, which is exercised by the Minister of Foreign Trade, is based on the communist policy of expropriation of every form of capital and capitalistic accumulation and on the treatment of private commerce as a source of unearned income and parasitism. Consequently no private person residing in the USSR is legally capable of concluding a foreign trade agreement on his own behalf; he may act only as a representative of the legal entities authorized by laws and statutes to carry on commercial operations. The operative enforcement of the State monopoly in this field is realized either by Soviet trade delegations (in the countries to which they are sent) or by the government corporations authorized for this purpose by the Ministry of Foreign Trade. The capacity of these corporations to enter into foreign commercial transactions is based on a decree of the USSR Council of People's Commissars of the 27th of July 1935, which provided as follows: "The People's Commissariat for Foreign Trade shall be permitted to authorise the export, import and mixed export-import, as well as transport, and trade combinations operating under its authority to enter, in the name of a given combination and within the limits of its charter, into legal transactions with foreign firms in the territory of the USSR and abroad, as well as to issue bills and notes to foreign firms and to accept bills and notes from them in pursuit of such transactions". (1) The Ministry's authorization is also indispensable for permanent commercial activities on Soviet territory by foreign firms. This matter was regulated originally by the decree of the 11th of March 1931, entitled: "On the procedure for admission of foreign firms to run commercial operations in the territory of the U.S.S.R." (2) According to Article 1 of this decree, a foreign firm wishing to carry on commercial operations in the USSR must first obtain a permit from the Ministry of Foreign Trade of the USSR. After this permit has been granted the foreign firm must comply with the laws and regulations of the USSR (3).

(1) Quoted from Gsovski, I, pp. 469-470.

(2) Sobranie Zakonov SSSR, 1931, no. 24, p. 197.

(3) Article 9 of the decree 1931.

In Article 12 of the same decree it is provided that foreign firms and foreigners concluding individual commercial transactions with Soviet commercial organizations are not bound to obtain a special permit. As Pereterskii put it: "If foreign firms come to the USSR in pursuit of an agreement with a Soviet trade organisation for carrying negotiations and for the conclusion of separate contracts, i.e., on short term, ...it is not required that the foreign firm should obtain a special permit or should be registered for admission to operation." (1)

The rule laid down in Article 12 of this decree is now replaced by Article 124 of the Fundamentals of Civil Legislation of the USSR, which provides that foreign firms need no permit to conclude contracts on Soviet territory with the competent Soviet organizations. Undoubtedly this does not mean that a foreign firm may establish a branch to conduct commercial operations on a permanent basis without a permit. Although the Fundamentals do not contain a provision similar to that of Article 1 of the decree of 1931, the conclusion cannot be drawn from this omission that no permit is required for more or less permanent foreign establishments on Soviet territory. From the general principles of the Soviet economic and legal systems, both notorious for their restrictive and protectionistic character, it can be inferred that the old rules requiring preliminary permission for permanent etablishments will be maintained in the future.

The power of the Soviet Ministry of Foreign Trade is not limited only to giving a general authorization for foreign commercial transactions. The Ministry is also empowered to issue or deny, to cancel or prolong a licence for each individual commercial transaction (2) guided by the interests of Soviet foreign policy alone. In this matter the decision of the Ministry is absolutely binding upon the parties, with the effect that a contract without a licence can produce no legal consequences. This was convincingly illustrated in an award rendered on the 3rd of July 1958 by the Foreign Trade Arbitration Commission in Moscow, on a claim filed by the Jordan Investment Ltd., an Israeli Company, (referred to as "the Company") against the Soviet All-Union Foreign Trade Corporation "Soiuznefteksport", (referred to as "the Corporation"). (3)

"In accordance with a contract concluded on the 17th of July,

(1) Pereterskii, Krylov, 1959, p. 90.

(2) For the view of Western lawyers that the export-import restrictions are part of a country's public policy, see e.g. Dölle, pp. 406-407.

(3) The Award is translated by Martin Domke: The Israeli-Soviet Oil Arbitration. In: Am. Journal of Intern.Law, 1959, pp. 800-806.

1956, in Moscow, between the (Israeli) Company and the (Soviet) Corporation; the Corporation undertook to furnish the Company, during the years 1957 and 1958 with 650 tons of heavy fuel oil F.O.B. Black Sea ports. On the 4th of August, 1956, the Corporation applied to the USSR Ministry of Foreign Trade, hereinafter referred to as the 'Ministry', for an export licence. On the 5th of November, 1956, The Ministry by letter advised the Corporation that the licences applied for in accordance with the above contract dated July 17th, 1956, would not be granted and that performance of the contract was prohibited. On the 6th of November, 1956, the Corporation informed the Company that the Ministry had advised the Corporation to the effect that export licences for shipment of fuel oil during the years 1957 and 1958 as per terms of contract, dated July 17th, 1956, would not be issued and that accordingly pursuant to the *Force Majeure Clause* (paragraph 7 of the Contract) (1), the contract was thereby cancelled...... On the 25th of October, 1957, the Company filed a complaint against the Corporation before the Foreign Trade Arbitration Commission...... . In its complaint the Company charged that the Corporation had unilaterally and illegally cancelled the contract of the 17th of July, 1956, and that as a result of such violation of the contract by the Corporation, the Company had been compelled to purchase fuel oil elsewhere in substitution for the quantities which the Corporation had undertaken to furnish in accordance with the contract, and that, furthermore, the Company had been compelled to conclude charter-parties for the shipment of the fuel oil thus purchased. The Company claimed damages to the amount of US$"2.396.440,69 and demanded payment of the amount by the Corporation. The Company further sought to establish its right to compensation for additional losses and damages in excess of the above amount which the Company had incurred or might incur due to the violation of the contract, and finally the Company asked that the Corporation be compelled to pay the Company all costs and expenses in the arbitration proceedings. In its brief filed with the Foreign Trade Arbitration Commission

(1) Force Majeure Clause provided: "Neither of the parties shall be liable for any damage or non-compliance with terms of this contract or any part of these terms, if this damage of non-compliance is due to one or more of the following events preventing one or the other party from performing its duties under the contract in whole or in part; natural disasters, fire, flood, war-like acts of any kind, blockades, strikes on the vessel carrying goods under this contract, acts or demands of the Government or other authoritative agencies of the country under whose flag the chartered tanker belongs (but excluding the Government and authoritative agencies of the State of Israel), due to any other cause of whatever nature beyong the control of the non-performing party."

in reply to the above complaint, the Corporation stated that it did not recognize the Company's claim and considered it completely unfounded. The Corporation pointed out that performance of the contract had become impossible as a result of the ban imposed by the Ministry. Therefore, in accordance with Article 118 and paragraph "d" of Article 129 of the Civil Code of the R.S.F.S.R. (1), the obligation of the Corporation to supply fuel oil to the Company should be considered as having completely ceased to exist. Accordingly and by virtue of paragraph 7 of the contract, the Corporation asked to be released from any liability..." The Foreign Trade Arbitration Commission, consisting of P.E.Orlovsky as Umpire and M.V.Nesterov and D.M.Genkin as Arbitrators, dimissed the complaint as unfounded.

There are two essential points in this award bearing on our topic: The imperative character of the Ministry's refusal of an export licence and the implied public policy considerations in the act of refusal. Both points were brought out in the objections of the Soviet Corporation to the complaint and were reaffirmed in the "Rationale" of the Award. "The prohibition by the Ministry", contended the defendant, "made it impossible for the Corporation to perform the contract...... In this case, such inability to perform could neither be anticipated nor could it be prevented through the efforts of the Corporation. Therefore... the Corporation must be released from any and all liability towards the Company. In this connection the Corporation *stresses the situation prevailing at the beginning of November 1956, and created by agression against Egypt,* in view of which conditions the licence was denied to the Corporation and performance of the contract was prohibited."

The continuation of export to Israel was considered by the Soviet government as detrimental to the interests of Egypt, at the time a friendly nation. (2)

Considering that the denial of a licence constituted one of the

(1) Article 118, RSFSR Civil Code of 1922: "Unless otherwise provided by law or contract, the debtor shall be relieved from liability for nonperformance, if he proves that impossibility of performance resulted from circumstances which he could not prevent, or that it came about owing to intentional design or negligence of the creditor."
Article 129, final paragraph: "An obligation shall terminate either in full or in part: .. by impossibility of performance for which the debtor cannot be held liable (Article 118)". See Gsovski, II, pp. 107, 110.

(2) These measures are reminiscent of a case of British public policy invalidating foreign trade transactions which are considered as compromising the international friendly relations of the country. Cf. Graveson, pp. 572-574; and Cheshire, pp. 138-139.

circumstances provided in the concluding words of Article 7 of the contract dealing with "force majeure" the Arbitration Commission maintained: "Denial of the licence and prohibition of performance of the contract..... on the part of the Ministry, being absolutely binding upon the Corporation, does in fact constitute such circumstances releasing the latter from liablity."

Whether we have to accept the Soviet legal device of separation between the fisc on the one hand and the Commercial Corporations or Arbitration Commission on the other, one thing is clear: neither of them can act contrary to the instructions of the Ministry of Foreign Trade because the ultimate authority for exercising foreign commercial or commercial arbitration functions is vested in the Ministry.

According to Soviet law, the foreign trade organizations are legal entities distinct from the State and, like all other Soviet State enterprises with legal personality, they are not liable for the State's debts; conversely, the State never accepts liability for obligations incurred by State enterprises (1). All such State enterprises conclude contracts on their own behalf and for their own account. Their capacity is limited only to special groups of commercial transactions clearly defined in their statutes. Lastly, they do not enjoy immunity of jurisdiction in contradistinction to Soviet Trade Agencies (torgpredstva), and they are liable for their debts to the extent of the assets allocated to them by the State with the exception of the means of production such as buildings, machinery, ships, etc.

An illustration of the peculiar character of Soviet Corporations as legal persons distinct from the State is shown in one of the earliest decisions of the Maritime Arbitration Commission in Moscow, to which attention has been drawn in Western literature. In Re Motorship "King Edgar" (1932) the Commission had to adjudicate in a dispute between the Soviet Merchant Fleet Corporation and English shipowners, the former claiming compensation for having rendered assistance to the latter's motorship King Edgar when aground in Soviet territorial waters. The defence of the shipowners that their ship had run aground owing to the negligence of the plaintiffs, as the Soviet maritime authorities had misleadingly placed the buoys in territorial waters, was rejected by the Commission with the following arguments:

"Sovtorgflot (Soviet Merchant Fleet Corporation) operates as

(1) The liabilities of Soviet State enterprises as legal persons are determined in a more general manner by Article 13 of the Fundamentals of Civil Legislation. This section has preserved the old principles unchanged. See also: Articles 32 and 33 of the RSFSR Civil Code, 1964.

an independent unit on the basis of separate economic accounting; that is, it constitutes an independent juridical person. The supervision of buoys is a function of the People's Commissariat for War and Maritime Affairs. By virtue of Article 4 of its charter of incorporation Sovtorgflot is not responsible for the debts of the State and of other enterprises and organizations, nor is the State responsible for the debts of Sovtorgflot. Consequently... no responsibility can be attributed to Sovtorgflot for any acts or omissions of other Soviet organisations" (1).

It has been mentioned above that Soviet Trade Agencies (Torgpredstva) are also authorized to conclude transactions in foreign commerce in the territories to which they are sent. A few words on their legal status are necessary.

An authority on private international law comparing "torgpredstva" with the ordinary Soviet foreign trade corporations highlights the following characteristic features of the former: Foreign Trade Agencies are not legal entities; they conclude commercial transactions on behalf of, and for the account of, the Soviet State and possess general capacity, i.e., they may conclude all kinds of commercial transactions; the State alone bears the material responsibility for such transactions, but in its capacity of Sovereign it claims immunity from jurisdiction so that the claims of foreign firms against the Trade Agencies are never enforceable in courts unless this immunity has been waived by agreement or a special unilateral act (2).

A word of explanation is necessary with regard to the Soviet claim of immunity from jurisdiction, which according to Levitin "derives from the principle of respect for State sovereignty and undoubtedly pertains to the fundamentals of the Soviet system", so that any non-recognition of this claim is contrary to Soviet

(1) Transl.: Pisar, p. 644; see also Lunts, 1949, pp. 180-181.

(2) Genkin, 1960, pp. 24,25. The principles governing the legal status of Soviet Trade Agencies and Soviet Commercial Organisations are reflected also in Article 8 of the French-Soviet Commercial Agreement of 1951, which provides:

"The commercial Representation of the USSR in France shall carry out its duties in the name of the USSR. The Government of the USSR shall only assume responsibility for commercial transactions concluded and guaranteed in France in the name of the Commercial Representations and signed by duly authorised persons.

Commercial transactions concluded without the guarantee of the Commercial Representation of the USSR in France, by any State Economic Organisation of the USSR, possessing, in terms of the law of the USSR the status of a distinct legal personality, shall only involve the responsibility of the above-mentioned organisation and execution shall be effected solely upon its effects. No responsibility shall lie either with the Government of the USSR in France, or with any other economic organisation of the USSR".

public policy. (1) The Soviet State claims the following immunities for her Trade Agencies:

1. Immunity from jurisdiction in general. (2)
2. Immunity from seizure of assets belonging to the commercial agencies as a measure of security.
3. Immunity from enforcement actions against the agencies' property pursuant to foreign judgements.

With regard to the first immunity, the following particuliarities should be borne in mind:
Immunity from jurisdiction is claimed only in cases where the Trade Agencies have to appear as defendants. They may, however, bring an action in a foreign court, i.e., as plaintiffs against foreign firms. In such a case, according to Soviet doctrine, the foreign defendant must abstain from advancing counter-claims unless the competent Soviet authorities have expressly consented to this. (3)

Soviet Trade Agencies may submit to the jurisdiction of a foreign court only with express consent for the case in issue or pursuant to an agreement between the USSR and the foreign country concerned. Section 4 of the regulations on the "Torgpredstva" (Trade Agencies) dated the 13th of September 1933 (4) reads: "As a defendant the Trade Agencies may appear before foreign judicial organs only in disputes arising out of commercial transactions concluded by the Trade Agencies in the foreign country and only in those countries with regard to which the Government of the USSR by means of agreement or unilateral declaration communicated to the Government of the State concerned, has expressed its consent to submission of the commercial agency to the local courts with respect to the mentioned disputes." A note added to this Section states that "the Government of the USSR may also give the Trade Agent in his official letters, permission to insert in the contracts which he concludes a clause of submission of disputes, arising out of these contracts, to the local courts."

In conformity with these regulations the Soviet Union has concluded with some countries agreements whereby it has waived its immunity of jurisdiction with regard to disputes arising out of commercial transactions concluded in the territory of the respective countries.

(1) Levitin, p. 226.
(2) Cf. Pereterskii, Krylov, 1959, pp. 197-206; Pereterskii, Krylov 1940, pp. 118-131; Lunts, I (1959), pp. 187-188; Boguslavskii, 1956, p. 58: Lisovskii, pp. 223-225.
(3) Lunts, 1949, p. 340; Pereterskii, Krylov, 1959, p. 203.
(4) See: Sobranie Zakonov SSSR 1933, no. 59, p. 354.

Even if the USSR waives its immunity of jurisdiction, it is submitted that it does not follow from this that all the rules of procedure in force in the country concerned apply to the Soviet Trade Agency. If the latter has submitted to the jurisdiction of a foreign court and a decision is rendered against the Soviet agency, the question of enforcement of this decision, for instance, remains open. It is maintained in Soviet writings that an immunity *sui generis* exists with regard to the enforcement of a judgement which is in no way affected by the general waiver of the immunity of jurisdiction (1).

As an illustration the agreement with Norway (1925), which provides that all disputes shall be resolved in accordance with Norwegian procedural law, is cited. A Soviet legal writer explains that since nothing is said in the agreement about security of action or about compulsory enforcement neither of the two measures may be taken against the property of Soviet agencies located in Norway. Such property is immune from enforcement, as it belongs to a Sovereign, unless this immunity also has been explicitly waived. (2).

Many foreign countries, being aware of the difficulties which the far-reaching immunity claims of Soviet Trade Agencies may cause, have required that their commercial agreements include a clause in which the Soviet Union explicitly waives the immunities of seizure and enforcement actions against assets belonging to her Trade Agencies.

As examples of such agreements we may mention:

The agreements on the legal status of Soviet Trade Delegations concluded with Sweden in 1927, with Great Britain in 1934 and with North Vietnam and Iraq in 1958; the commercial agreements with Rumania of 1947, with Austria of 1955, with the Korean PR of 1960, etc.

Each of these agreements varies slightly in its provisions on the matter at issue, but what they have in common is that a judgement rendered against the Soviet Trade Agency may be en-

(1) Pereterskii, Krylov, 1959, p. 206; Lisovskii, 1955, p. 224; cf. also Pereterskii, Krylov, 1940, p. 124.

(2) The same opinion has been expressed by French "Cour d'appèl d'Aix (4e Ch)" 9-XII-1938, which refused execution of a judgement against a foreign Sovereign with the following motivation:

"Mais attendu qu'en admettant que l'Etat étranger ait laissé une jurisdiction francaise trancher le litige le concernant, le bénéficiaire de la sentence ne pourrait acquérir de ce fait le droit de l'exécuter sur l'Etat condamné, par la saisie de ses biens, qu'ils appartiennent au domaine public ou privé car semblable exécution constituerait, hors le cas d'une renonciation expresse de l'Etat à ce privilège, un act de violence incompatible avec la souveraineté et l'indépendence des Etats. "Cf. Journal du Droit International 1939, no,3-4, p. 599.

forced against its assets with the exception of the property necessary for the carrying out of its official functions, which remain immune and may not be the object of enforcement measures.

In default of an agreement, the general rules are expected to apply. From the very beginning of its existence the Soviet State has claimed an absolute immunity from jurisdiction for its officials. Theory has faithfully followed practice, while recent legislation takes for granted the principles stated above. In contradistinction to the old Soviet practice and theory, which were concerned with the immunity claims of the Soviet State rather than with rules on foreign States' immunities in the USSR, the Fundamentals of Civil Procedure of 1961 followed a quite different and more appropriate method. Foreign States are granted *absolute* immunity (1), and in the absence of reciprocity, and only then, the Soviet Government *may* provide corresponding measures for restricting the immunities of a foreign State. The matter is dealt with by Article 61 of the "Fundamentals", which provides:

"Filing of a suit against a foreign country, securing collection of a claim and attachment of property of a foreign country located in the USSR may be permitted only with the consent of the competent organs of the country concerned.

Diplomatic representatives of foreign countries accredited in the USSR and other persons specified in the relevant laws and international agreements shall be subject to the jurisdiction of the Soviet court in civil cases, only within the limits determined by the rules of international law or agreements with the countries concerned.

In cases where a foreign country does not accord the Soviet State , its representatives or its property the same judicial immunity which, in accordance with the present Article, is accorded foreign countries, their representatives or their property in the USSR, the council of Ministers of the USSR or other authorized organ may impose retaliatory measures in respect of that country, its representatives or the property of that country."

Although the principle of reciprocity is not explicitly provided for in respect of the immunity of a foreign State, it seems improbable that the Soviet government will fail to answer with retaliation whenever the absolute immunity of the Soviet State is not respected. The law itself, however, provides only the possibility of recourse to retaliation by the Soviet government. Whatever the extent of the Soviet rule relating to the absolute

(1) Lunts, 1962 (in: Novoe...), p. 64.

immunity of foreign States may be, one thing remains beyond any doubt: that the claim of the Soviet State to an absolute immunity from jurisdiction pertains to the domain of Soviet public policy and that no decision or act of a foreign State's authority ignoring this claim will ever be recognized in the USSR.

In many Western countries, courts and legislatures are inclined to recognize foreign State's absolute immunity without discrimination (1). Such a non-discriminatory approach, followed by the courts of the Netherlands (2), is not always justified, because, as Fensterwald says: "Communism and State socialism as practical realities are new factors which were not seriously considered when the rules of sovereign immunity were crystallized". The treatment of the Soviet State in Western courts on an equal footing with States having a free economy may lead to results detrimental to innocent firms concerned. The economic and legal system of the USSR is so flexible that nobody can say in advance precisely where the Sovereign functions of the Soviet State begin and where they end. An example given by Kiralfy and based on "in Re Motorship 'King Edgar' quoted above, shows how complicated this problem can be: "Soviet public corporations are distinct from the Soviet State, but clame to share its immunity. The results are interesting. If a warship of the Russian navy negligently damages a foreign vessel, the Russian mercantile shipping administration may nonetheless recover salvage claims for saving it as the two agencies are not to be identified. On the other hand the administration would, it is insisted, be entitled to rely on the immunity of a foreign sovereign if one of its vessels negligently damaged a vessel belonging to a Western firm". (3)

Regulations as to the form. The foregoing comments reflect the basic rules governing the Soviet State monopoly of foreign trade and the legal status of persons charged with its practical realization. Considering the foreign trade monopoly as a sovereign function of the Soviet Union, Soviet lawyers maintain that the legal capacity and the form of the transactions in this domain

(1) Among the supporters of absolute immunity may be mentioned e.g. Great Britain, The Netherlands and until 1952 also the USA. The USA changed its attitude in 1952 when the Department of State announced that "with respect to its own action regarding requests from foreign governments for a grant of immunity from suit, it would follow the restrictive theory" developed in the civil law countries led by Belgium and Italy, and providing that with respect to her acts of a private character a State is held to be properly subject to suit before the local courts in the same way as private persons (Cf. Setser, pp. 291-316. See also: Fensterwald, pp. 614-642).

(2) See Fensterwald, p. 636 and the decision which he quotes of the Amsterdam court of appeal in the case Weber v. Promsyrioimport, where the USSR was involved. 30th April 1942, (1942) Nederlandsche Jurisprudentie, no. 757.

(3) Kiralfy, p. 122.

are also manifestations of this sovereign function, and that they are therefore imperatively binding (1).

More recently, following attempts made in the West (2) to qualify the rules under consideration and speaking exclusively in terms of private international law, Lunts made the following additional explanation:

"There are questions which are decided only on the basis of Soviet law, irrespective of any foreign element which may be found in the situation underlying the transaction. For instance, regulations prescribing the method of signing contracts of foreign trade made by Soviet organizations are closely connected with the State monopoly of foreign trade and are governed exclusively by Soviet law, these regulations being - to use a French expression, - 'lois d'ordre public'." (3).

Thus the problem of the application of foreign law arises only in connection with the substance of a foreign trade transaction. The form and the procedure for the signing of such transactions, when Soviet organizations are parties to them, are always governed by Soviet law. In particular, the requirement of the written form is imperative - Soviet organizations have no right to make contracts in oral form. This rule is now incorporated in Article 125, paragraph 2, of the Fundamentals of Civil Legislation, which states:

"The form of foreign trade transactions concluded by Soviet organizations, and the procedure governing their signature, regardless of the place where such transactions are concluded, shall be determined by the legislation of the USSR; while, according to Article 14, paragraph 4, of the Fundamentals: "non-compliance with the form of foreign trade transactions and the procedure governing their signature (Article 125 of the present Fundamentals) shall entail invalidation of the transaction."

The main rules governing formalities in foreign trade transactions are laid down in the Resolutions of the 13th of October 1930, the 26th of December 1935 and the 8th of December 1936, issued by the Central Executive Committee and the Council of

(1) Lunts, 1961, p. 273; Ramzaitsev, 1957, p. 51; Pereterskii, Krylov, 1959, pp. 126-130; Ramzaitsev. 1964, pp. 142-143.

(2) Bringing Soviet initial opinions to their logical conclusion, the writer of this paper qualified the Soviet formality rules as early as 1964 as being of a public policy character. (See my article "Soviet private international law relating to carriage by sea." In: The Modern Law Review, 1964, no.4, p. 415). Schmitthoff also admitted the possibility of considering these rules as pertaining to Soviet order public, without taking a personal attitude on this matter. (See: Schmitthoff, p. 10).

(3) Lunts, 1965, pp. 15-16.

People's Commissars of the USSR. They may be summarized as follows.

As a rule all contracts in foreign trade, promissory notes, warranties and money obligations of all kinds must be signed by two persons. The particular persons capable of signing vary, depending on the contracting party they have to represent. The contracts made on behalf of the Trade Agencies abroad must be signed in the first place either by the Trade representative or by his deputy or, on authorization of the Trade representative, by a person leading a division of the Trade Agency; in the second place it must also be signed by a member of the staff of the Trade Agency whose name appears on a special list approved by the Ministry of Foreign Trade.

The lists of persons authorized to sign contracts on behalf of the Trade Agencies of the USSR and their divisions, are communicated to the Governments of the countries concerned and published in the corresponding organs of the press.

By way of exception to this rule a Trade representative may also validly sign a contract with a single signature quite independently if the contract involves a sum up to 400,000 rubles (= 40,000 new roubles) and with a permit from the Minister of Foreign Trade or his deputy if the contract involves a higher amount of money.

On behalf of a Soviet economic organization a contract must be signed by two persons duly authorized by the management of the organization. In particular, the contracts of All-Union Foreign Trade Combines have to be signed by the President of the Combine in all cases where the place of contracting is outside Moscow (e.g. abroad or in another Soviet town.) If, however, the contract of a Foreign Trade Combine is to be made in Moscow, the signature of the President of the Combine or his deputy is required, together with the signature of a person authorized for this purpose by the President; in cases where promissory notes and other money obligations with respect to foreign trade are issued or undertaken in Moscow, the second signature must be that of the accountant-general of the combine. It should also be noted that only those persons are considered duly authorized to sign foreign trade contracts whose names are published in the official organ of the Ministry of Foreign Trade "Vneshniaia Torgovlia". Furthermore, the control of the Ministry of Foreign Trade is made all-pervasive by the requirement that all authorizations for foreign trade (with the exception of those issued by the State Bank, and the Bank of Foreign Trade) be made with a special permit issued by the Ministry or the cor-

responding Trade representative abroad (1).
The Foreign Trade Arbitration Commission in Moscow (F.T.A.C.) invoked the rules of form for the first time in its Award of 1937 rendered in the case Shenker v. All-Union Organization "Raznoimport".

The plaintiff, a French firm, claimed compensation for transport expenses at a rate higher than that agreed in the written contract, basing its claim on an oral promise allegedly given to it by the representative of the defendant (the Soviet firm). F.T.A.C. rejected the claim of the French firm with the following motivation.

"If we assume that the assertion of the plaintiff is correct that the president of "Raznoimport" has promised to pay a rate increased in accordance with the devaluation of the Franc, such promises and statements cannot be considered as a consent and obligation of the defendant (All-Union organization "Raznoexport"). Soviet law (Resolution of the USSR C.E.C. and the C.P.C. of the 13th of October 1930, changed by the Resolution of the 26th December 1935) has established a special procedure for the signing of foreign trade contracts, non-compliance with which makes a contract void.... According to the obvious meaning of the law, the same procedure must also be complied with in cases of modification of already concluded foreign trade contracts... Therefore according to private international law, the Resolutions of the Supreme authorities of the USSR already mentioned also have to be applied in those cases where the contract concerned is to be governed by the law of another country" (2).

The legal basis of this claim has been strongly criticized by the American lawyer Samuel Pisar (3). "The imperative operation of the special Soviet formality law - writes Pisar - is postulated by the Soviet doctrine as a principle of private international law binding extraterritorially upon foreign courts just as much as upon domestic courts... the juridical basis of this claim, however, is very doubtful. Its starting point is the public nature of the USSR's foreign-trade activities. A refusal on the part of a foreign court to apply the special law is considered to be tantamount to an infringement of the sovereign rights

(1) See: Vilkov, pp. 130-131; Ramzaitsev, 1957, pp. 51-52; Lunts, II(1963), pp. 158 et seq. Gsovski, I, pp. 470-471.
(2) See: Lunts, 1949, pp. 236-237; Ramzaitsev, 1957, p. 53. Legal provisions of a public policy character regarding form are also to be found in the West-European legislations, but they have a more limited scope of operation, than in Soviet law. Cf. e.g. Frankenstein, 1930, p. 322 and Louis-Lucas, pp. 425-426.
(3) Pisar, p. 654.

of the Soviet State." Pisar rightly observes further that "from the point of view of Soviet conflict of laws this claim discloses a basic inconsistency" because Soviet foreign commercial corporations cannot be at the same time both legal persons separate from the State and "governmental agencies performing a sovereign function".

The rule stated above applies also to the legal capacity of Soviet foreign trade organizations, as well as to mandates and powers of attorney given by such organizations to their representatives and agents abroad. These are always determined by Soviet law irrespective of whether the proper law of the principal contract is Soviet or foreign (1).

Merchant Shipping. Public policy manifested itself very conspicuously in the domain of merchant shipping. It was a policy of a rigid protectionism of an economic branch too weak at the time for competition in international commerce. This policy motivated the abnormal competence which was given to Soviet law by virtue of the one-sided conflict rules contained in Article 4, paragraph "b", of the Soviet Merchant Shipping Code.

The principal preoccupation of the Soviet legislature when drawing up the Merchant Shipping Code of 1929 (2) was to guarantee the widest possible scope of application. This has been realized by laying down a few application rules imperative in character and extraterritorial in effect. By virtue of these rules, which demonstrate a combination of territoriality and nationality principles, the majority of sea transport cases have to be decided by the Soviet substantive law. This fact is explicitly admitted in the Soviet literature.

"The conflict rules of the Soviet maritime law are directed towards the application of the Soviet law; its function is to ensure the proper application of the Soviet maritime law" (3). Undoubtedly, this principle is not applied in cases where it does not serve the interest of the Soviet State efficiently, because, as was stated in a recent publication devoted to Soviet maritime law, "the State participating in merchant shipping, lays down conflict rules which take into account the protection of its interests" (4).

(1) Genkin, 1960, p. 7 et seq., p. 19 et seq.: Lunts 1961, p. 274.

(2) The articles of the Merchant Shipping Code quoted in this paper are translated by Szirmai and Korevaar unless otherwise indicated.

(3) Keilin, p. 18.

(4) Shmigel'skii, Iasinovskii, p. 25.

In fact the Soviet Merchant Shipping Code does not contain a conflict rule for determining the proper law of a contract for carriage by sea. It lays down only some application rules which clearly define the domain which the Soviet law reserves for itself to the total exclusion of any foreign law. The principles so established are not to be interpreted in the sense that by implication they determine which foreign law shall apply in cases which do not come within the sovereign control of the Code. The latter cases are governed by the general rules of Soviet private international law.

According to the Code, its provisions concerning carriage by sea are applicable to contracts of carriage between the ports of the USSR, from Soviet ports to foreign ones and also when the dispute is dealt with by a judicial institution of the USSR or a Union Republic as concerning a contract of carriage from abroad to the ports of the USSR. In addition, the provisions of the Code apply to contracts of carriage by sea between two foreign ports, if one or both parties are citizens or legal entities of the USSR (1). These rules are incorporated in Article 4, paragraph "b", of the Merchant Shipping Code of the USSR, which provides literally:

> "the provisions contained in parts A and B of Chapter V (on contracts of carriage by sea) apply to contracts of carriage by sea between ports of the USSR and to those from a port within the USSR to a foreign port; they also apply to contracts of carriage by sea from abroad to a port of the USSR when the dispute is dealt with by a court of the USSR or of a Union Republic, as well as to contracts of carriage by sea from one foreign port to another, provided that one or both of the parties are Soviet citizens or legal entities of the USSR" (2).

With regard to the last category of carriage by sea, viz. that between two foreign ports, Soviet authorities explain that by virtue of the nationality principle accepted in the Soviet Code it applies both to the case in which Soviet cargo is carried on foreign ships and when Soviet ships carry foreign goods (3).

The nationality principle is also used as a criterion for the application of the Code's provisions dealing with time charters. Pursuant to Article 4, paragraph "e", the provisions of the Soviet Code laid down in Chapter V, Part B, and relating

(1) Keilin, p. 18; Lunts, 1949, pp. 279-280; Avsov, Egorev, Keilin, p. 98. See also Dobrin, p. 252.

(2) This translation of Article 4, paragraph "b", is in slight deviation from the one made by Z. Szirmai and J. Korevaar.

(3) Avsov, Egorev, Keilin, p. 98.

to time charters "apply to contracts in which both parties or one of them are citizens or legal entities of the USSR".

Generally speaking the rules laid down in Article 4, paragraph "b", of the Soviet Merchant Shipping Code are given an extensive sphere of operation. They purport to cover not only cases of carriage under bills of lading, but also those effected under charter parties. On the other hand they have a restrictive legal effect as to the Code's articles which must be complied with by the parties entering into such contracts. Apart from the several imperative rules contained in the Code which may not be departed from by the contracting parties, the rest of the provisions bearing only a directive character may be dispensed with or replaced by other rules, provided that the parties agree to that effect. If, however, there is no such agreement, the whole contract has, by virtue of Article 4, to be governed by the Code. In such a case at least the Soviet courts will apply not only the mandatory rules of the Code, but also its directive ones (1).

The scope of application of the Soviet Maritime Code has been illustrated by one of the pre-war decisions of the Maritime Arbitration Commission at the All-Union Chamber of Commerce in Moscow (2). The arbitrators appointed in accordance with paragraph 30 of the Statute and Articles 5 and 7 of the regulations of the Maritime Arbitration Commission considered at a public sitting on the 28th of November 1936 a claim for damages filed by the All-Union Corporation for the Export of Petroleum "Soiuznefteksport", Moscow, against the French company "Courtages et Transports", Paris. Being confronted with a case containing international elements the Commission had first of all to decide what was the applicable law. The facts of this case (cited as Re Breach of Charter of the Steamship "Phoenix") are as follows:

According to a charter party of the 6th of November 1935, made in Moscow, the defendants had accepted several thousand tons of benzine, and other petroleum products, for carriage from a Soviet port to Istanbul. When the goods were unloaded in Turkey they were found to have been damaged as a result of some defects in the ship. The Commission, applying the Soviet Code, accepted the claim for damages advanced by the Soviet corporation for the following reasons:

"The contract for the charter of the Steamship Phoenix (sailing under French flag) was concluded in Moscow between

(1) See Pisar, p. 621.

(2) Re Breach of Character of the Steamship "Phoenix". See also: Pisar, p. 620.

Soviet foreign trade Combine 'Soiuzneftеksport' and the French company 'Courtages et Transports' for carriage of goods from a Soviet port to a foreign destination. Paragraph 13 of the charter provides for submission of the contract to the law of the flag, viz. French law. By virtue of Article 4, paragraph b of the Merchant Shipping Code of the USSR Soviet law is applicable to contracts of carriage by sea from a port in the USSR to a foreign port. This provision is of a mandatory character and cannot be excluded by the parties. At the same time according to Article 5 of the Merchant Shipping Code of the USSR it is admissible to stipulate the application of a foreign law within the limits in which the parties are allowed to depart from the rules laid down by the Code. The contractual relations between the parties arising out of the charter of Steamship Phoenix in all matters concerning the mandatory rules of the Soviet law are therefore governed by that law. With regard to questions which in Soviet law are governed by directory rules, French law may be applied" (1).

Foreign exchange and currency regulations(2). The imperative rules which form the legal expression of the economic foundation of the Soviet system govern also the foreign exchange regulations. The basic rules governing this matter are laid down in the Joint Resolution of the Central Executive Committee and Council of People's Commissars of the USSR of the 7th of January 1937, which proclaimed a State monopoly over transactions in foreign exchange (3).

Article 1 of this Act provides for "the exclusive right of the USSR State Bank (4) within the territory of the USSR to enter into legal transactions involving gold, silver, platinum and metals of the platinum group, in coin, bullion and ingots (raw materials) as well as foreign exchange and instruments reciting payment in foreign exchange (bills and notes, checks, money orders, etc.) and foreign securities (stocks, bonds, coupons, etc.)..." By this instrument it is established further that pay-

(1) There was no recent decision on the matter under consideration available to the writer of this paper. Therefore it is only fair to note that modern Soviet lawyers are inclined to deny the binding authority of the above award. Lunts for instance, commenting on Article 4, paragraph "b", of the Merchant Shipping Code at a colloquium of the Summer Session of the Hague Academy of International Law, 1965, declared that the present Soviet courts give a more liberal interpretation of the Article, admitting greater autonomy of the parties than was done in the award.

(2) On the public policy character of similar regulations cf. e.g. Valery, p. 198; Dölle, pp. 405-407; Maury, 1952, pp. 63-64; Neumayer, p. 64; Deelen, pp. 172-173.

(3) Translation: Gsovski, II, p. 49.

(4) At present this right is shared by Soviet Foreign Trade Bank. See Smirnov, chapter II, Lunts II(1963), pp. 231 et seq.

ments in foreign exchange shall be permitted in Soviet territory only for the purpose of foreign commerce. Exceptions can be made by law or in individual cases by special permission of the USSR Ministry of Finance (Articles 2 and 4). Payments and the acceptance of payments have to be made exclusively through the intermediary of the USSR State Bank (Article 2 in fine) (1).

From this Resolution and especially from Article 24 of the RSFSR Civil Code of 1922 (2) it was inferred that a legal presumption existed to the effect that all transactions in foreign exchange were forbidden with the exceptions mentioned. Payments and the acceptance of payments in foreign currencies in performance of obligations based on contracts to which a Soviet citizen is a party are also inadmissable on Soviet Territory. At present this rule is also laid down in Article 175 of the RSFSR Civil Code of 1964, which reads: "Debts must be expressed and paid in Soviet currency. The expression of debts and payments of debts in foreign currency is only permitted in the cases and by the procedures laid down by the legislation of the USSR" (3).

The imperatively binding force of Soviet foreign exchange regulations in all private international law cases is recognized and insisted upon by Soviet writings. The opinions in this respect are summarized in the following conclusion of Lunts (4).
"The effect of these rules extends also to legal relations which according to Soviet conflict law are governed by a foreign law; the submission of a legal relation to a foreign law cannot serve as a ground for any exception from the binding force of Soviet currency restrictions concerning this legal relation."

As illustration Lunts gives the following examples:

A debtor in a foreign trade transaction cannot pay his debt in the USSR in Soviet rubles instead of the agreed foreign currencies, notwithstanding the fact that the law to which the transaction was submitted admits such a substitution. In fact the substitution of money obligations was prohibited implicitly by the Resolution of 1937. Paragraph 3 of the Resolution provides: "Where the financial obligations arising from legal transactions in foreign commerce are in terms of foreign exchange, the making of payment in USSR currency is permitted only if

(1) See note 4 of the preceding page.

(2) According to Article 24 of the RSFSR Civil Code of 1922, the foreign exchange objects, as enumerated in Article 1 of the 1937 Resolution, "may be the objects of private legal transactions only in the manner and within the limits established by special laws." See text in: Gsovski, II, p. 48.

(3) Transl. by Kiralfy.

(4) Lunts II(1963), pp. 216-217.

such manner of payment is provided for by the terms of the transaction."

The second example put forward by Lunts relates to succession to valuables. According to him, the Soviet legal rules concerning the transmission of foreign exchange values to an heir living abroad will be applied independently of the rules of succession. The question of the transmission of money pertaining to the inherited property will always be decided in the USSR according to Soviet law, irrespective of whether the succession itself will be decided according to Soviet or foreign law.

"Infringement of currency regulations" and also speculation in currency or "documents of value" are punishable according to the USSR Law on the Criminal Responsibility for Crimes against the State (Section 25) and the laws of the Union Republics (see for instance Article 88 of the RSFSR Criminal Code). The punishments vary from 3 to 15 years imprisonment, while in especially grave cases the death penalty is incurred. In most cases confiscation of the foreign currencies is the sanction.

All sorts of transactions, such as sale/purchase, gift, deposit, exchange, etc., can constitute an infringement of the foreign exchange regulations if the object of the transactions is one of the valuables enumerated in the law, as being under State monopoly. Commodities, objects and ornaments made of gold, silver etc. may be transferred by contract as long as there is no intention to derive a profit. Individuals who become involved in transactions in similar objects with the purpose of making a profit are punishable as perpetrators of a state crime (Article 88 of the RSFSR Criminal Code) - speculation in foreign exchange (1).

Precious stones and pearls constitute a special category of foreign exchange valuables in the USSR. In spite of the fact that they are not placed under the system of State monopoly as described above, they may not be used by private persons as a means of effecting international payments. This conclusion may be inferred inter alia from the decision of the Military Collegium of the Supreme Court of the USSR in the case "Rakitianskii and others", where two of the accused were found guilty of infringement of Soviet foreign exchange regulations by secretly taking abroad and selling in East Germany diamonds and other valuables. The court gave the following elucidation:

"... The Decree of the CEC and CPC of the USSR dated the

(1) See: Mikhailov, p. 22. Article 154 of the Criminal Code of the RSFSR defines "speculation" as "the buying up and reselling of goods or any other articles for the purpose of making a profit".

7th of January 1937 and relating to Contracts in foreign exchange valuables and payments in foreign currency, the Statute of the State Bank, Section 137 of the RSFSR Civil Code of 1922 and Section 137 of the RSFSR Civil Code of 1964 enumerate only those foreign exchange valuables which are within the exclusive monopoly of the State Bank.

The monopoly of the State Bank does not extend to precious stones and to products derived from them in form of consumer goods, and they may be the object of any legal transactions in the territory of the USSR. This does not mean, however, that precious stones and their products are not considered by the State as foreign exchange valuables. In cases where they are used as a means of international payment and for this purpose are taken from the USSR to another country or from abroad to the USSR, they are considered as foreign exchange valuables.

This conclusion is based on the Decree of the Council of Ministers of the USSR dated 25th January 1948 "On the procedure of export, import exchange and sending abroad or from abroad to the USSR of currencies and foreign exchange valuables", as well as on the Instruction of the Ministry of Finance of the USSR dated the 1st of April 1949, no. 463, concerning the application of the Decree.

In paragraphs 9 and 10 of this Decree it is expressly provided that precious stones, pearls and products thereof pertain to the foreign exchange valuables just as gold, silver, platinum and metals of the platinum group (in bullion, scraps and manufactured articles) and may be taken abroad only according to the norms and the procedure established by the Ministry of Finance of the USSR and on the condition that they are for personal use..." (1)

In principle the keeping of foreign exchange objects is not prohibited unless they have been obtained by criminal acts. However, the possession of a significant amount of valuables always implies the assumption that these valuables have been obtained through the commission of a crime, because it is universally known that there is no legal way in the USSR of making a fortune (2).

The foreign exchange rules relating to contracts in valuables, to payments in foreign and national currencies and to the transfer of money from the USSR to a foreign country and vice versa are imperatively binding upon citizens and foreigners alike. Penal law sanctions are incurred by all persons committing on

(1) Biulleten' Verkhovnogo Suda SSSR, 1966; 1, pp. 33-37.

(2) Cf. e.g. the case Zakharii Zhdanov extensively quoted in: Fomin, pp. 200 et seq.

Soviet territory any infringement of these rules (1).

3. THE LAW OF PROPERTY

In the preceding pages it has been pointed out that, by virtue of the Articles 122 and 123 of the Soviet Civil law Fundamentals, aliens living in the USSR cannot enjoy more extensive civil rights than Soviet citizens. In particular, all restrictions imposed on the property rights of Soviet citizens are equally binding on aliens. These imperative requirements have also prompted the acceptance of the *lex rei sitae* as a basic conflict rule in Soviet private international law. We therefore agree with Lunts that property rights in the Soviet Union are governed by the combined effect of the principle that the Soviet national regime also applies to foreigners and the principle of *lex rei sitae*. (2) However, we cannot ignore the fact that in this combination the provisions contained in Articles 122 and 123 are primary and decisive, while the invocation of *lex rei sitae* is used only as a supplementary ground for the justification of Soviet property claims in private international law. The conflicts rule *lex rei sitae* is here intended to accentuate and reinforce the internationally binding force of Soviet municipal law. In addition it is used as a legal ground for the claim that Soviet citizens abroad should enjoy all property rights admissible under the *lex rei sitae* even when they have no such rights at home. (3)

In short the rules set out above, whether operating separately

(1) In exceptional cases, aliens are expelled from the Soviet Union for foreign exchange transgressions instead of being punished with deprivation of liberty. This was the case with the Italian citizens Cezarin (brother and sister), employees of the U.S. and Turkish Embassies respectively, who were accused of speculation in American dollars and gold watches, i.e. of selling such valuables to Soviet citizens. (Quoted in: Mikhailov, pp. 31-32).

(2) Lunts, II (1963), p. 76.

(3) In its Circular Letter no.329 of the 23rd of October 1929, the Soviet People's Commissariat for Foreign Affairs, referring to a previous, more general Letter, no.42 of 1922, gave the following explanation of this matter: "..........the objective of Circular Letter no.42 was to clarify a rule to the diplomatic representatives of the Soviet Republics abroad ....by which the protection of property rights of their fellow citizens abroad must be extended even in instances in which the rights of these citizens are based upon the civil law of the countries where the representatives are stationed, when these rights are not in conformity with their domestic legislation.

or jointly, serve Soviet economic interests exclusively and in discharging this function they form an expression of Soviet public policy. In this connection we should also mention two special one-sided conflict rules contained in the Soviet Civil Law Fundamentals:
"The form of transactions relating to structures located in the USSR shall be governed by the legislation of the USSR. and the Union Republic concerned." (Article 125, paragraph 3).
"Inheritance of structures located in the USSR shall in any case be determined by Soviet law. The same law shall determine the capacity of a person to make or revoke a will, and also the form of the latter, where a structure located in the USSR is bequeathed." (Article 127, paragraph 3).
According to Lunts, these Articles can be given one of two alternative interpretations: they can be seen either as exceptions to the main conflict rules contained in the preceding paragraphs of the Articles or as one-sided conflict rules sanctioning the principle of *lex situs*. Of the two possible interpretations Lunts recommends the second (1). In my own opinion the Soviet courts need not choose between these two modes of interpretation, which of course do not exclude each other but only concern two different aspects of these provisions. In the light of the general spirit of Soviet private international law, both paragraphs imply the rule that immovables (in the USSR only structures) are governed by *lex rei sitae*. In the light of the preceding paragraphs of the corresponding Articles, however, the provisions under consideration form rigid exceptions to two normal conflict rules: the rule of *locus regit actum* of Article 125, paragraph 1, and the rule contained in Article 127, paragraph 1 and 2, according to which the deceased's or testator's permanent residence is decisive in the matter of succession. Evidently, however important this point of discussion may be for inheritance of foreign estates, it is of no great practical significance, as far as Soviet structures are concerned. Under both possible inter-

For example, a Soviet consul may assist a Soviet citizen in the exercise of his rights of ownership of land located in the country where the consul is stationed, although within the confines of the USSR private ownership of land is abolished. Consequently, here, it is merely clarified that the Soviet citizen may exercise outside of the confines of the Soviet Union rights based upon foreign laws and that, insofar as such rights may be violated in contravention of these laws, the Soviet diplomatic and consular representatives may render assistence to such citizen in the protection of his rights........." (Transl.: Gsovski, I, pp. 306-307.)

(1) Lunts, 1962 (in: S.G. i Pr.), p. 105; Lunts, II (1963), pp. 82; 284-285; Lunts, 1963 (in: Ocherki), pp. 107-108.

pretations, the provisions of Article 125, paragraph 3, and Article 127, paragraph 3, reveal the distinctive features of a legislative public policy which preclude any foreign law from application. (1)

After this brief outline of the conflict rules, which mandatorily lead to the application of Soviet law, special consideration must be given to some important substantive rules whose mandatory character has greatly contributed to the homeward orientation of the conflict rules.

There is no doubt that most significant legal provisions pertaining to Soviet legislative public policy emanate from the State monopoly of the basic means and instruments of production and economic activity. This monopoly embraces *inter alia* land, waters, mines, factories, mills, banks and the means of international transport and international commerce in general (2).

Soviet State ownership has always been considered by communist officials and lawyers as a sovereign right. They have, on many occasions, insisted that foreign States and courts must also recognize all the measures of the Soviet government through which its status of owner has been realized, and have claimed an absolute immunity from jurisdiction, seizure and enforcement actions for State property. Such measures affecting territorially and extraterritorially the property rights of foreigners and citizens alike, constitute a part of Soviet legislative public policy *par excellence*. The attribution of such an extensive binding force to these rules could be justified only by public policy considerations of the highest order, as no normal conflict rule can authorize such an excessive competence. To these measures belong the series of nationalization decrees enacted by the Soviet government as a result and major purpose of the October revolution(3). Pursuant to these Acts, the State acquired the exclusive ownership of land and all kinds of enterprises considered as capitalistic with any property attached thereto. The nationalization decrees, confiscatory by nature, involved many foreign countries either because the interests of their nationals were affected or because their territory was in issue being the *situs* of some nationalized property (4). In all these cases the Soviet authorities claimed an unrestricted extraterritorial effect to their measures. Their claim was usually based on the priciples of international

(1) Of the Western lawyers who consider the legal rules relating to immovables as being of a public policy character cf.: Weiss, p. 394; Louis-Lucas, p. 399; Valery, p. 197; Kosters-Dubbink, p. 340.

(2) Article 6 of the Constitution and Article 21 of the Fundamentals of Civil Legislation.

(3) For some nationalization legal sources see: Gsovski, pp. 10-11.

(4) See supra, under "Soviet criticism of Western public policy".

law as understood in their own country (1).

In my opinion the extraterritorially binding force of the decrees under consideration could be based rather on strictly legislative policy. It was implied in the economic and political purpose which the nationalization decrees were designed to serve, viz. the creation of the economic fundamentals of a communist State. In other words, all legislative measures of expropriation and monopolization of the basic means and instruments of production or economic activity were a direct implementation of Soviet public policy. This opinion finds support also in Soviet literature where "ordre public" is sometimes considered as a synonym for the foundation of Soviet society (2).

The original revolutionary Acts which created the Soviet economic foundations were the expression of supreme ideological imperatives binding on all subsequent law-giving authorities. They cannot be set aside as long as the dominating political forces remain faithful to their original ideology. Illustrative in this respect are the nationalization decrees of the 26th of January 1918 and the 13th of April 1930, according to which all sea-going vessels were declared to be in governmental ownership. The basic rules of these decrees are still in force and they were restated on several occasions in laws concerned with this matter (3). Accordingly, any sea-going ship of significance, being at present State property, may not be transferred into private ownership, may not be mortgaged nor be the object of enforcement measures for the satisfaction of creditors' claims (4). This has been pointed out as an example of public policy also in Soviet literature. "Soviet courts or arbitrations", said Lunts, "could not for instance recognize the legal force of a foreign law which would restrict the effect of Soviet laws on the nationalization of vessels and which would impede the implementation of the Soviet legal rules laying down that the Soviet sea-going vessels are withdrawn from civil commerce." (5)

The above rules apply with an equal validity to all kinds of basic means of production and economic activity. The general provision in this respect is contained in Article 22 of the

(1) Pereterskii, Krylov, 1959, pp. 114 et seq.; Lunts, II (1963), pp. 74-75.

(2) Pereterskii, 1924, pp. 31-32; Levitin, 1960, p. 523. See also above, under "Soviet legal writers on their own system".

(3) See e.g. Article 6 of the Soviet Constitution and in particular Article 10 of the Merchant Shipping Code.

(4) Article 176 of the Merchant Shipping Code.

(5) Lunts, 1949, p. 121.

Fundamentals of Civil Law, according to which "State enterprises, buildings, structures, plant and other property constituting the fixed assets of State organizations... shall not be subject to alienation to citizens, with the exception of some property, the sale of which to citizens is permitted by the legislation of the USSR and the Union Republics". The State property here referred to may not be the object of mortgage, nor may it be attached to answer the claims of creditors. (1)

Public policy considerations have also brought about the rules relating to ownership in land. As already mentioned, only the State has the right to own land. Private persons are barred from such ownership. This principle applies with equal force to foreigners and citizens, to Soviet and foreign organizations. The only right with regard to land which may be allowed to persons is the right to use plots of land for agricultural or housing purposes. In a Soviet textbook the following case is quoted as typical in this respect:

> "A certain Mr. M., resident of Canada, claimed that he was the brother and sole heir of a man who had owned some land in the Western Ukraine untill the year 1939 and was now deceased. This claim could not be allowed, because land in the USSR is State property and cannot become the property of heirs, whether Soviet or foreign citizens." (2)

Among the general rules relating to State property which should be mentioned in this study is the rule laid down in Article 28, paragraph 4, of the Civil Law Fundamentals: "State property, and also the property of kolkhozes and other co-operative and mass organizations unlawfully alienated by any means whatsoever, may be recovered by the organizations concerned from any holder." This provision, according to Lunts, has an extraterritorial effect and admits of no exception. "The *lex situs*, which in principle governs the rights of a *bona fide* possessor, is restricted in this case by considerations of public policy." (3)

Finally a word should be said about some supplementary legal provisions which under Soviet conditions are aimed at further restricting the property of individuals. Such are for instance the rules governing ownerless property which apply imperatively to every object to be found on Soviet territory, whether its

(1) See also Articles 96 and 98 of the RSFSR Civil Code, 1964, where these rules are restated. Cf. also the above-considered immunity from jurisdiction (under "Foreign Trade".)

(2) Boguslavskii, Rubanov, op.cit. 1959, pp. 56-57; idem, 1962, p. 56.

(3) Lunts, II (1963), p. 81.

original owner was a citizen or a foreigner. "Property which has no owner or whose owner is unknown (ownerless property) passes into the ownership of the State after a decision of the court pronounced in a suit brought at the end of one year after registration of the property" (Section 143 RSFSR Civil Code of 1964) (1). This Section, being a restatement of a rule in operation in the USSR also under the RSFSR Code of Civil Law of 1922, can be interpreted in the light of previous Soviet court practice. According to a Ruling of the Presidium of the RSFSR Supreme Court, of the 13/14th of Agust 1934, "Property may be declared ownerless if its owner is unknown, is an absentee, or the property is in escheat".... "But no property, in particular a building, of owners whose whereabouts are precisely known, may be declared ownerless. If no care is taken to safeguard a building and it is threatened with destruction or pillage, the village Soviet may institute proceedings by filing in court a civil suit for declaration of the building as ownerless, which suit shall be decided by court under the civil code..." (2).

The second paragraph of this Ruling which was based on Article 1 of the RSFSR Civil Code of 1922 and the Decree of the 14th of May 1923 (3) is at present incorporated in Article 32 of the Fundamentals of Civil Legislation and Section 141 of the RSFSR Civil Code of 1964. Its internationally binding force can be illustrated by the following case quoted in the Soviet Yearbook of International Law for 1961 (4).

"The Swiss citizen Iren Graf owned a house in Tallinn. In 1940 she moved to Switzerland and settled there in permanent residence, while the management of her house was entrusted to a representative. The Executive Committee of the Tallinn rayon soviet decided in 1952 to incorporate the house into the public housing facilities on either of two legal grounds: as mismanaged or as ownerless. Two years later (1954) as a result of the appeal of the owner, the Executive Committee of the Tallinn town soviet cancelled the earlier decision and returned the confiscated house to the legal owner. The reasons for the second decision were that the grounds for the confiscation measure 'mismanagement' or 'absence of the owner' were not present: the address of the owner was well known and the latter had properly provided

(1) Transl. by Kiralfy, 1966.
(2) See Gsovski, II, p. 76.
(3) Gsovski, I pp. 288-289.
(4) Korobov, Sokolov, pp. 365-366.

for a manager for the house" (1)

Although the final decision in this case has annulled the preceding confiscatory measure, it is quite clear that the rules under consideration were mandatory in character for the purpose both of internal and of private international law.

The right to own a house, being the most important personal right admitted in the USSR, deserves special consideration. Having already discussed the general aspects of the individuals' capacity to own property (2), here we have to make only a few additional observations respecting the right of ownership of dwelling accommodation. It would be no exaggeration to say that all legal rules pertaining to Soviet housing law are a matter of public policy. Some of them restrict the capacity of the owners, others, the powers inherent in the right of ownership, all of them being intended as impediments to capital accumulation.

The basic rule relating to dwelling houses is laid down in Article 25, paragraph 2, of the Fundamentals of Civil Law, and provides as follows:

"Every citizen may have one dwelling house in his personal ownership. Cohabiting spouses and their minor children may have only one dwelling house which is owned by right of personal ownership by one of them, or which is owned as common property. The maximum size of dwelling house which may be in the personal ownership of a citizen, the terms and manner of lease of premises in such a house shall be established by the legislation of the Union Republics."

By virtue of Article 122 and Article 123 of the Civil Law Fundamentals, this legal provision is equally binding on nationals and aliens as to their ownership of houses situated on Soviet territory. The same legal force is given also to the corresponding legal provisions in the Civil Codes of the Union Republics, to which Article 25 of the Fundamentals refers. A number of elaborate imperative rules are contained for instance in the RSFSR Civil Code, some of which are noteworthy as characteristic in this field.

Restating the rule of Article 25 of the Fundamentals that a family cannot have more than one house in personal ownership, the RSFSR Code postulates further that such a house or a part of a house may not exceed 60 square metres of living space. For greater space, special permission is needed from the Executive Committee of the region or town soviet (Section 106). Dwelling accommodation exceeding the maximum size must be

(1) For the recent developments in this domain of Soviet law see Bloembergen, pp. 42 et seq.
(2) See above under "capacity regulations and the position of foreigners in the USSR".

sold, bequeathed or otherwise alienated within a year. In default of voluntary or compulsory alienation the accommodation will be confiscated and transferred to state ownership (Section 107).

Although the right to lease dwelling premises in houses belonging to private persons is admitted by the law (1) and therefore recognized as conforming to the ideological basis of Soviet housing law, all kinds of restrictions with regard to the exercise of this express the ideological imperative that "the personal property of citizens may not be used to derive unearned income" (2) To this category belongs for instance the provision laid down in Article 57 of the Fundamentals and Section 430 of the RSFSR Civil Code, according to which payment for the use of dwelling space owned by private persons may not be higher than the maximum rates established for such houses by the legislation of the Union Republic concerned. Noncompliance with this requirement may constitute a ground for confiscation provided, of course, that the other conditions required by the law for confiscation are also present (3).

(1) Article 56 of the Fundamentals of Civil Law; and Section 298 of the RSFSR Civil Code, 1964.

(2) Article 25 of the Fundamentals of Civil Legislation

(3) Section 111 of the RSFSR Civil Code requires as a condition for confiscation that the owner systematically extracts from his house unearned (untoiled-for) income. In the case of lease the income is unearned if it is obtained by letting a dwelling space at a rate exceeding the legitimate one.. For more details about Soviet housing law see: Rudden, pp. 231-262. It should be noted that Soviet imperative housing law is not an isolated phenomenon. Post-war difficulties in housing as well as requirements of social justice have also prompted the introduction of many restrictive housing measures in Western Europe. Notwithstanding the difference in the ideological backgrounds between Soviet and Western European laws on leases, the imperative rules of both kinds of laws pertain to the same legal category, viz: they are laws of public policy. (Comp. e.g. the Netherlands law: "Wet van 13 October 1950 (Stbl. no. K 452), houdende regelen nopens de huurprijzen van onroerend goed en de bescherming van de huurders, (Huurwet)".

Soviet private international law does not contain any written conflict rule on torts. In the early years of Soviet history, marked by a policy of isolation and mistrust of everything and everyone coming from abroad, this legislative omission was interpreted as an implicit exclusion of any foreign law from application in this domain. Thus Soviet local law was considered imperatively binding irrespective of whether the tort was committed on Soviet or on foreign territory. This was also the opinion of two leading authorities of that time, viz. Pereterskii (1) and Goichbarch (2). This was usually explained by the alleged essential difference between Soviet law and the laws of non-communist countries. At present, as does modern Soviet writing, we must take it for granted that the general spirit of Soviet legislation requires that in principle torts be governed by the *lex loci delicti commissi*, i.e. this is considered to be the normally applicable law. There are, however, several questions relating to torts which are governed by Soviet law under all circumstances. This abnormal application of the local law is motivated by public policy considerations. In the words of Lunts, "many Soviet legal provisions in the domain of torts are considered as a matter of principle and they must be observed by the Soviet court also in cases with foreign elements. In terms of private international law, it might be said, that here is a question of public policy rules which cannot be set aside by a reference to foreign law". (3)
The rules susceptible of being included in this category are the following. The question of whether an act has to be considered as unlawful or not must be decided according to Soviet law. Soviet lawyers consider it contrary to the fundamentals of the Soviet system to impose payment of damages for an act done abroad which is not unlawful according to Soviet law. (4)

1) Pereterskii, 1924, pp. 105-106.
2) Giokhbarg, 1928, p.98.
3) Lunts, II (1963), pp. 237-238.
4) See Pereterskii, Krylov, 1940, p.132, idem 1959, p.146; Lunts, II (1963), p.237. This rule is comparable to the English "first Rule" in Phillips v. Eyre, according to which "no tort alledged to have been committed abroad gives rise to a liability according to English law unless the act was actionable according to English law". (Kahn-Freund, p.49. For details of the English solution see: Dicey, Morris, pp.919 et seq.). A similar public policy rule is to be found also in Article 12 of the German EGBGB. However, in contradistinction to the English and Russian solution, which applies indiscriminately to nationals and aliens, the German rule purports to give a kind of protection to German defendants.

This is an old maxim underlying the Soviet law of torts since the revolution. It was evaluated by Makarov in the following manner: "La notion du délit est à tel point étroitement liée en droit soviétique a l'ordre public qu'il est impossible d'admettre que le tribunal soviétique reconnaisse le caractère délictuel d'un fait reconnu comme délit par la loi du lieu où il s'est produit, mais qui au point de vue du droit soviétique n'est pas un délit" (1).

On the other hand, if an act done abroad is lawful according to *lex loci delicti* but unlawful according to Soviet law, in cases of personal damages, Soviet courts must apply their own law even against a foreign tortfeasor if he happens to be in the USSR and the detrimental consequences have occurred on Soviet territory. This relates at least to cases where the physical integrity of a person has been so gravely affected that his ability to work has been lost or diminished (2).

A specific restriction of the application of the *lex loci delicti*, mentioned by Lunts (3) as pertaining to Soviet public policy, is contained in paragraph 2 of Article 93 of the Fundamentals of Soviet Civil Legislation. It relates to the amount of damages payable: "The court may reduce the amount of compensation for injury caused by a citizen, depending on his property status". The powers given to the Soviet courts by this provision can be used irrespective of the place where the tort has been committed.

Another question closely connected with the amount of damages is that concerning the manner of their payment. This matter is governed in principle by the *lex loci delicti*. An imperative exception is made, however, with regard to compensation payable by foreign shipowners. It is formulated by Soviet lawyers as follows:

"When cases are heard regarding compensation to be paid by foreign shipowners in respect of injury or death caused to citizens of the USSR, the court may, in accordance with the ruling of the Plenary session of the Supreme Court of the USSR, of the

only. The related Article 12 provides: "Aus einer im Ausland begangenen unerlaubten Handlung können gegen einen Deutschen nicht weitergehende Ansprüche geltend gemacht werden, als nach den deutschen Gesetzen gegrundet sind". As the German legislator requires here legal comparison and evaluations we may conclude that this rule pertains to German judical public policy.

1) Makarov, 1933, p.305.

2) See Pereterskii, Krylov, 1959, p.146.

3) Lunts, II (1963), p.237.

22nd of February 1932, decide that the full sum of compensation shall be paid into court. The competent authority will periodically pay out instalments from these sums to the victim or his relatives" (1).

In cases of damage caused by a Soviet citizen to the Soviet State, to a Soviet organization or to a fellow citizen, the Soviet law of torts (2) applies exclusively and the liability provided for by that law will be the same as that for purely domestic cases. Thus for tortious acts where only Soviet physical or legal persons are involved the *lex loci delicti* is superseded entirely by Soviet law. This solution does not constitute a normal conflict rule based on the common nationality of the parties to the tort action, because it relates to Soviet citizens only and does not extend to cases involving foreign citizens. Here the Soviet legislator, *a priori*, though implicitly, has declared the *lex loci delicti* inoperative, considering national interests as absolutely dominating (3).
Soviet courts are also bound to apply their own substantive law in cases where Soviet citizens sent abroad to provide technical aid are injured and owing to circumstances beyond their control cannot bring an action against the foreign tortfeaser. A decision to this effect was made by the Civil College of the Supreme Court of the RSFSR in the case "Rudnev v. Krasnogorsk Construction Works".

1) Boguslavskii, Rubanov, 1959, p.114; see also Lunts II (1963), p.242; For the ruling of the Supreme Court see: Sbornik postanovlenii Plenuma Verkhovnogo Suda SSSR, 1924-1963, Moscow 1964, p.25.
2) The basic substantive rules relating to torts are contained in chapter 12 of the Fundamentals of Soviet Civil Legislation and can be summarised as follows. It is provided that injury caused to the person or property of a citizen and also injury caused to an organization, shall be subject to full indemnity by the person causing the injury. The person causing the injury shall be absolved from indemnification if he proves that the injury was not caused by his fault (Article 88). Indemnity is due even without fault when the injury is caused by "Sources of increased hasard". This relates to damage caused by transport organizations, building enterprises, owners of motorcars, etc. These can be exempted from liability only when they prove that the injury was the result of force majeure or intent on the part of the injured person. Another provision of particular importance is contained in Article 93 of the Fundamentals and regards the reduction of the indemnity for injury in accordance with the fault of the injured person and the property status of the party causing the injury. The court may reduce the amount of compensation where gross negligence on the part of the person injured has contributed to the occurrence of or an increase in the severity of the injury. On the other hand the amount of compensation may also be reduced when the person causing the injury has not sufficient means to compensate the damage. (See also chapter 40 of the RSFSR Civil Code, 1964, Sections 444-471).
3) See: Pereterskii, Krylov, 1940, p.132; idem 1959, p.146; Lunts, 1949, p.175; Lunts II (1963), pp.237 et seq.; Zvekov, pp.133-134.

"Rudnev, a transient employee of the Krasnogorsk Construction Works of the Prokop'evsk Mine Construction Trust, was sent by the All-Union 'Tiazhpromeksport' Combine on a foreign assignment for a period of two years to provide technical aid in the construction of a coal mine. While working in the mine, Rudnev had an accident as a result of which he fractured his left hip and was subsequently declared an invalid of the second group.
In this connection Rudnev brought an action against the Krasnogorsk Construction Works to recover damages for injuries to his health.
The People's Court of the Rudno Ward of Prokop'evsk upheld the claim and gave judgment against the Krasnogorsk Construction Works in favour of Rudnev in the amount of 693 rubles, payable monthly.
The Kemerovo Provincial Court set aside the judgment of the People's Court and remanded the case for a determination of the proper defendant. The Presidium of the Kemerovo Provincial Court set aside the judgment of the People's Court and the decision of the Provincial Court and dismissed the case.
The Civil College of the Supreme Court of the R.S.F.S.R., on protest by the Deputy Prosecutor General of the USSR, by a decision of September 13, 1960, set aside all the judicial decisions in the case and remanded it for a new trial. At the same time the College declared as follows:
The Presidium of the Kemerovo Provincial Court based its dismissal of the case on the ground that the Soviet courts were without jurisdiction, since a foreign enterprise- the mine where the accident occurred- should have been brought in as a defendant.
The agreement on the conditions of the assignment of Soviet specialists for the rendering of technical aid and other services, entered into between the USSR Government and the Government of the particular foreign state, does not, however, provide for liability on the part of the economic agency of that state for accidents involving Soviet specialists.
For these reasons, Iniurcollegia (1) did not consider it possible to bring an action on behalf of Rudnev.
At the same time the fault of the management of the foreign enterprise, which had failed to provide for the observance of technical safety rules in connection with the construction of the mine, in connection with Rudnev's accident was confirmed by the official report of the accident and by the conclusions of the technical expertise.
Since Rudnev could not, in view of circumstances over which he had no control, bring an action for damages for injuries to

1) A college of barristers for cases with foreign elements.

his health against the organisation for which he had been assigned to work, it must be concluded that the liability for the harm in the instant case must be imposed on the All-Union Combine "Tiazhpromeksport" which had assigned Rudnev abroad and which had paid him his salary during the whole period of his foreign assignment.
In view of these circumstances the dismissal of the case by the courts was error. Upon a new trial of the case, the combine 'Tiazhpromeksport' must be brought in as co-defendant under Article 166 of the Code of Civil Procedure of the R.S.F.S.R. and the case decided in accordance with Article 413 of the Civil Code of the R.S.F.S.R." (1).

A special rule of legislative public policy with a wide scope of operation as to the persons involved is to be found in the Soviet Merchant Shipping Code. By virtue of Article 4, of the Code, the rule (Article 177) according to which "a shipowner's liability shall be unlimited in respect of claims by workers for damages for loss of limb or life" (2), must be applied by Soviet

1) Sovetskaia Iustitsiia, 1961, no. 4, p. 28. Transl. in English by John Hazard and Isaac Shapiro, in: The Soviet legal system, New York 1962, part III, pp. 94-95.
Article 413 of the old RSFSR civil code referred to in the above decision provides: "The person or enterprise making insurance payments for the injured person under social insurance provisions shall not be liable to repair injury caused by the happening of the insurable event.
However, where the injury is caused by a criminal act or omission on the part of the entrepreneur, the social insurance agency which satisfied the injured person shall have a claim against the entrepreneur to the extent of the compensation paid to the injured person (subrogation).
In such case, the injured person who has not received full reparation of his injury under social insurance has additional claim against the entrepreneur."
Articles 166 of the old RSFSR Code of Civil Procedure referred to in the same decision provides:
"If it appears, in the course of the proceedings, that the complaint has been filed by a party other than he who has the right to sue in the case, or against the party other than he who should be the respondent, the court, without dismissing the case, may permit the substitution of proper plaintiffs of defendants for the original plaintiffs or defendants in the case."
(Transl.: Gsovski: II.).

2) Transl. by Szirmai and Korevaar. For the private international law rules contained in this code see my article: Soviet private international law relating to carriage by sea. In: Modern Law Review, 1964, no. 4, pp. 412-433. The provision of Article 177 of Soviet Merchant Shipping Code does not differ essentially from the corresponding provisions of the Netherlands Maritime Law (Articles 522-524), which declare null and void stipulations limiting or ecxluding the carrier's liability for loss or damage sustained by a traveller.

courts under all circumstances. Lunts also considered this rule in the light of Soviet public policy and drew the following conclusion: "The principle of unlimited liability of the shipowner regarding claims of workers for damages or death, even when caused by the fault of the crew, must be considered as an imperative rule which cannot be restricted by reference to a foreign law" (1).

The imperatively binding force of these rules was prompted by political considerations in the strictest sense of the word. The major purpose was to create and fortify the conviction among working people that only the Soviet legal system was granting them a truly human treatment, whilst non-communist laws on torts were directed against their interests. Or as Lunts put it: "The laws of the bourgeois States restrict in every possible way the liability in cases of causing injury to a person. These restrictions, established in the interest of the employers and directed against the interest of the toilers, cannot, of course, receive recognition in a Soviet court" (2).
Although these chauvinistic motivations cannot inspire a serious legal discussion even among Soviet lawyers, they have been prevalent under the operation of the RSFSR Civil Code of 1922 and have survived in recent interpretations of the Fundamentals of Soviet Civil Legislation of 1961. This is hardly surprising, bearing in mind that the basic political principles, which both laws were created to serve, have never changed.

1) Lunts, 1949, p.121.
2) Ibid., p.275; The same opinion is also to be found in: Zvekov, p.118.

5. SUCCESION

Although the Soviet law of succession has undergone several important changes (1) since the revolution, these have not had any substantial effect on communist public policy in this domain. Throughout the entire Soviet history the legislative public policy rules relating to succession have purported to defend the economic foundations of the USSR. Together with the corresponding rules relating to ownership, they were and remain directed against any intrusion of foreign law in matters relating to the basic means of production, including land, machinery and all kinds of structures situated in the USSR. They also purport to defend the economic monopolies of the Soviet State, for instance by preventing the accumulation of private capital on Soviet territory. This is the *raison d'être* of the imperative rules governing succession in the USSR. Their operation in the domain of private international law is justified, from the point of view of Soviet lawyers, by the fundamental functional difference between communist and non-communist laws. This difference is usually conceived as follows: "The Soviet socialist law of succession is diametrically opposed to the law of succession of the capitalist countries. The basic purpose of the capitalist law is the consolidation of the inequality of ownership, the preservation of the instruments and means of production in the hands of the exploiters' class....... In the Soviet Union succession does not have and cannot have an exploiting character ... it is directly connected with the protection of the personal ownership (2) in the USSR". (3)

The changes which have occurred in Soviet private international law on succession with the introduction of the Fundamentals of Civil Legislation of 1961, although the public policy of the USSR has not been affected, have nevertheless brought about some significant modifications in the methods and the means by which this policy is realized. Under the operation of the RSFSR Civil Code of 1922 and the corresponding codes of the other republics there was no written general conflict rule on succession. The

(1) For the principal stages in the development of Soviet legislation on this matter, beginning with the prohibition of succession in the USSR and ending with the formal acceptance of the conventional modes of inheritance, see e.g.: Gsovskii,I, pp.623 et seq: Szirmai, p. 19.

(2) On the concept of "personal ownership" see above under "The law of property".

(3) Pereterskii-Krylov, 1959, pp.176-177. See also Lunts 1949, p. 309; Lunts, II (1963, p.267; Rubanov, p. 162. For similar opinions see also; Gsovski, I, pp.619-620.

prevailing doctrine and practice (1), however, supported by Section 42 of the Consular Regulation of the USSR (2) and Section 4 of the RSFSR Code of Civil Procedure (3), interpreted this ommission as a tacit exclusion of the foreign laws in successoral matters affecting Soviet economic interests in one way or another. Consequently, it was taken for granted that succession to the estates of Soviet citizens wherever they had died and of foreigners who had died in the USSR were to be governed exclusively by Soviet law. By this rule the Soviet legislator intended to defend both the economic order of the country and the interests of its citizens domiciled abroad. That this abnormal extension of the competence of Soviet law by means of conflict rules was not at all necessary for the attainment of the declared purpose has become clear from the new Fundamentals of Soviet civil legislation. The Fundamentals laid down some classic conflict rules based on the notion of the permanent residence of the deceased (4) and let the public policy function be performed by universally known special conflict rules and imperative substantive legal provisions. Accordingly, the Soviet legislator submitted the successoral rights and obligations

(1) Krylov, 1930, pp. 242, 250; Lunts, 1949, pp. 177-178; Lunts, II (1963), p. 281; Pereterskii, Krylov, 1959, pp. 177-178; 181-184. Cf. also: Szaszy, Budapest 1964, p. 366, note 3; Grzybowski, pp. 134-135.

(2) Section 42 of the Consular Statute provides:
" In cases of death of citizens of the USSR in the confines of the consular district, the consul shall take all measures for the preservation of the property left by the deceased. The subsequent measures of the consul relating to the inheritable property shall be determined by corresponding agreements between the USSR and the Goverment of the country of the consul's residence or by the practice established with respect to this question in the mutual relations between the USSR and that country.
If, according to an agreement or established practice, all inheritable property or a part thereof is transferred to the consul to proceed with it according to the laws of his country. the consul shall be guided in the measures to be taken with respect to the transferred property by the laws of the USSR and of the Union Republic of which the deceased was a citizen" (Quoted from: Vilkov, p. 243).

(3) According to this provision, if there is a gap in the law Soviet courts will be guided by "the general principles of Soviet legislation and the general policy of the goverment of workers and peasants".

(4) "Relations arising from the succession shall be determined by the law of the country where the deceased had his last permanent domicile. The capacity of a person to make and revoke his will and also the form of bequest and the act of its revocation, shall be determined by the law of the country in which the testator had his permanent domicile at the moment of making the act. However, a will or its revocation may not be deemed invalid by reason of non-compliance with the form, if the latter satisfies the requirements of the law of the place where the act was made or the requirements of Soviet law" (Article 127, paragraphs 1 and 2, of the Fundamentals of Civil Legislation).
In my opinion the words "permanent domicile" in the official translation should be understoo as "permanent residence". This expression corresponds better to the original Russian wording "postoinnoe mesto zhitel'stva".

to the law of the deceased's last permanent residence (1), the capacity to make and revoke a will to the law of his permanent residence at the time of making the act, and the form of the will and its revocation to the law of the testator's permanent residence, the *lex loci actus* or Soviet law.

Apart from these main rules, the legislator has provided several imperative exceptions the first of which is the one-sided conflict rule of Article 127, paragraph 3, of the Fundamentals. This provides: "Inheritance of structures located in the USSR shall in all cases be determined by Soviet law. The same law shall determine the capacity of a person to make or revoke a will, and also the form of the will, where a structure located in the USSR is bequeathed."

The primary concern of the Soviet authorities in drafting this legal provision was to obtain an effective maintenance of the restrictive ownership system in their territory. As already pointed out, Soviet law is directed against any accumulation of private capital in the territory of the USSR and against the use of property for the extraction of unearned profit. Inheritance, being an important if not the only source of private capital accumulation in the USSR, would have been inadmissible if the danger inherent in this institution were not neutralized through the operation of the numerous restrictive substantive and formal measures, the most important of which relate to the ownership of immovables. That is the reason why the Soviet legislator has submitted the inheritance of structures exclusively to Soviet law. Thus the whole matter of the inheritance of such structures was thoroughly dominated by public policy considerations. Even without the provision of Article 127, paragraph 3, it was quite clear to Soviet judges that in general no deviation was possible from the internal law relating to immovables, even through the medium of inheritance of estates of owners who had died abroad. From this point of view it does not make any difference whether we see Article 127, paragraph 3, as an expression of the *lex rei sitae* principle (2) or an exception to the main conflict rules on succession (3).

(1) According to the prevailing opinion in Soviet legal literature, the question whether the de cuius had his permanent residence in the USSR or abroad must be decided according to Soviet law. Thus, in this respect, lex fori classification is insisted upon. (Cf. Lunts, II(1963), p. 283; Rubonov, p. 219. The definition of the notion "residence" is to be found in the Civil Codes of the Union Republics and in particular in Section 17 of the RSFSR Civil Code, which runs as follows:
"The place of residence of a citizen is the place where he lives permanently or habitually". (Transl. by Kiralfy).

(2) Lunts, II (1963), p. 285; See also Lunts' comments on the corresponding Sect. 567 of the RSFSR Civil Code, in: Nauch.-prakt.Komm. GK, 1966, p. 635.

(3) Rubanov, pp. 219-223.

The difference in interpretation concerns only the question whether the inheritance of structures located in foreign countries will be governed by the *lex rei sitae* or by the *lex domicilli*. Whatever interpretation the Soviet courts may choose, Soviet public policy relating to inheritance will never be affected.

Furthermore, it should be noted that by virtue of Article 127, paragraph 3, the whole complex of legal provisions on inheritance, as laid down by the Fundamentals of Civil Legislation and by the Civil Codes of the Union Republics (1), is charged with the performance of a public policy function whenever the inheritance of a house or another structure located in the USSR is at issue. Accordingly, if, for instance, a testator whose last permanent residence was in England bequeathed a house located in the USSR, the validity (formal and substantive) has to be determined according to Soviet law; his bequest will in any case be declared invalid if it is not notarially certified, if it is detrimental to the compulsory shares of the heirs enumerated in Soviet law, etc. Soviet law of succession must also determine when and whether

(1) The most characteristic substantive provisions laid down in the Fundamentals of Civil Legislation are the following. "Where inheritance is by operation of law, the children (including the adopted children), the spouse and the parents (adoptive parents) of the deceased shall be heirs of the first turn, in equal shares"....(Article 118, paragraph 1). "Persons who are unable to earn and who had been dependents of the deceased for not less than one year prior to his death shall be heirs-at-law. In the presence of other heirs they shall take equally with heirs of the turn upon whom the estate devolves" (Article 118, paragraph 4). "Children of the deceased (including adopted children) who are minors or who are unable to earn, shall inherit, regardless of the content of the testamentary disposition, not less than two-thirds of the portion which would have been due to each of them under intestate succession (portio legitima)...." (Article 119, paragraph 2).

"Where there are no heirs-at-law or testamentary beneficiaries, or none of the heirs accept the inheritance, or are disinherited by the testator, the property of the deceased shall pass to the State by the right of succession" (Article 117, paragraph 3).

As to the formalities required for the validity of a will in general and a will regarding structure in particular, the following sections of the RSFSR Civil Code of 1964 are of major significance.

"A will must be drawn up in writing with a statement of the time and place of execution, signed by the testator personally and notarially authenticated" (Section 540).

"The following wills are treated as equivalent to notarial wills:

(1) wills of servicemen, certified by the headquarters of the military unit in question;
(2) wills of citizens aboard sea-going or riverine ships plying under the flag of the USSR, certified during the voyage by the captain of the ship;
(3) wills of citizens under treatment of hospitals, field hospitals, sanatoria and other institutions for in-patients and also in invalid homes certified by the head or senior doctor or duty-doctor;
(4) wills of citizens participating in exploration or Arctic, etc. explorations, certified by the leader of the expedition" (Section 541). (Both Sections of the RSFSR Civil Code are translated by Kiralfy).

a structure located in the USSR escheats to the State; it can happen that the bulk of the deceased's estate situated in his last permanent residence devolves upon distant relatives not recognized by Soviet succession law (1), while the deceased's house in Moscow escheats to the State. It goes without saying that the capacity to be a heir to a house located in the USSR is also determined by Soviet law. Accordingly, if such a house is bequeathed to a church, the bequest will be declared invalid because, in contradistinction to other social organizations, the church in the USSR is not capable of being an heir (2).

The right of inheritance of dwelling-houses located in the USSR is greatly affected by the imperative restrictions to the related right of ownership of such houses. It has already been noted in connection with the law of property that, pursuant to Article 25, paragraph 2, of the Fundamentals of Civil Legislation and Articles 106 and 107 of the RSFSR Civil Code, no one may keep more than one house in personal ownership (3). Accordingly, if a person, irrespective of whether a citizen or an alien, comes into possession of two houses in the USSR by mean of succession, he is obliged to sell one of them within a year. If he fails to do this voluntarily, a compulsory sale will follow, and if there is then no buyer, the house will pass into State ownership without any compensation (4).

The compulsory modification of the object of the heir's right to a house or the eventual confiscation cannot be precluded by the invocation either of the law of decedent's last permanent domicile or of the personal law of the heir. The legal ground of this conclusion is to be found in the combined effect of Article 127,

(1) As Rubanov rightly observes, the circle of heirs is narrower under Soviet law than under the laws of countries with a free economy. (Rubanov, p. 116); See also Rubanov's interpretation of Article 127, paragraph 3, of the Fundamentals, ibid, pp. 219 et seq.)

(2) See: Serebrovskii, p. 101; Rubanov, pp. 110-111).

(3) According to Section 106 of the RSFSR Civil Code, 1964, the house in personal ownership may not exceed sixty square metres of dwelling space.

(4) The particuliarity of Section 107 of the RSFSR Civil Code, which also contains the basic elements of Section 106 of the code and Article 25 of the Fundamentals, necessitates its partial quotation. Section 107 provides as follows:

"If, on grounds permitted by law, more than one dwelling-house is individually owned by a citizen or spouses living together and their minor children, the owner has the right to elect which of these to keep. Within the course of a year the other dwelling-house or dwellings must be sold, given away or otherwise disposed of. The period of one year for voluntary transfer of such dwelling or dwellings is reckoned from the date on which title accrued to the other dwelling or dwellings.

If, within one year the owner fails to dispose of the dwelling in some form, the house becomes liable, after a decision of the executive committee of the regional or city council paragraph 3, just discussed, and Article 122 of the Fundamentals limiting alien's civil law capacity to that of Soviet citizens (1).

The right of inheritance of a second house and its transformation into a right to the value of the house is comparable to another restricted right of inheritance in the domain of Merchant shipping affecting exclusively foreigners' interests. According to Article 12 of the Merchant Shipping Code of the USSR of 1929, if a ship sailing under Soviet flag devolves by way of inheritance to a person who is not a citizen of the USSR, the Ministry of Water Transport can, within a period of 6 months, buy up such a ship. The same right of redemption is given, by virtue of Article 13 of the Code, to any Soviet citizens who may be co-owners of a ship. When a part of a jointly owned ship devolves by right of inheritance to a foreigner, the co-owners, having Soviet citizenship, have the right within a period of 3 months to buy up that part. Only where the right of redemption is not exercised within the fixed period, may the foreign heir take the inherited ship, but then the latter must sail under the flag of another country because according to Article 6 of the Code only the ships of Soviet organizations and citizens (2) may sail under the flag of the USSR. There is no doubt that the *raison d'être* of these provisions is the protection of the interests of the Soviet State and its citizens

of workers's deputies to compulsory sale by the procedure laid down by the Code of Civil Procedure of the RSFSR for the execution of judicial decisions. The former owner receives the proceeds of sale after deduction of the costs connected with the compulsory sale. In cases in which the compulsory sale does not take place for lack of buyer, the house passes into State ownership, after a decision of the local council, without any payment..." (Translation by Kiralfy).

(1) See supra, under "Capacity regulations and the position of foreigners in the USSR."

(2) The kinds of ships which may be owned by Soviet citizens are determined by Article 8 of the Merchant Shipping Code which provides:
"Citizens of the USSR and legal entities not mentioned in Sect. 7 may, on an ownership (property)-basis, operate only:
a. Ships with a carrying capacity not over 50 tons;
b. ships with engines of not more than 15 IHP, and in certain areas, the list of which will be published by the Ministry of Sea Navigation of the USSR, of not more than 20 IHP;
c. ships used for sport, with the exception of ships and boats fitted with motors of over 10 IHP;
d. any type of ship used in the fishing or hunting trade with the exception of engine-driven ships of more than 20 gross.reg.tons. Nobody may own more than one ship of the categories mentioned in paras. "a" and "b" of this section.
Note 1. Sailing ships fitted with an auxiliary motor, which on a calm sea, when sails are not set, gives the ship a speed not exceeding 6 miles an hour, are not considered engine-driven vessels within the meaning of this section.
Note 2. The CPC of the USSR may grant exemptions from the provisions of this section. (Transl. by Szirmai and Korevaar.).

as against those of aliens, the latter being of secondary concern. While agreeing with Rubanov's statement (1) that there are in Soviet law some formal safeguards that foreign heirs will receive the price of the ship or part of it when redeemed (2) it must also be admitted that this is not the main point. What matters here is the fact that a foreigner cannot choose between the ship and its price as Soviet citizens are empowered to do. Thus the former are not treated on equal footing with the latter. In addition, it will be of interest to note that special restrictions of the kind just discussed also exist with regard to inheritance in foreign estates. Although Soviet citizens may have the right to inherit every kind of property located in foreign countries, even the means of production which in the USSR can neither be owned nor inherited, this right can only be exercised without limitations abroad and according to the corresponding foreign laws granting the right. If, however, the heir wants to exercise right of ownership to the property so acquired in Soviet territory, the admissibility of such a right will be governed by Soviet law. A Soviet-lawyer recently gave the following explanation of this question.

"In a capitalist country a Soviet citizen may become an heir to objects such as machines, equipment, apparatus of a productive character, building materials, etc. Such property is to be used in production processes. However, under the property relations system, existing in this country a private person cannot be the owner of a manufacturing enterprise; therefore, the heir cannot use such property for its purpose. In this connection, such property, even when acquired by way of succession, is not permitted to pass the frontier if addressed to a private person. Soviet citizens receiving such property by way of succession may sell it abroad and transfer the money received without restriction to the USSR in the manner described above" (3).

The public policy exceptions to the main conflict rules on succession as to structures are closely connected with those concerned with the titel to land in the USSR. Land, belonging exclusively to the State, constitues, according to a Soviet lawyer, the very basis of the imperative rules relating to suc-

(1) Rubanov, pp. 50-51.

(2) In respect of the price, Article 12 of the Soviet Merchant Shipping Code provides that if the value of the ship is disputed, it shall be determined in accordance with Article 11 of the Code, by a commission consisting of representatives of the Ministry of Sea Navigation of the USSR, of the Commission of Foreign Trade of the USSR, and of the Ministry of State Control of the USSR.
Article 13 on the other hand provides that if the value of the ship jointly owned is disputed, it shall be determined by the court.

(3) Rubanov, p. 104.

cession to structures, and to all property relations connected with them (1). Pursuant to Article 6 of the Constitution of the USSR and Article 21 of the Fundamentals of Civil Legislation, land is not capable of passing into private ownership. This holds good for every classic mode of acquisition, including succession. Thus no person, whether an alien or a citizen, living in the USSR or abroad may inherit land on Soviet territory as no deceased's estate contains such property (2).

Public policy considerations also dominate the rule of characterization regarding successoral rights on Soviet territory. The rule, both under the RSFSR Civil Code of 1922 and the Fundamentals of 1961, is to the effect that Soviet substantive law is the only competent law to determine whether a certain right relating to properties situated in the USSR is to be considered as a right of inheritance, or not. With respect to this Lunts wrote: "The application of the foreign inheritance laws is excluded when a given right to acquire property upon death of a person cannot be recognized as a right of inheritance from the point of view of the Soviet law" (3).

Thus the operation of the general conflict rules, which otherwise would have given competence to a foreign law, will be precluded with regard to the following issues.

The share of a farming household member in the common property of the household is not capable of being inherited either by the operation of law or under a will (4) as long as the household remains. After the death of such a member his share devolves upon the remaining members as a whole and the question of inheritance does not arise at all. (Section 560 paragraph 1, RSFSR Civil Code of 1964). The property of the household may become an object of inheritance only when the de cuius is the last member of the household (Section 560, paragraph 2, RSFSR Civil Code of 1964) and probably when the collective farm to which the household pertains ceases to exist, for instance when it is transformed into a "Sovkhoz" (a State farming enterprise) (5).

(1) Rubanov pp. 219-221.

(2) For a decision to this effect see above under "The Law of Property".

(3) Lunts, 1949, p. 316; see also Lunts, II, (1963), pp. 286-287.

(4) See Lunts, 1949, p. 316; Lunts, II (1963), p. 286. See also Grzybowski, p. 136.

(5) Cf. Ioffe, Tolstoi, p. 439.
The corresponding Section 560 of the RSFSR Civil Code provides:
"No succession to household property occurs in the event of the death of a member of a collective farm household or separate peasant household. If on death of a member of a collective farm or separate peasant economy, no other members of the household are left, the rules of this Part of the Code apply to the property of the household" (Trans. by Kiralfy).
On the interpretation of this Section see also: Nauch.- prakt. komm. GK. 1966, p. 625.

Soviet court practice has provided a number of illustrations of this problem. For instance, the case "Korotkova and others v. A.A. Tatarkina" seems noteworthy.

"A notary public refused to give to Korotkova, Fomicheva, Kozlova and Vlasova a certificate of succession to a house that was left after the death of their mother E.M. Tatarkina in the village of Biserovo, district of Moscow. The refusal was based on the fact that after the death of Tatarkina the succession could not take place because there was still one remaining member of the kolkhoz household of which she had been the head: the daughter in-law of the deceased, A.A. Tatarkina. Korotkova, Fomicheva, Kozlova and Vlasova brought an action in court against A.A. Tatarkina for the recognition of their right of ownership of the house, alleging that their mother was the last member of the kolkhoz household and that therefore by virtue of Section 418 of the RSFSR Civil Code (1922) they were her heirs-at-law. Furthermore, the mother left a will by which she bequeathed all her property to her daughter Korotkova.

The Moscow district court rejected the claim of Korotkova and others, and nullified the will.

The civil law division of the Supreme Court of the RSFSR, having considered the appeal of the plaintiffs, reaffirmed by a resolution of the 7th of March 1961 the decision of the Moscow district court and rejected the complaint on the following grounds.

According to Section 65 of the Land Laws Code of the RSFSR, a household is a family-labour organization of persons keeping a peasant household. The court established that E.M. Tatarkina kept a peasant household in Biserovo. In 1922 the defendant A.A. Tatarkina married the son of E.M. Tatarkina and became a member of the household. Insofar as the daughters of E.M. Tatarkina are concerned, they left the household when they reached the age of majority and married. It is clear from the materials of the case that E.M. Tatarkina, her son and the defendant were members of the kolkhoz in the village Biserovo and took part in its production through their labour.

In 1946 the defendant, together with her husband T.S. Tatarkin and their children, went to Kaliningrad to take up permanent residence and in 1948 received a part of the apportioned household property. In 1955, however, the defendant and her husband returned to Biserovo and since then had been living with E.M. Tatarkina, keeping a common household with her. In the land-register of the village soviet they were listed as members of the kolkhoz household whose head was E.M. Tatarkina, and the kolkhoz alloted to them additionally 0.12 hectares of garden plot, as the result of which the garden plot of the household increased to 0.20 hectares. The chairman of the Iurov village soviet Barakin, and the witnesses Shcherbakov, Miakoshina and others testified that the household of E.M. Tatarkina was a Kolkhoz household. Her son, T.S. Tartarkin, worked till his death in the kolkhoz, while the defendant took part in the production of the kolkhoz. Under these circumstances the court correctly came to the conclusion that the deceased, E.M. Tatarkina, was not the last member of the household and no opening of succession took place after her death, since A.A. Tatarkina remained as a member of the household" (1).

A second case where no right of succession arises is mentioned in Section 561 of the RSFSR Civil Code, 1964 (2). When a depositor in a State Savings Bank or a State Bank of the USSR leaves an instruction to the Bank to the effect that in the event of his death the deposit should be paid to a certain person, this deposit will form no part of the estate. Only when the depositor has made no special instruction to the above effect will his deposit pass to the heirs according to the general rules of succession (3). Nor does any right of succession arise in cases of life insurance. Lunts gave the following explanation for these exceptions. "Il n'est pas douteux que le droit du bénéficiaire d'une assurance est fondé sur une stipulation pour autrui. Nous en dirions autant du droit du destinataire d'une dépot en banque ou en caisse d'épargne, selon l'article 561 du Code Civil. Il en résulte qu'il n'est pas possible de leur appliquer les règles de conflit de l'article 127 des Principes, et qu'ils sont entièrement assujettis au droit soviétique interne" (4).

From Soviet court practice we can deduce at least one more case where no succession takes place This relates to outstanding pension claims of the *de cuius*.

"Fedotkina requested the first office of the Penzen notary public to issue a certificate respecting her right of succession to the outstanding pension claims of her deceased husband I.A. Fedotkin. After the expiry of a 6-month period from the opening of the succession the senior notary public officer issued the certificate to the wife of the deceased pensioner. However, according to Section 179 of the Regulation of the procedure for the granting

(1) Sovetskaia iustitsiia, 1961: 12, p. 28. A similar decision was rendered in the "Kozhinov's Kolkhoz household" case, Sovetskaia iustitsiia, 1964: 18, p. 30.

(2) See also the corresponding provision of Section 436 of the RSFSR Civil Code of 1922.

(3) See: Lunts, 1949, pp. 316-317; Lunts II (1963), pp. 286-287; Korobov, Sokolov, p. 366. This interpretation was confirmed also by the Supreme Court of the USSR in its Ruling no. 6 of the 1st of July 1966. (Biulleten' Verkhovnogo Suda SSSR, 1966: 4, p. 22, paragraph 9).

(4) Lunts, 1964, p. 644.

and payment of State pensions as approved by a Decree no. 1044 of the USSR Council of Ministers of the 4th of August 1956, pension amounts due to a deceased pensioner before his death are not included in the inheritable estate and are payable to those members of the family which are provided for by a pension for the lose of the breadwinner. For all this, the parents and spouse have the right to receive these sums irrespective of whether they are unable to work and whether they were dependent on the deceased" (1).

Finally a word should be said about the successoral rights to foreign exchange, valuable works of art, antiques, etc. Such rights can be based on foreign laws by virtue of Soviet conflict rules only insofar as their recognition is concerned. Their practical realization, however, especially when consisting of the conveyance of valuables from the USSR to foreign countries, is exclusively governed by Soviet foreign exchange and customs regulations. Thus, the right to acquire the inherited valuables does not pertain to the complex of successoral rights of the heir, and due to the cultural, economic or financial importance of the objects concerned, they are placed under the exclusive application of Soviet internal law (2). Some of the provisions of Soviet law are of a formal character and they also have to be complied with by foreign heirs in order to obtain the inherited valuables (3). Others are substantive and often amount to an absolute prohibition of the transfer of certain items, such as paintings, antiques, etc., abroad. In these cases the foreign heir will be precluded altogether from the realization of his successoral right outside the Soviet Union (4).

(1) Sovetskaia iustitsiia, 1961: 16, p. 31.

(2) Lunts, 1949, p. 317; Lunts, II (1963), p. 287; Pereterskii, Krylov, 1959, p. 178. See also above, under "Foreign exchange and currency regulations".

(3) For some of these provisions cf. Gsovski, I, pp. 629-630.

(4) Pereterskii, Krylov, 1959, p. 178: Rubanov, p. 81.

6. FAMILY LAW

Preliminary Remarks. We here enter a domain where Soviet legislative public policy is tending towards absolute domination. Or as Szászy has recently put it, "in the Soviet Union rules of family law are in general qualified as belonging to public policy" (1). Soviet lawyers are also used to justifying this exuberant claim by the invocation of some fundamental differences between the communist and non-communist families. An analysis of these differences as exposed in Soviet literature and legislation will therefore be our first task. In the course of history, they have appeared either as imaginary differences, being a mere reflection of the communist preconceptions against the families of Western civilization and the chauvinism with which thė Soviet families are viewed, or as real ones based on the law. It is maintained that whatever changes may have been introduced in Soviet Family law, it still remains different from and superior to the law of the bourgeois countries, mainly because of the difference in the economic basis which the families under two systems have and the purpose they are called to serve. In particular, the non-communist family is conceived as an institution of the bourgeois social-economic system based on private ownership of the means of production; it is therefore a union of capitals (2) or business transaction establishing the power of a man over a woman (3). The communist family on the other hand is presented as being based on ideal personal relations where inequality and subjugation are altogether excluded (4).

Such differences imagined by the communist politician have strongly influenced the formation of the conflict rules in Soviet family law, most of which are shaped as rules of public policy. They have nothing or very little to do with the real differences based on the substantive legal provisions of the two social systems. There is much to be said, of course, about the typical communist rules, drafted and experimented with for a long time after the revolution, which were cardinally opposed to the related rules of the majority of non-communist countries. As most of them

(1) Százy, Budapest 1964, p. 341. The qualification of family law as a matter of public policy is not limited to Soviet legal system. It is current also in some European and American systems, cf. e.g. Wolff, 1950, pp. 313 et seq.; Rabel, I, pp. 215 et seq.

(2) Lunts, 1949, p. 299; Lunts II (1963), p. 304.

(3) Pereterskii, Krylov, 1959, p. 158.

(4) Lunts, 1949, p. 299; Lunts, II (1963), p. 305; Pereterskii, Krylov, 1959, p. 157.

belong entirely to the past however, we shall limit our selves to mentioning some of them.

Before the reform of the 8th of July 1944 (1), which brought the Soviet family law system very close to the traditional pattern of the West, there were, in this system, two basic principles which were susceptible of provoking the well-known statement of an English judge that "What Russia calls a marriage is no marriage in the Christian sense" (2).

Firstly, *de facto* marriages were treated on an equal footing with registered marriages with the sole difference that the registration constituted conclusive evidence of the existence of the marriage (3). The basic principle was implied *inter alia* in Section 133 of the Code of Laws on Acts of Civil Status, Marriage, Domestic Relations and Guardianship, RSFSR (1918), which provided:

"Birth itself shall be the basis of the family. No differentiation whatsoever shall be made between relationship by birth in or out of wedlock" (4).

The same rule we find reflected in the original text of the RSFSR Code of 1926, Section 25, and more specifically in Section 6 where a *de facto* marriage was considered as an impediment to the registration of another marriage.

The ease of dissolving a marriage was the second characteristic feature of the Soviet system prior to 1944. It was provided that either the mutual consent or the unilateral declaration of one of the spouses would be sufficient to dissolve the mar-

(1) The most important provisions of the Edict of the Supreme Soviet of the USSR of 8th July 1944 were contained in Sections 19 and 23 relating to marriage and divorce respectively. Subsequently they were incorporated in the family Codes of the several Union Republics. For instance Sections 1 paragraph 2 of the RSFSR Code of Laws on Marriage, Family, and Guardianship, which corresponds to Section 19 of the Edict, provides: "Only a registered marriage creates the rights and obligations of spouses provided for in the present Code" (as amended April 16, 1945, Vedomosti, 1945, no. 26).

Section 18 of the same Code (restating section 23 of the Edict) provides: "During the lifetime of both spouses, the marriage may be dissolved only by means of a divorce granted by the court upon petition of one or both parties". (As amended April 16, 1945, Vedomosti 1945, no. 26).

(2) Quoted from: Wolff, 1950, p. 14.

(3) RSFSR Family Code, Section 2.

At present there is only one case in which a de facto marriage entered into before 1944 is treated like a registered marriage. If a spouce has died without having registered the marriage as provided by the Edict of 8th July 1944, the other spouse has the right to obtain from the people's court a certificate stating that he or she has been legally married to the deceased (Section 1 paragraph 3 of the RSFSR Family Code. This was also the final decision in the case "The de facto marriage of Zaustinskaia E.M. and Durov G.G." See: Biulleten' Verkhovnogo Suda SSSR, 1961, pp. 24-26).

(4) Quoted from: Gsovski, I, p. 111.

riage (1). Such a dissolution could be entered in the Civil Registry Record, but, as Gsovski put it, "just as Soviet marriage was merely a registration of existing marriage, the Soviet divorce was not a divorce but a registration of the fact that cohabitation was discontinued" (2).

Since 1944 there have been no anomalous phenomena of the kind just considered except for the Edict of 5th February 1947, which prohibited marriages between Soviet citizens and aliens (3). This severe encroachment upon the personal rights of foreigners and citizens alike was abrogated, as mentioned elsewhere, by the Decree of the Supreme Soviet of the USSR, of the 26th of November 1953.

Of the differences between present Soviet family law and the laws of the West we should mention that relating to the impediments to marriage. In particular, consanguinity as a legal impediment is limited according to Soviet law only to relatives of the direct line of descent and brothers and sisters (4). This consanguinity circle is indeed considerably narrower than that under the majority of Western legal systems (5).
The difference, however, is not an absolute one because the related Soviet provision is neither alone in the world nor an absolute imperative for all communist countries. German family law contains a fairly similar provision, as far as consanguinity is concerned (6). On the other hand, many East European communist laws provide a broader circle of kinship in the collateral line than the Soviet law does.

Other differences of similar relative significance include the following: The Soviet Union is one of the few countries where marriage does not imply the obligation of husband and wife to have a com-

(1) Section 18 of the RSFSR Family Code, 1926.
(2) Gsovski, I, p. 122.
(3) Vedomosti Verkhovnogo Soveta SSSR, 1947, no. 10. See also Lunts, 1949, p. 302.
(4) Section 6 of the RSFSR Family Code. The above provision is also reflected in Section 10 of the Principles of Legislation of the USSR and the Union Republics concerning Marriage and Family of 27th June 1968, hereinafter refered to as "Principles of Family Legislation".
(5) For instance the difference between the Soviet provision and the corresponding provisions of Dutch law, is conspicuous. Beside the marriages between relatives of the direct line of descent and between brothers and sisters the Civil Code of the Netherlands prohibits, with some reservations, also marriages between uncle and niece, aunt and nephew etc. (Civil Code, Sections 87 and 88).
Impediments similar to those of Dutch law are to be found in the legislations of many other countries in the West.
(6) Article 4 paragraph 1 of German family law provides: "Eine Ehe darf nicht geschlossen werden zwischen Verwandten in gerader Linie, zwischen vollbürtigen und halbbürtigen Geschwistern sowie zwischen Verschwägerten, in gerader Linie, gleichgültig, ob die Verwandschaft auf ehelicher oder auf unehelicher Geburt beruht".

mon residence (1). This is usually seen by Soviet lawyers as an expression of the equality between man and woman. In my opinion the totalitarian character of the Soviet State provides an additional explanation for this phenomenon. The State interests as determined by the Communist party have dictated that natural family ties must not stand in the way of citizens in the fulfilment of their duties toward the State.

The obligation of the spouses to support each other depends under Soviet law on inability to work and need of support on the one hand and the ability to render support on the other; this principle applies during the marriage as well as after divorce.

In contradistinction to many legal systems of the West, Soviet family law does not know concrete specified grounds for dissolution of marriage. Instead, it provides that "if it is established by the court that the further common life between the spouses and the preservation of the family have become impossible, the regional (town) people's court shall decree dissolution of marriage" (2). This general ground for divorce is erroneously considered by some Soviet writers as a specific communist solution distinct from the system of exhaustive legal enumeration of grounds" characteristic for the legislation of all bourgeois countries" (3). In this connection attention should be drawn to Section 142 of the Swiss Civil Code which provides: "Chacun des époux peut demander le divorce lorsque le lien conjugal est si profondément atteint que la vie commune est devenue insupportable. Si la désunion est surtout imputable à l'un des conjoints, l'action ne peut être intentée que par l'autre".

Preserving the above ground for the dissolution of marriage as the only one in court proceedings, the Principles of Family Legislation of 1968 have with some restrictions reintroduced the old ground of Soviet law before 1944, the mutual consent of the spouses, as a ground for divorce effected by the civil status officers. This is provided in Section 14 of the Principles in the following wording:

"If spouses which have no children under age mutually agree on the dissolution of their marriage, the dissolution is effected by the organs for the registration of acts of civil status. In these

(1) Section 9 of the RSFSR Family Code; Section 11 of the Principles of Family Legislation.

(2) Decree of the Presidium of the Supreme Soviet of the USSR of 10th December 1965. In: Vedomosti Verkhovnogo Soveta Soiuza SSR, 1965, no. 49, text 725. The above provision can be considered as a legal crystallization of the previous Soviet court practice in this matter. Cf.: Postanovlenie Plenuma Verkhovnogo Suda SSSR, 16 Sept. 1949. For more details on the recent development of Soviet divorce law see: Vondracek, pp. 237-248. At present the rule under consideration is incorporated in the Principles of Family Legislation, Section 14.

(3) Orlova, 1966, p. 163.

cases, the official registration of the divorce and the handing over to the spouses of the certificate of the dissolution of their marriage will be made after a period of three months from the day on which the spouses filed their divorce petition" (1).

Finally, a word should be said about the functional difference between Soviet family law and the laws of non-communist countries. It is repeatedly emphasized in Soviet legal literature that the family in a communist country is called to fulfil a messianic function alien to the family of Christian morality. "It is a natural foundation of social development, and promotes communist upbringing and mutual assistance in everyday life. It is a vital factor in the development and consolidation of the Socialist society, in the advance of the Soviet State to communism" (2). Therefore, "The norms of Soviet law are intended actively to promote the development of the Socialist family relationships into communist relationships" (3).

What practical significance the ideological function as ascribed to Soviet family law has, is difficult to say. In any case, if we may take as a criterion the necessity for an extensive control exercised by Soviet administrative organs, volunteers' brigades and other social organizations over the family's private life, we may venture the conclusion that many Soviet families are as unconscious of their mission of communist upbringing as many Western families are of their task to provide generations of free citizens.

Marriage. The basic conflict rule and at the same time the main instrument of Soviet public policy, before the Principles of Family Legislation of June 1968, was the rule laid down in Section 136 of the RSFSR Family Code and the corresponding sections of the Family Codes of the other Union republics. It reads as follows:

"Marriages between aliens and Soviet citizens, as well as marriages between aliens, contracted within the territory of the USSR

(1) Furthermore, Section 14 of the Principles of Family Legislation provides that "the organs for the Registration of acts of civil status may also dissolve a marriage concluded with: a person declared missing according to the rules established by law.

a person declared incapable in consequence of mental illness or feeble-mindedness according to the rules established by law;

a person who has been found guilty of committing a crime and has been sentenced to deprivation of liberty for a period of not less than three years.

In the event of disputes between the parties in these instances, dissolution of marriage is effected in court proceedings". (Translation: G.P. v.d. Berg).

(2) Sverdlov, p. 358.

(3) Orlova, 1966, p. 139. The last paragraph of the introduction to and Section 1 of the Principles of Family Legislation, 1968, are drafted in the same spirit.

shall be registered in accordance with the general rules.

Note: On the basis of reciprocity, registration of marriages between aliens by consular offices and diplomatic missions of the countries concerned acting within the territory of the USSR shall be permitted provided there is observance of the conditions set out in Part One, Chapter II of the present Code" (1).

This legal provision has a general scope of operation with respect to marriages contracted in Soviet territory. It relates to formal as well as to substantive requirements of such marriages, although its binding force is not quite the same with regard to each of them.

To begin with the form, first of all it should be observed that Soviet law, like many Western laws, now provides that only marriages registered at the civil status office are recognized as validly concluded (2). In this respect neither cohabitation nor ecclesiastical celebration produces any legal effect. This is an imperative rule equally binding on Soviet citizens and aliens wishing to be married in Soviet territory. There is no doubt that in the USSR, as in many Western European countries (3), secular marriage as a compulsory formal requirement constitutes an expression of the public policy of that country.

When proclaiming that marriages between aliens and between citizens and aliens shall be registered in accordance with the general rules, the RSFSR legislature had in mind Soviet municipal law only and not the general rules of private international law. This is further made quite clear by the codes of White Russia and the Ukraine where it is plainly provided that marriages within the respective territories must be contracted according to the local laws (4).

Only one exception to this rule is admitted, viz. that concerned with the so-called "consular marriages": on the basis of reciprocity foreigners are permitted to register their marriage at the consular office or diplomatic mission of their country. This exception, is limited to marriages between aliens of the same nationality only (5). Marriages between persons of different national-

(1) The text is based on the present law as changed by a Decree of the Supreme Soviet of the RSFSR of 21st January 1954 and the law in force prior to 1954 as translated in: Gsovski, II pp. 288-289. As to the interpretation of this legal provision, it seems that there is no difference of opinion among the Soviet lawyers. Cf. for instance: Lunts, 1949, pp. 300-301; Lunts II (1963), pp. 311-313; Pergament, pp. 171 and 179; Pereterskii, Krylov, 1959, pp. 159-161; Orlova, 1966, pp. 203, 204, 211 et seq.

(2) RSFSR Family Code, Section 1, paragraph 2; See also The Family Code of White Russia, Section 1, paragraph 2; and the Ukrainian Family Code, Section 104; Section 105, paragraph 2.

(3) Rabel, p. 233. See also Wolff, 1950, p. 341.

(4) Family Code of White Russia, Section 10, paragraph 1; Family Code of the Ukraine, Section 107, paragraph 2.

(5) Orlova, 1966, p. 204.

ities must be recorded in all cases by a Soviet civil officer.

As has been seen from the Sections 136 of the RSFSR Family Code, the Soviet legislature has been even more inexorable with respect to the material conditions of marriage. Soviet law was declared exclusively competent to determine the substantive prerequisites for the validity of a marriage, contracted in Soviet territory, and here no exception is tolerated. The legal significance of this rule was to the effect that neither the Soviet civil officer nor the consuls and ambassadors of foreign countries were permitted to consult any law other than Soviet law to determine the intrinsic conditions of a marriage.

Thus, reference to the *lex patriae* or the *lex domicillii* was excluded altogether by Soviet law. That was also the meaning of the reservation made in the note of Section 136 of the RSFSR Family Code, according to which, by contracting a consular marriage "the conditions provided for in Part One, Chapter II, of the present Code" must be observed. In that chapter the conditions governing the registration of marriages are laid down: mutual consent, marriageable age, which under the Russian Code is fixed at 18 (1), and the absence of a legal impediment, such as the existence of a previous marriage, insanity and consanguinity (3).

At present the function of Section 136 of the RSFSR Family Code and the corresponding provisions of the Codes of the other Soviet Republics is taken over by Section 31 of the Fundamentals of Family Legislation except for the substantive requirement relating to consular marriages, which can be considered as repealed.

The new legal provision runs as follows:

"Marriages of Soviet citizens with aliens as well as marriages of aliens with aliens are concluded in the USSR according to the general provisions.

(1) RSFSR Family Code, Section 5. As to the marriageable age in the other Union Republics, the situation as presented by Gsovski as follows "The marriageable age is not uniformly regulated in the Soviet Union. It is eighteen not only in the RSFSR but also in the Byelorussian, Latvian, Lithuanian, Estonian, Karelian and Kazak republics. In all these republics, the local administrative authorities may reduce the marriageable age for a woman in a given case to seventeen. Marriageable age is eighteen for men and sixteen for women in the Ukrainian, Moldavian, Uzbek, Turkoman, Tadjik, Georgian, Armenian and Azerbaijan Republics. In the Ukrainian and Moldavian republics a marriage between persons who are six months under the required age may be registered in rural localities". (Gsovski, II, p. 241).

(2) A marriage contravening the most important legal prerequisites entails punishments by imprisonment and forced labour. Such punishments are provided e.g. by RSFSR Criminal Code against a person using force to get a marriage contracted, concluding a customary agreement to marry a person under age or being guilty of bigamy. (The Criminal Code of the RSFSR, Sections 233-236).

Marriage of a Soviet citizen with an alien does not bring about loss of the citizenship.
Marriages among aliens concluded in the USSR at the embassy or consulate of a foreign State are considered valid in the USSR on condition of reciprocity if such persons at the time of concluding the marriage were citizens of the State that appointed the ambassador or consul". (1)
The imperative character of Soviet law in the matter under considation was clearly underlined in a decision rendered by the Court of Odessa (Ukraine) in 1959.

"The plaintiff C. (a woman of French nationality) went to the Ukraine for her university education. In Odessa she married the Soviet citizen L., but after some time returned to France and wrote to ask the Court of Odessa to declare her marriage invalid. She based her request on the fact that at the time of her marriage she had been under age and had not had the consent of her parents as required by French law. In the Court decision it was indicated that the law of the Ukrainian SSR, which determined the conditions for contracting marriage, did not provide such a ground for invalidation. The marriage could be dissolved by divorce in the manner established by Soviet legislation" (2).

In justification of the imperative application of Soviet law with respect to the material requirements of marriage Lunts gave the following explanation: "Reference to the personal law of the marrying foreigners with regard to the conditions for contracting a marriage is impossible because it would signify, for instance, a refusal to register, in particular cases, marriages for religious or racial reasons, etc., thus it would entail the application on our territory of foreign laws which essentially contradict the basic principles of our law laid down in the Stalin Constitution. Marriages of foreigners in the USSR are therefore governed exclusively by Soviet law" (3).
A peculiar explanation, indeed, bearing in mind that Soviet courts and civil officers are empowered to use a general clause of reservation against any repugnant foreign legal provision! With this weapon at their disposal the Soviet authorities do not need a total exclusion of foreign laws to serve the imperatives of Soviet public policy.

Although legislation and doctrine recognize the formal validity of marriages contracted by Soviet citizens abroad according to

(1) Translation: Z. Szirmai.
(2) Quoted from: Orlova, 1966, p. 217.
(3) Lunts, 1949, pp. 300-301. See also Orlova, 1960, p. 151.

the *lex loci celebrationis* (1), there are indications that not all Soviet courts have been inclined to accept this solution. Lunts, for instance, reported the following two decisions to this effect.

"On 2nd February 1958 the People's court of Kirovgrad refused to grant the request of the Soviet citizen K. for the recognition of her marriage to the citizen K.: the marriage was concluded in China 1957, according to the Chinese law then in force, in an orthodox church but without registration at the Soviet consulate. The Presidium of the Regional court of Sverdlovsk, by a ruling of 23rd April 1959, annulled the decision of the People's court with the following reasoning: "Deciding the above case, the court did not take into consideration the fact that marriages concluded in China in the form established in that State are also recognized as valid in the territory of the USSR and that therefore the recognition of such a marriage in judicial proceedings is not required".

The second case is as follows:

"The Soviet citizen D. being in Teheran in 1937 concluded a marriage with the Iranian girl Amalia P. In 1958, D., having returned to the USSR, married there Raisa Sh. In 1960 D. died, and Amalia P. brought an action in the People's court of the Tskhakal rayon (Georgia) for invalidation of the second marriage of D. On 22nd March 1963, the People's court rendered a decision in favour of the plaintiff, recognizing therewith the validity of the first marriage concluded in accordance with the formal requirement of the foreign law. This decision was annulled by a decree of the Civil division of the Supreme court of the Georgian SSR dated the 23rd of April 1963, which ordered a new trial by the People's court of the Tskhakal rayon for the reason that the People's court in its decision of 22nd March 1963 did not es-

(1) According to Section 107 paragraph 1 of the Ukrainian Family Code and the corresponding sections of some other Republican Codes, marriages of foreigners and of Soviet citizens with foreigners are recognized as validly concluded if they comply with the law of the place of celebration or Soviet law. This rule is considered by Soviet lawyers as a general conflict rule of form of the whole Union. Cf. Pereterskii, Krylov, 1959, pp. 161-162, Pergament, pp. 173-174. Lunts, II (1963), pp. 315-317; Orlova, 1966, pp. 202-203.
This problem is now definitely settled by Section 32 of the Principles of Family Legislation, according to which Soviet citizens may conclude their marriages abroad either at Soviet embassies and consulates or before the competent authorities of a foreign country. In particular, paragraph 3 of the said Section 32 provides as follows:
"Where marriages among Soviet citizens and marriages between Soviet citizens and aliens are concluded abroad in compliance with the form of the marriage established by the law of the place of celebration, such marriages are recognized as valid in the USSR if there are no impediments arising from Sections 10 and 15 of the present Principles".
(Translation by Z.Szirmai with slight modification by the author.)

tablish whether the marriage of D. with Amalia P., concluded in Iran, had been registered in the embassy of the USSR in Teheran, for only in that case might the marriage be recognized as valid". By its decision of the 2nd of July 1963, the People's court rejected the claim of Amalia P. on the ground that her marriage had not been registered in the Soviet embassy.

By its ruling of the 4th of May 1964, the Presidium of the Supreme court of the Georgian SSR quashed the decision of the People's court of the 2nd of July 1963 and the decree of the Civil Division of the Supreme court of the Georgian SSR of the 23rd of April 1963, confirming thereby the legal force of the first decision of the People's court rendered on 22nd March 1963 for the invalidation of the second marriage of D. with Raisa Sh. - a decision which was based on the assumption that the first marriage concluded in Iran according to the law there in force, was valid also in the USSR" (1).

Soviet lawyers unanimously insist on the extraterritorially binding force of Soviet law in respect of the material conditions of marriages of Soviet citizens (2). This claim is usually based on Section 57 of the Consular Statute of the USSR, according to which "the consul is authorized to officiate at the civil status acts of citizens of the USSR living abroad; for this purpose the consul shall be guided by the laws of the respective Union republics on the Acts of civil status and by the instructions of the People's Commissariat of Foreign Affairs" (3).

Soviet lawyers have given a quite extensive interpretation to this legal provision to the effect that a Soviet citizen cannot contract a valid marriage abroad if he (or she) does not satisfy the material conditions laid down in the corresponding Soviet family code; this rule is considered binding not only with respect to marriages contracted before a Soviet consul, but also with regard to marriages recorded by a foreign civil officer.

The principles of Family Legislation of June 1968 have resolutely reaffirmed this interpretation of the above special provision by providing in Section 32, paragraph 3, that marriages among Soviet citizens and marriages between Soviet citizens and aliens, if concluded abroad according to the local law, may not be contrary to Sections 10 and 15 of the Principles containing the material conditions of marriages and the rules of invalidation.

As to the marriages of Soviet citizens at the embassies and consulates of the USSR in foreign countries, these are governed

(1) Quoted from: Lunts, III (1966), pp. 104-105.

(2) Lunts, 1949, p. 305; Lunts, II (1963), p. 315; Pergament, p. 173; Peretersku, Krylov, 1959, pp. 161-162; Orlova, 1966, pp. 214-215.

(3) Quoted from: Vilkov, p. 211.

in all respects by Soviet law. The rules in this respect as laid down in Section 32 paragraphs 1 and 2 are as follows:
"Marriages of Soviet citizens who live outside the borders of the USSR shall be concluded at the embassies or consulates of the USSR.

When a marriage is concluded or other act of civil status is performed at embassies and consulates of the USSR abroad, the laws applied shall be those of the Union Republic whose citizens are the interested persons.

If the interested persons are citizens of different Union Republics or it is not established which Union Republic's citizens they are, then the laws are applied of a Union Republic agreed upon by the parties or, in case of disagreement, as decided by the official who records the act" (1).

Effects of marriage. The fact that Soviet law does not contain conflict rules on the effects of marriage has been interpreted by Soviet lawyers as a deliberate exclusion of any foreign law from application in this matter. It is maintained that when dealing with disputes relating to personal or property relations between spouses, Soviet courts must apply only Soviet municipal law, irrespective of whether the parties are citizens of the USSR or of a foreign country and of whether they are domiciled in the USSR or abroad (2).

The legal provisions having an absolute application to husband-wife relations are contained in Chapter III (Sections 7-16) of the RSFSR Family Code and in the corresponding chapters of the other republican codes. They can be summarized as follows. The spouses have the right to choose between preserving their pre-nuptial surnames and the acceptance of that of the husband or the wife as a common surname (Section 7). The marriage does not entail changes in the nationalities of the spouses (Section 8). Both husband and wife are at liberty to choose their occupations or professions, and each of them may have a separate residence as the wife is not obliged to follow her husband when he changes his place of abode. (Section 9). Each of the spouses retains ownership of property possessed prior to the marriage, while property acquired during marital life is considered as common property (Section 10). Agreements between the spouses purporting to limit the property rights of the husband or the wife are invalid (Section 13). Only a spouse unable to work and destitute

(1) Based on the translation of Z. Szirmai.

(2) Pereterskii, Krylov, 1959, pp. 163-164; Lunts II (1963), p. 327; Orlova, 1966, pp. 223-224.

is entitled to receive alimony from the other spouse (Section 14). This right can be exercised both during the marriage and after its dissolution, provided that the inability to work has come about during the marriage or not later than a year after the dissolution. The alimony may be restricted in amount or duration, or be denied altogether by the court if the marriage has lasted only for a short time or if the plaintiff has behaved during the marriage in an unworthy manner. In any case, the right to support is extinguished on remarriage. (Section 15 as amended on February 12, 1968.) (1).

The above rights to maintenance were in a way further extended by Section 13 of the Principles of Family Legislation of June 1968 which provided as follows:

"The spouses must support one another financially. If such support is not forthcoming, the spouse unable to work and in need of financial support as well as the wife while she is expectant and within one year of childbirth, are entitled to claim in court maintenance (alimony) from the other spouse if the latter is able to provide it. This right is preserved after divorce.

The divorced needy spouse also has a right to maintenance if he or she becomes incapable of working within one year of the divorce. If the spouses were married for a long time, the court may also award maintenance to the divorced spouse if he or she will reach pensionable age not later than 5 years of the time of the divorce.

In specific cases the spouse may be relieved of liability of maintaining the other spouse or his or her liability may be limited to a certain period of time. The premises under which the court may grant relief to the spouse from his or her liability to provide maintenance for the other spouse or limit it to a certain period of time are established by the legislation of the Union Republics" (2).

Most of these rules are considered by Lunts as an expression of the principle of equality between man and woman laid down in the Soviet Constitution. According to Lunts, they pertain to the fundamentals of the Soviet State system, i. e. to its public order. Their binding force cannot be weakened by admitting a reference to foreign law even then when the case is one of spouses -aliens living abroad. Thus, if a Soviet court has to deal with a question concerning the relations of such spouses no reference to a foreign law should be admitted unless this reference could

(1) Vedomosti Verkhovnogo Soveta RSFSR, 1968: 7.

(2) Based on the translation of Z. Szirmai.

be based on an international agreement concluded by the USSR" (1).

Divorce. Annulment of marriage. The solutions of the conflict of law problems in divorce do not differ essentially from those relating to the matter just discussed. Here again they are based on a general legislative public policy. The courts therefore feel themselves absolutely bound to apply Soviet substantive law to the exclusion of any foreign legal provision in cases of divorce. Of course, they are not authorized to deal with the dissolution of every marriage containing international elements, for instance with cases where both spouses are aliens living abroad, but if they declare themselves jurisdictionally competent, no foreign law is taken into consideration. This applies to matters of form as well as to the substantive conditions or grounds for divorce, irrespective of whether the case involves foreign citizens or is of a purely internal character (2).

The above imperative conflict rule is incorporated at present in Section 33, paragraph 1, of the Principles of Family Legislation in the following wording:

"Dissolution of marriages of Soviet citizens with aliens as well as of marriages of aliens with aliens in the USSR is effected according to the general provisions" (3).

Once again it should be noted, as elsewhere in this paper, that the expressions "according to the general provisions" or "according to the general rules" signify that in the corresponding cases Soviet material law should be applied.

As already mentioned in the preliminaries of this chapter, Soviet divorce law rests upon the following principles. A marriage can be dissolved during the life of the spouses by means of divorce effected either by the court or by the civil status officer. The dissolution of the marriage can be effected by the civil status officer by mutual consent of the spouses, provided that they have no children under age. The only ground on which a divorce decreed by the court can be based is the factual disintegration of the marriage. Thus, instead of compiling a list of specified grounds each sufficient in itself to justify a divorce, the legislature has left it to the discretion of the court to decide whether there is a reasonable and healthy basis for the continuation of the com-

(1) Lunts, II (1963), p. 327. For the attitude of a Soviet notary public on the matter at issue see above under "capacity regulations and the position of foreigners in the USSR".
(2) Lunts, 1949, p. 304; Lunts, II (1963), p. 323; Pereterskii, Krylov, 1959, p. 166; Cheburakhin, p. 109; Orlova, 1966, p. 235.
(3) Translation: Z.Szirmai.

mon marital life or not (1). However, the Soviet courts are bound to follow the following directive of the Plenum of the Supreme Court of the USSR in matters of divorce. "....The judges must bear in mind that a temporary discord in the family and conflicts between the spouses provoked by incidental and transient causes as well as the unwillingness of one or both of the spouses, not motivated by serious reasons, to continue the marriage, cannot be considered as a sufficient ground for dissolution of the marriage. Only, when in the case under consideration, the court comes to the conclusion that the bringing of an action for divorce is provoked by well-grounded motives and that further preservation of the marriage would contradict the principles of communist morals and could not create normal conditions for a common life and for the raising of children, may the court dissolve the marriage...." (2).

Of the court decisions in divorce cases with international elements reported in Soviet legal writings, the following seem to be of interest.

> "Upon a petition of the wife X., a citizen of the USSR, the Moscow town court in 1956 dissolved her marriage with a Belgian living in Belgium. In its decision the Court indicated that the family could not be restored as the spouses lived separated for a long time owing to the unwillingness of the petitioner X. to leave the Soviet Union".
>
> "The District Court of Ternopol' in 1959 dealt with the petition of B., who married his Russian wife in the USSR in 1927. In 1929 B. went to Canada and lived there as a Canadian citizen. There were no children of this marriage. The court decreed the dissolution of the marriage, pointing out that the family had long ago disintegrated as the spouses had lived separated for 30 years" (3).

It appears that the presence of the spouses during the divorce proceeding is not strictly necessary (4). In particular, when both spouses are Soviet citizens living abroad, they may apply to the Moscow city court to dissolve their marriage in their absence. Two cases of this kind have been reported (5). By its

(1) For recent legislation relating to divorce see above under "Preliminaries" of this chapter.

(2) Postanovlenie Plenuma Verkhovnogo Suda SSSR ot 16 sentiabria 1949g., no.12/8/u.

(3) Quoted from: Orlova, 1960, pp. 161-162.

(4) According to Ruling no. 13, 1965 of the Plenum of the USSR Supreme Court, the parties in a divorce proceeding may be absent only in exceptional cases and provided that the court has issued a reasoned decision to this effect. (Biulleten' Verkhovnogo Suda SSSR, 1966: 1, pp. 16-17).

(5) Cheburakhin, p. 110.

decisions of the 9th of May 1956 and the 29th of March 1957 the Civil Collegium of the Moscow City Court granted divorces to two couples with Soviet nationality living in Czechoslovakia and Hungary respectively.

In the decision of 1956 the Court gave the following reasons:

> "The family has in fact been disrupted for a long time. The parties have not lived together since 1947. During that time they have not tried to restore the family, nor are there premises for a restoration in the future, and therefore, the marriage may be dissolved".

In the reasoning of the second decision we read:

> "The request of the petitioners should be granted, as the parties have not created a lasting family, and having lived together for a short time, they have discontinued nuptual relations. The parties have lost their mutual respect and confidence; therefore, there are no grounds to assume that there is a possibility of restoring the marriage".

The absolute application of Soviet law is also insisted in cases of annulment of marriage. The rule is that marriages between foreign citizens as well as those between aliens and Soviet citizens can be declared invalid by the courts of the USSR only on grounds provided for by the family codes of the Soviet republics concerned (1). In particular, such a ground is always present when the marriage contravenes one of the conditions enumerated in Part One, Chapter II of the RSFSR Family Code viz. mutual consent, marriageable age, absence of a marriage previously concluded by one of the spouses, absence of feeble-mindedness or insanity affecting one of the parties, and non-existence of near kinship as described above (2). In any case a Soviet court will never take a ground for annulment into consideration which is unknown to the law of a Union Republic.

Mutual relations of parents and children. According to Soviet private international law, as developed by legal writers and court practice, mutual relations of parents and children cannot be af-

(1) See Orlova, 1966, pp. 216-217. For a decision see above under "Marriage".

(2) See also Section 15 of the Principles of Family Legislation.

A marriage contravening the material requirements may be annulled only if the ground for annulment is present at the moment the action is brought. For instance a bigamous marriage cannot be annulled if the first marriage, although existing at the time the second marriage was concluded, had already been dissolved when the action for annulment was brought. This was made clear by the decision of the USSR Supreme Court in the case "Frolov v. Frolova" (Biulleten' Verkhovnogo Suda SSSR, 1967: 2, pp. 36-37) and the decision of the RSFSR Supreme Court in the case "Alekseev v. Alekseeva N." (Biulleten' Verkhovnogo Suda RSFSR, 1967: 8, pp. 4-5.)

fected by foreign law. Internal relations as well as relations containing international elements are governed in the USSR exclusively by Soviet law (1). The reasons for the exclusion of foreign law from this particular field are not different from those evoked by Soviet lawyers on other similar occasions: fundamental differences between Soviet law and the laws of non-communist countries on the one hand and a deliberate abstention of the legislature from referring to a foreign legal system on the other. The rule that Soviet municipal law is alone competent to govern the mutual relations of parents and children does not only cover persons residing in the USSR, but also the parent-child relations of Soviet citizens residing abroad. Moreover, it applies to the moral as well as to the material rights and duties based on these relations, including the mutual obligations of support and maintenance.

The basic principles of parent-child relations before the entry into force of the Principles of Family Legislation of June 1968 were laid down in the RSFSR Family Code (2) and the Codes of the other Union Republics and can be summed up as follows:

The origin of a child is the one indicated in the Civil Registry Record, but it can be contested in a judicial proceeding. (Section 25). The mother has no right to sue in court for the establishment of paternity and payment of alimony for support and maintenance of a child born out of wedlock (Section 29) (3). The child bears the common parental surname, if any; if there is none, the surname is that agreed upon by the parents, or that of the mother if she has not entered into a registered marriage. (Sections 27, 34). The child has Soviet nationality whenever at least one of the parents is at the time in the USSR. If both parents live abroad and one of them is Soviet citizen, the nationality of the child may be determined by agreement of the parents (Section 35). If the parents live apart, the residence of the child is determined by agreement of the parents and, failing such agreement, by the people's court (Section 40). The parental rights must be exercised exclusively in the interests of the

(1) Lunts, 1949, pp. 306-307; Lunts, II (1963), pp. 330-333; Pergament, 1963 (in: Ocherki), p. 95-96; Pereterskii, Krylov, 1959, pp. 168-170; Orlova, 1966, p. 242; Averin, 1966, p. 159.

(2) RSFSR Family Code, Moskva 1961; the texts are also in accordance with the translation by Gsovski, II.

(3) There was one exception to the rule that no action was granted for the payment of alimony for the support and maintenance of a child born out of wedlock, Such an action, according to the Supreme Court of the USSR, should be granted if the defendant although not having a registered marriage with the mother of the child has lived together with her, has kept with her a common household and has taken part in the support and upbringing of the child. (Antipina V.D. v. Emel'ianov S.A. Biulleten' Verkhovnogo Suda SSSR, 1961: 1, pp. 7-9.)

children. If they are not so exercised or if the parents fail to fulfil their duties toward the children, the court may deprive the parents of their parental rights and entrust the children to a guardianship or a curatorship agency without relieving the parents of their duty to support the children (Sections 33, 46, 51). In particular, the parents have the right and duty to protect the personal and the proprietary interests of their minor children, for which purpose they are authorized to represent them in courts and other institutions (Section 43). Both parents have a duty to care for the children, to raise them, to prepare them for socially useful activity and to provide them with maintenance even when grown up but unable to earn a living (Sections 41, 42, 48). On the other hand, if the parents are unable to work and destitute, their grown-up children owe them support and maintenance (Section 49). They may be released from this duty only if it is proved in court that the parents have not fulfilled their parental obligations (paragraph 2 added to Section 49 on 12th February 1968) (1).

The above legal rules, in so far they are not contrary to the Principles of Family Legislation of June 1968, will remain in force in the future. However, the provisions, relating to the origin of a child, the establishment of paternity and payment of alimony for the support of children born out of wedlock must be considered as repealed, as they are contrary to Sections 16 and 17 of the said Principles. Section 16 provides:

"The mutual rights and duties of parents and children are based on the descent of the children, ascertained in established legal procedure.

The descent of a child from its parents joined in marriage is ascertained by the registration of the marriage of the parents. The descent of a child from parents not joined in marriage is established by a declaration made in common by the father and mother of the child before the State authorities for the recording of acts of civil status.

If the child was born of parents not joined in marriage, and if no common declaration of the parents is available, paternity can be established in court proceedings.

In establishing paternity the court will be guided by (the following facts): that the mother of the child and the defendant had lived together and had a common housefold before the child was born, that they had brought up the child together or provided (in common) for its maintenance, or by other evidence reliably confirming the recognition of the defendant, as being the father of

(1) Vedomosti Verkhovnogo Soveta RSFSR, 1968: 7.

the child" (1).

None of these rights and duties may be diminished or excluded by private agreements. This has been made quite clear, for instance, in the case "Contractual discharge of payment of alimony" dealt with by a Soviet notary public.

"The spouses A. applied to the notary public to legalize their signatures under a statement according to which they divided the children between themselves and declared that after the divorce they would not claim from each other alimony for the children's maintenance. The notary public refused to legalize the signatures of the spouses on the ground that their statement, having the character of a friendly arrangement, was contrary to the law. Furthermore, according to the law such an agreement cannot deprive a spouse of the right to demand that the court order the other spouse to pay alimony for maintenance of a child" (2).

In particular, suits of a private international law character filed against parents for the maintenance and support of children are decided in Soviet courts in accordance with Section 51a of the RSFSR Family Code and the corresponding sections of the other Republican codes. Section 51a provides as follows:

"If alimony for the maintenance of one child is awarded, one quarter of the defendant's pay may be attached; for the maintenance of two children, one third, and for the maintenance of three or more children, one half of the defendant's pay" (3).

Accordingly, the Haapsalu Regional Court of the Estonian SSR decreed the attachment of 25% of the income of the Soviet citizen Radi Edgar, residing in Estonia, as alimony for the maintenance and support of his daughter living in Sweden; while the Regional Court of Dubnovo in the province of Roven awarded in 1958, the alimony of 50% of the whole income of the Soviet citizen A.I. Lebed' for the maintenance of his three daughters living in Czechoslovakia (4).

(1) Based on the translation of Z.Szirmai and G.P. v.d. Berg.
As to the manner in which the entering of the names of the parents of children born out of wedlock should be effected, see Section 17 of the Principles of Family Legislation.
Under the above rules the establishment of paternity can be effected in court proceedings only in respect of children born after the coming into effect of the Principles. For the other cases special rules are provided in the Law of the USSR, approving the Principles of Legislation of the USSR and the Union Republics concerning Marriage and Family, of 27th July 1968, and the Decree of the Presidium of the Supreme Soviet of the USSR of 20th September 1968, published in Izvestiia on 21st September 1968, on the manner of putting these Principles into effect.

(2) Sovetskaia iustitsiia, 1962: 7, p. 30.

(3) Translation: Gsovski, II, p. 256.

(4) See: Cheburakhin, p. 111.

Two cases concerned with the legal assistance between the Soviet Union and the other East-European countries seem to be of particular interest, mainly because of the assertion of communist legal writers that public policy plays no role in the legal conflicts between these countries.

In the first case, which is primarily concerned with the recognition of a foreign judgment on the basis of the Soviet-Czechoslovak Agreement on legal assistance, it is indirectly indicated that Soviet law relating to the maintenance of children applies imperatively unless there is a treaty provision to the contrary.

"On the 11th of January 1946, the Czechoslovakian citizen I. Slavikova gave birth to a daughter whose father (according to the birth and christening certificate) was the Soviet citizen Zhuskovskii-Iatsenko K. A ground for the indication of the name of the father was an excerpt from the record of the regional court of Tanvald (Czechoslovakia) dated the 27th of November 1945, personally signed by Zhukovskii-Iatsenko and acknowledging that he was the father of the as then unborn child.

Slavikova maintained that her marriage with Zhukovskii-Iatsenko was registered on the 26th of October 1945 in Wroclaw (Poland) without being able to present a document confirming this assertion. In 1947, it became clear that Zhukovskii-Iatsenko had earlier concluded another marriage which had never been dissolved. In its decision of the 21st of January 1953 the city court of Prague declared the marriage of Slavikova and Zhukovskii-Iatsenko invalid, basing its decision on the fact that in 1945, according to both Czechoslovakian and Polish law, the only legal form of marriage was celebration in church in the presence of two witnesses and preceeded by an agreement. The court also indicated that the fact of the conclusion of the marriage had not been proved by any document and that therefore the daughter of Slavikova must be considered as born out of wedlock.

According to Czechoslovakian family law (Law no. 265/1949) (1), a child of persons not having entered into registered marriage has the right to receive alimony from its father if paternity has been established. Proceeding from the fact that Zhukovskii-Iatsenko himself had admitted that he was the father by a declaration at the court of Tanvald, Slavikova asked the court to order the defendant to pay alimony for the maintenance of the child.

The Czechoslovak court considered that the dispute in this legal relationship was exclusively within its jurisdiction and that, by virtue of Section 27 of the Soviet-Czechoslovak Agreement

(1) The law then in force.

on Legal Assistance, the law of the child's nationality, i. e. the corresponding norms of the Czechoslovak law, should be applied to the case.

However, -continues the reporter of this case-according to paragraph 'a' of Section 45 of the Agreement, the said Section 27 cannot be applied in this case: the Agreement came into force on the 10th of May 1958, while the child was born on the 11th of February, 1946. Therefore, the jurisdiction and the choice of law with respect to the legal relations between the daughter of Slavikova and the defendant should be determined not on the basis of Section 27 of the Agreement, but according to the rules provided by Soviet legislation.

The present Soviet legislation does not contain a rule by virtue of which Slavikova could bring an action in a Soviet court In accordance with the Decree of the Presidium of the Supreme Soviet of the USSR dated the 14th of March 1945 a claim for alimony against a citizen with whom the mother has not entered into a registered marriage may be advanced if the child was born before the publication of the Decree of the 8th of July 1944 (1) and if at the recording of the birth the defendant was indicated in the civil status register as the father of the child" (2).

In a second case a Soviet court refused to apply a provision of the agreement on legal assistance between the USSR and Poland as being contrary to Soviet substantive law relating to maintenance.

"The district court of Ivan-Franko (Ukraine) received a request for the enforcement of a decision rendered by the regional court of Zabsze (Poland) on the claim of the Polish citizen J. Krasii against the Soviet citizen V. Krasii for payment of alimony for maintenance of two children at the rate of 350 zloty for each child. As the salary of the defendant was 92 Russian Rubles per month the requested payment was equal to 45 rubles and 78 kopecs, i. e. 50% of the monthly earnings. Though the Civil Division of the District Court of Ivan-Franko took into account the fact that paragraph 2 of Section 31 of the Soviet-Polish Agreement on legal assistance submitted the legal relationship to the law of the State of which the child was a citizen, it nevertheless, considered that it could not grant compulsory enforcement of the judgment as it contradicted Section 31 of the Ukrainian Family Code" (3).

(1) See note 1 p. 113 "Fam. law".

(2) The case is reported by Averin, pp. 160-161. No mention is made of the Soviet authority which rejected the request for the enforcement of the Czechoslovak judgement.

(3) Quoted from: Averin, p. 179.
Section 31 of the Ukrainian Family Code corresponds to Section 51a of the RSFSR Family Code quoted above.

Adoption. Before the coming into force of the Principles of Family Legislation of June 1968, Soviet legislative public policy relating to adoption found its expression in the note to Section 59 of the RSFSR Family Code as well as in Section 45 of the Consular Statute of the USSR. Both legal provisions operate as one-sided conflict rules referring exclusively to Soviet law.

The first rule as laid down in the note of Section 59 of the Family Code reads as follows:

"Adoption of children of Soviet nationals by foreign nationals (subjects) residing in the USSR territory shall be permitted, provided that the rules laid down in the present chapter are observed, and provided further that special permission is obtained in each individual case from the regional (provincial) executive committee".

According to unanimous interpretation by the Soviet doctrine (1) based on the general practice, this rule applies not only with regard to adoptions of Soviet children by aliens living in the USSR, but also in cases when the adopters live abroad. Furthermore, Soviet law also applies to adoptions of foreign children by Soviet citizens whenever this is to take place in the USSR. In the latter case, according to Lunts, the foreign consul concerned is as a rule consulted, but this formal inquiry does not affect at all the imperative force of the Soviet law.

According to the second rule contained in Section 45 of the Consular Statute, the Soviet Consul abroad is charged with the effectuation of adoptions when the adopter and the adoptee are Soviet citizens living abroad. In such a case the consul effectuates and registers the adoption in accordance with the law of the Soviet republic of which the adoptee is a citizen (2).

The Soviet authorities interpreted these legal provisions to the effect that adoptions abroad involving Soviet citizens (as adopters or adoptees) must comply with the material conditions provided by Soviet law. With respect to such adoptions, an extraterritorial effect was claimed for Soviet law, which means that even the adoption effectuated by foreign authorities must comply with the defined material conditions. Moreover, when the adoptee was a Soviet citizen the foreign act of adoption would never be recognized in the USSR if the permission of the appropriate Soviet executive committee, as required by Sect. 59 of the RSFSR Family Code, had not been obtained. The purpose of this extraterritorial requirement was in the opinion of Lunts "to exclude

(1) Lunts, 1949, pp. 307-308; Lunts II (1963), pp. 334-335; Gorodetskaia, Voprosy usinovleniia, pp. 144-148; Boguslavskii, Rubanov 1962, pp. 118-119.
(2) As presented by Lunts, II (1963), p. 334.

the recognition of a foreign act of adoption purporting to prevent the Soviet citizens considered as displaced persons from returning to the USSR" (1).
This is an explanation difficult to understand and one which would seem to have nothing to do with the problem under consideration.

At least in one respect the Principles of Family Legislation of June 1968 have brought about a drastic change in the previous legislation and practice relating to adoption. For the recognition of adoptions effected in foreign countries it is not longer required that such adoptions comply with the material conditions of Soviet law. The requirement of prior permission for the adoption of Soviet children will remain in force, however. This matter is dealt with in Section 34 of the Principles, which provides:
"Adoption of children having Soviet citizenship and living outside the borders of the USSR is effected in the embassies or consulates of the USSR. If the adopter is not a Soviet citizen, then permission of the competent organ of the Union Republic is required for the adoption.
The adoption of a child that is a Soviet citizen, before the authorities of the State in which it is living, will also be valid if the permission of the competent authority of the Union Republic has been obtained in advance.

The rules for the adoption of children who are Soviet citizens, by aliens, on the territory of the USSR are established by the legislation of the Union Republics" (2).

The basic substantive provisions relating to adoption as contained in Chapter III of the RSFSR Family Code are the following: Only minors and juveniles may be adopted, i.e. persons under the age of eighteen. (Section 57, in connection with Section 11 of the RSFSR Civil Code of 1964).
Normally, the consent of the legally capable parent is required for a valid adoption. This consent is not necessary if the parents do not live together with the children, do not take part in their upbringing and maintenance and their address has been unknown for more than a year. The consent of parents whose address is

(1) Lunts, II (1963), p. 335. For adoption abroad involving Soviet citizens see also: Gorodetskaia, Voprosy usinovleniia, p. 150; Boguslavskii, Rubanov 1962, p. 119.
These rigid rules regarding the material conditions of the adoption of Soviet citizens abroad are somewhat mitigated in the Principles of the legislation of the USSR and the Union Republics on Marriage and Family. According to Section 34, paragraph 2, of the Principles, the adoption of a Soviet child effected abroad by the authorities of a foreign country shall be recognized in the USSR if the competent organ of the Soviet republic concerned has given its permission. No other condition for the validity of such an adoption is required.
(2) Based on the translation of Z.Szirmai.

known may be dispensed with if their neglect of the children has lasted longer than a year in spite of a warning by the guardianship and curatorship agency (Section 61 and Section 61^{I}, which was added in February 1968) (1).
If the child is above the age of ten, his consent is also necessary (Section 63).
The adopters must satisfy the following requirements.
They must not have been deprived of parental rights or of the right to vote by a court decision. Their interests must not be opposed to those of the adoptee and they must not be on hostile terms with him. They must have attained the age of majority (Sections 58 and 77). If the adopter is married, the consent of his or her spouse is also required (Section 62).

According to Section 57 of the RSFSR Family Code the adoption must be exclusively in the interests of the child.

If the above requirements are met, the adoption is granted by a resolution of a guardianship and curatorship agency, whereupon the act has to be registered at the Civil Registry Office (Section 59).
The mutual relations of the adoptive parents and the infant as well as their rights and duties are the same as those of parents and children by blood (Section 64).

An adoption can be cancelled only in the interests of the infant. The cancellation is effected either by a resolution of the guardianship and curatorship agency on a petition of parents who have not given their consent for the adoption or by a court decision upon an action brought by any person or institution (Sections 65 and 66).
The following decision has been reported on this matter:
"The Soviet citizen K. adopted in Beregovo (Ukraine) in 1947 the Czechoslovak girl Tatiana F. residing in the USSR. The parents of Tatiana addressed a petition to the Soviet authorities to cancel the adoption, alleging that they had not given their consent to it, as required by the legislation of the Ukrainian SSR. Upon a request by the public procurator this adoption was cancelled be the Executive Committee of the Zakarpatian district Soviet" (2).

Guardianship and curatorship. The final confirmation of the thesis that Soviet family law is dominated by public policy considerations is provided by the complex of imperative legal provisions governing guardianship and curatorship. That this subject-matter

(1) For Section 61^{I} see: Vedomosti Verkhovnogo Soveta RSFSR, 1968: 7.
(2) Quoted from: Gorodetskaia, Voprosy usinovleniia, pp. 148-149.

is also a matter of public policy for Soviet lawyers, can be seen in the general observation of Gorodetskaia that "in the USSR the institution of guardianship and curatorship bears a State character" (1). Proceeding from this assumption, the Soviet authorities have interpreted the absence of a classic conflict rule in this branch of law as an indication that Soviet municipal law claims absolute application in the territory of the USSR even in cases with international elements (2). Thus, neither the nationality nor the domicile of the persons involved (as guardians, wards, etc.) is ever taken into consideration in the appointment of guardians or curators on Soviet territory and in determining the rights and duties based on the corresponding legal relations.

The situation with respect to guardianship and curatorship of Soviet minors abroad is the same. Here again, Soviet municipal law claims unrestricted application both from a formal and from a substantive point of view. The matter is governed by Section 45 of the Consular Statute of the USSR, according to which "all children of a citizen of the USSR who dies within a Consular District and also persons under his guardianship, come under guardianship of the Consul, or of persons whom he shall appoint in accordance with the procedure laid down by the legislation of the USSR and the corresponding Union Republics and by the agreements concluded by the USSR and the country in which the Consul is stationed" (3).

Accordingly, in the absence of an international agreement to the contrary, the Consul is bound to establish a guardianship or curatorship as provided by Soviet law. The Consular Statute and the RSFSR Family Code speak of a "procedure" (poriadok) to be complied with, but according to the unanimous interpretation by Soviet lawyers the substantive prerequisites and the legal consequences of these institutions must also be determined by Soviet law (4). Soviet substantive law claims in this respect an extraterritorial effect, which means e.g. that no foreign act relating to guardianship or curatorship over Soviet minors shall be recognized in the USSR if it contradicts the relevant Soviet

(1) Gorodetskaia, voprosy opeki, p. 339.

(2) Pereterskii, Krylov, 1959, p. 170; Gorodetskaia, Voprosy opeki, pp. 338-339; Boguslavskii, Rubanov, 1962, p. 120; Lunts, II (1963), p. 341.

(3) Quoted from: Vilkov, p. 211. A similar provision is also contained in Section 85 of the RSFSR Family Code, which reads: "Representatives of the USSR abroad shall attend to matters involving guardianship and curatorship regarding USSR citizens residing or possessing property outside of the USSR. The procedure for the institution of the guardianship over property left abroad after the death of USSR citizens shall be determined by special rules." (Translation: Gsovski, II, 1949, p. 271.

(4) Pereterskii, Krylov, 1959, pp. 170-171; Gorodetskia, Voprosy opeki, pp. 333-334; Lunts II, p. 340.

legal provisions (1). Of course, the question of recognition of such foreign acts will only arise in cases where the Soviet Consul is materially or legally prevented from exercising his functions in the territory concerned.

Among the basic principles relating to guardianship and curatorship as laid down in Part III of the RSFSR Family Code and in the Law concerning Guardianship and Patronage of Children Who Have Lost Their Parents, of 1943 (2), the following are of particular interests.

The purpose of the institution of Guardianship or curatorship is "to protect a person incapable of entering into legal transactions, his lawful rights and interests, as well as to safeguard his property in cases provided for by law" (Section 68).

Guardians may be appointed only over minors who have not reached the age of 14 years and over persons duly declared feeble-minded or mentally deranged. Guardianship may be instituted also for the safeguarding of property belonging to absentees and dead persons (Section 69). Curators are provided for minors between the age of 14 and 18 years, and for adults who "by reason of their physical condition are incapable themselves of protecting their interests" (Section 70). Guardians and curators are appointed only if there are no parents who can effectively fulfil the functions of natural guardians and curators. (Section 71). Or as Section 24 of the above-mentioned Law Concerning Guardianship and Patronage has put it "every child who is not in the custody of his parents or a proper children's institution shall be placed under guardianship", while "in event of the death of both parents, the institution of guardianship shall be mandatory". The same section provides for guardianship also in cases when both parents are alive: "a) if the parents have been deprived by a court of their parental rights and the custody of their child .... etc.; b) if the parents are not able to attend to the upbringing of their child for a considerable period of time (e.g. are in hospital, in confinement, on the road for a long period of time, etc.); c) if the parents are feeble-minded and have been placed under guardianship or in an appropriate medical institution..."

The guardians or curators charged with the immediate exercise of guardianship or curatorship are appointed by the presidia of the regional and provincial executive committees, the circuit, district, county and city executive committees or the village

(1) Gorodetskaia, Voprosy opeki, p. 335; Lunts, II (1963), p. 341.

(2) For the translation of this law and the corresponding provisions of the RSFSR Family Code, see: Gsovski, II, pp. 262 et seq.

soviets, which according to Section 72 of the RSFSR Family Code function as guardianship and curatorship agencies.

The same agencies are empowered to remove the guardians and curators if they neglect or abuse their powers (Section 92). The acceptance of an appointment is considered as a public duty and it can be declined only for reasons strictly defined by law: age over sixty, subjective or objective impediments to the discharge of such functions, bringing up of more than two children, having a child under eight or the discharge of another guardianship or curatorship (Section 78). On the other hand, the following persons may not be appointed as guardians or curators: (a) Persons deprived by a court of the right to vote; (b) persons deprived by the court of parental rights; (c) Persons whose interests are opposed to those of the prospective ward, as well as persons who are on unfriendly terms with him; (d) persons under age. (Sections 77).

The duties performed by the guardian or curator are gratuitous except when the ward has income-bearing property, in which case the guardianship and curatorship agency may allow a renumeration not exceeding 10 per cent of the income derived from such property. (Section 81).

Besides the general duty of the guardian as provided by Section 79 to attend to the upbringing of the ward, his education, medical care and training for socially useful activity, as well as the general authorisation of the guardian and curator to appear before all institutions, including courts, in the protection of the minor's interests (Section 91), the following more specific rights and duties should be mentioned:

The guardian or curator may enter into any legal transaction on behalf of the minor with or without the consent of the guardianship and curatorship agency, depending on the importance of the transaction (Sections 86 and 90). The guardian may not enter into legal transactions with his ward or may he represent him in transactions and lawsuits between the ward and the guardian's spouse or next-of-kin, nor may he acquire instruments of debt under which the ward is liable (Sections 88). It is further provided that minors between the age of fourteen and sixteen and other persons placed under curatorship may without permission enter into legal transactions involving articles and sums of money acquired by their personal labour. For other transactions the permission of the curator is strictly required (Section 90).

II SOVIET JUDICIAL PUBLIC POLICY

Preliminary Remarks. Judicial public policy, as already indicated, is a complex of ideological imperatives adressed to the judge, civil status officer, notary public, etc., by virtue of which a foreign legal provision normally applicable, must be discarded if its application would be detrimental to the political, economic and moral conceptions of the forum. These imperatives, quite indispensable to every legal system, are also to be found in Soviet law. They appear in Article 128 of the Fundamentals of Civil Legislation of 1961, in the Civil Codes of the individual Union Republics (1), in the Statute on the State Notary of the RSFSR and other laws. Article 128 of the Fundamentals and the corresponding articles of the Civil Codes of the Union Republics provide that:
"A foreign law shall not apply where its application contradicts the fundamental principles of the Soviet system".
In Section 84 paragraph 2 of the Statute on the State Notary we read: "The State Notary shall accept documents drawn up in accordance with the requirements of a foreign law and shall make legalisation in the form prescribed by a foreign legislation as far as this does not contradict the fundamental principles of the Soviet system" (2). In addition, mention should be made of Article 5 of the Fundamentals of Civil Legislation, which purports to reinforce the general clause of reservation in respect of civil rights to be exercised in Soviet territory.
"Civil rights shall be protected by law, except insofar as they are exercised in contradiction to their purpose in socialist society

(1) See for instance Civil Code of the RSFSR (1964), Section 568; Civil Code of the Ukrainian SSR (1963), Section 571; Civil Code of the UzSSR (1964), Section 621, etc. These legal provisions are in the same wording as Article 128 of the Fundamentals.

(2) See: Ukaz Prezidiuma Verkhovnogo Soveta RSFSR ob utverzhdenii Polozheniia o gosudarstvennom notariate RSFSR, 30 sent. 1965 g. (Decree of the Presidium of the Supreme Soviet of the RSFSR for the approval of the Statute on the State Notary of the RSFSR, 30-IX-1965). Published in: Vendomosti Verkhovnogo Soveta RSFSR, 1965, no. 40 (7th Oct. 1965).
Soviet notaries are comparable to a certain extent with the notaries in civil law countries. They are State officers with Soviet citizenship who have had higher education in law. In exceptional cases legal education is not required, provided, that the candidates have worked at least 3 years as judges, public prosecutors, legal advisers or barristers (Section 13 of the Statute). The educational or specialised requirements relate only to notaries of State notarial offices. In places where there are no such offices some of the notarial functions are carried out by the chairmen, secretaries or members of the Executive Committees of the regional or local Soviets, in which cases no legal education or practice is required (Section 5, paragraph 2 of the Statute).

in the period of communist construction".

In view of the fact that family law under the Soviet system forms a separate branch of law it has also been found necessary to provide a public policy clause in the Principles of Family Legislation. This is laid down in Section 36, paragraph 1, of the Principles and runs as follows:

"The application of foreign laws on marriage and family or the recognition of civil status acts based on these laws, can not take place if such application or recognition were contrary to the fundamentals of the Soviet system." (1)

In the preceding pages it has been made clear that the field of application of foreign laws on Soviet territory is rather restricted owing to the imperative application of the *lex fori*. Under these circumstances it is quite natural to expect that Soviet judicial public policy will play a far less significant role than its counterparts in the West. Nevertheless, there are still a great number of hypothetical cases in which the Soviet authorities should have recourse to this touchstone for the admissibility of foreign laws. Among the cases where such recourse will be necessary we could cite not only those where the application of a foreign legal provision would lead to results detrimental to society, but also those involving legal institutions absolutely unknown to the forum or vested rights acquired under the operation of a foreign law which are repugnant to Soviet conceptions. Of course this matter is too pragmatic to put into general terms. Its essential characteristics can be seen better in the light of living practice, and where this is lacking, in the light of some comparative examples. We should proceed from this premise in our further discussion.

1. OBLIGATIONS

Although neither the Fundamentals of Soviet Civil Legislation nor the Civil Codes of the Union Republics contain explicit conflict rules relating to the substantive validity of obligations in general, we may assume that the basic principle developed by Soviet courts and legal writers under the operation of Section 7 of the RSFSR Code of Civil Procedure (old) is intended to retain its applicability. This rule is to the effect that the intrinsic validity of obligations is determined by *lex loci contractus*. This conclusion is also based on Article 126 of the Civil Law Fundamentals, according to which the rights and duties of parties to a

(1) Translation by the author. Also in accordance with the translation of Z. Szirmai.

foreign trade transaction shall be determined pursuant to the law of the place where it is concluded. Moreover, it is in accordance with the authoritive statement of Lunts that the conflict rules relating to foreign trade have, to some extent, the character of general principles for the various civil law contracts with foreign elements (1).

As to the *capacity of a physical person to undertake obligations*, there is a tendency in Soviet practice to apply either the *lex patriae* or the *lex loci contractus* (2), of course with numerous imperative exemptions in favour of Soviet law which have already been discussed.

Notwithstanding these general conflict rules, Soviet authorities are bound to disregard the foreign legal provisions and the legal rights based thereon if they are repugnant to the moral, social and political conceptions of the USSR. The following examples, most of which have been suggested by Soviet legal writers, are pertinent:

The restrictions on the foreigner's legal capacity to contract or to undertake obligations in general are recognized in the USSR only on grounds known also to Soviet law. Thus restrictions based on difference of race, nationality, religion or sex are considered as contrary to the fundamentals of the Soviet system and therefore have no legal effect in the USSR (3).

A legal provision pertaining to this group was contained in Article 223 of the French Code Civil before 13th July 1965 (the date when this article was changed.

"La femme peut exercer une profession séparée de celle de son mari, á moins que ce dernier ne s'y oppose.

Les engagements pris par la femme dans l'exercise de cette profession sont nuls à l'égard du mari si les tiers avec lesquels elle contracte ont personnellement connaissance de l'opposition au moment où ils traitent avec l'épouse.

Si l'opposition du mari n'est pas justifiée par l'intérêt de la famille, la femme peut être autorisée par la justice à passer outre, auquel cas les engagements professionels qu'elle a pris depuis l'opposition sont valables" (4).

In a treatise on French Civil law we find the following inter-

(1) See: Lunts, II (1963), pp. 103-104; see also Grzybowski, pp. 122-123.

(2) See for instance Section 36 of the Soviet Statute on Cheques; Lunts, II (1963), pp. 32-33, 35.

(3) Lunts, II (1963), pp. 33, 37; See also! Pereterskii, Krylov, 1959, p. 56.

(4) Article 223 of the French Civil Code as changed on 13th July 1965 provides as follows: "La femme a le droit d'exercer une profession sans le consentement de son mari, et elle peut toujours pour les besoins de cette provision, aliéner et obliger seule ses biens personnels en plein propriété".

pretation of this legal provision (now repealed).

"...Donc la femme, au cas d'opposition du mari, est frappée d'incapacité mais seulement pour ses engagements professionels. Comme le plus souvent il y aura contrat de travail passé par la femme, ce contrat sera frappé de nullité, s'il s'agissait de l'exercice d'une exploitation agricole ou artisanale ou d'une profession libérale, la nullité s'étendrait à tous les actes que la femme aurait faits en vue de cette exploitation" (1).

From the point of view of Soviet law, if a French actress had entered into a contract in Paris in 1964 with a Russian organization to give a performance in Moscow in spite of her husband's objections, she would have to fulfil her obligations. Any nullity action on the part of the French husband before a Russian court would never have a chance of success. It would be declared inacceptable *ad initio*, because the very admission of such an action would amount to an indirect recognition of the inequality of husband and wife, i.e. it would be contrary to Soviet public policy as expressed in the constitution:

"Women in the USSR are accorded equal rights with men in all spheres of economic, governmental, cultural, political and other public activity" (Section 122).

An assertion by the husband that he exercised his authority exclusively in the interests of the family would be immaterial. Even the right of the wife, which she probably had under French law, to invoke her incapacity as an excuse for non-performance would never be recognized. What matters here, is not the personal interests or values, but the fundamental principle of the Soviet system regarding equality, which may not be brought into discredit by the application of foreign laws.

For these reasons the Soviet judge would also refuse to recognize the legal effect of Article 167 of the Swiss Civil Code containing a restriction on the wife's capacity similar to that of the repealed Article 223 of the French Civil Code.

Another example regarding the capacity restriction of a married woman is provided by Belgian law. According to that law, if the spouses have not explicitly stipulated in a marriage contract that their property relationship will be under the system of "biens séparés", the wife may not alienate e.g. her own house, pertaining to her dowry, without the consent of her husband; neither may she collect money accruing from the lease of that house without the authorization of the husband, because the fruits of the wife's property are considered as a contribution to

(1) Ripert, Boulanger, p. 808.

the husband for meeting marital expenses (1).

Let us imagine a case where a Belgian wife, married without a contract for the separation of property, owns a house in Brussels, which she has let to a Russian tourist for a period of three months. Owing to the absence of the husband, the wife acted without any authorization. Subsequently she joined her husband on holiday in Spain. A month later the Russian tourist was robbed of all his money and returned to Russia leaving only a letter of apology and a promise to pay the rent as soon as he was in a position to do so. If the Belgian husband tried to recover the money owed by the Russian in a Soviet court, his claim would be found inadmissible and his right to collect the income of his wife's property repugnant to Soviet public policy. The only alternatives left to the disappointed husband would be either to ask for authorization from his wife and proceed as her representative or to let her recover the debt herself.

Among the *contracts which in substance would be intolerable to Soviet public policy*, we may mention in the first place those which are considered to distort economic and social relations on Soviet territory. Pereterskii, Krylov use the following example: "If a contract provides for the transfer on the territory of the USSR of things which, according to our legislation, are *res extra commercium*, this contract, though valid from the point of view of the *lex loci contractus*, cannot produce on Soviet territory the intended legal results" (2). The point at issue here is that the transfer of basic means of production (machinery, sea-going vessels, etc.) in the territory of the USSR in favour of private persons residing there is contrary to Soviet public policy. Of course, the regular commercial transactions between duly authorized Soviet organizations and foreign firms are not affected.

There are other obligations based on foreign laws which will not be recognized or carried out in the USSR because of their being unknown or simply immoral under Soviet law. That would be the fate e.g. of contracts made in accordance with paragraph 72 of the German Marriage Act of 1946, which provides:
"Die Ehegatten können über die Unterhaltspflicht für die Zeit nach der Scheidung der Ehe Vereinbarungen treffen. Ist eine Vereinbarung dieser Art vor Rechtskraft des Scheidungsurteils getroffen worden, so ist sie nicht schon deshalb nichtig, weil sie die Scheidung erleichtert oder ermöglicht hat; sie ist jedoch nichtig, wenn die Ehegatten in Zusammenhang mit der Vereinbarung

(1) Cf. Articles 1530-1536 of the Belgian Code Civil. See also above, under "Capacity regulations and the position of foreigners in the USSR."
(2) Pereterskii, krylov, 1959, p. 125.

einen nicht oder nicht mehr bestehenden Scheidungsgrund geltend gemacht hatten oder wenn sich anderweitig aus dem Inhalt der Vereinbarung oder aus sonstigen Umständen des Falles ergibt, dass sie den guten Sitten widerspricht."

If a German court, basing its divorce decree on the agreement between the spouses, has entrusted the children to a spouse whose way of life would be detrimental to their interests, or has refused to grant payment of alimony by a capable spouse to the destitute one, such legal consequences could not be recognized or enforced in Soviet territory (1).

If a German girl abandoned by her Russian fiancé, tried to enforce a German judgement for payment of damages in a Russian court she would be told that such damages are unknown to Soviet law and contrary to the Russian conception of marriage as a union by free will, although the engagement itself as an agreement is known in Russia and contains nothing repugnant to Soviet public policy (2).

It would probably be in the general spirit of Soviet private international law to allow the law of the place of contracting decide the consequences of the invalidity of "a transaction effected under the influence of fraud, violence, threats, dishonest collusion of an agent of one party with the other party or under the impact of pressing difficulties" (3). However, if the *lex loci contractus* does not know such grounds of invalidity, Soviet municipal law will take its place to annul the contract and determine the consequences of the annulment (4). In contradistinction to other cases of international economic intercourse, where Soviet public policy is usually based on the supremacy of the interests of society, here, according to Soviet lawyers, "the veritable protection of the individual's interests effectuated by Soviet law" is the reason for non-recognition of the contract and non-application of the foreign law (5).

(1) See also Lunts, II (1963) p. 322.
On this matter Soviet public policy is comparable e.g. with Englich public policy, by virtue of which an agreement between spouses to facilitate divorce and for the abandonment by the husband of the custody of the children to his wife would not be recognized. (See: Dicey, Morris, pp. 737-738.

(2) For the operation of Netherlands public policy in this matter, see Van Brakel, 1953, pp. 85-86.

(3) As mentioned in Section 58 of the RSFSR Civil Code, 1964 (Transl. by Kiralfy).

(4) Cf. Lunts, 1949, 123; Pereterskii, Krylov, 1959, p. 126.

(5) Pereterskii, Krylov, 1949, p. 126.
A similar motivation is also to be found in the explanations of the public policy of other countries. It is certainly implied in the statement of Martin Wolff that according to English public policy "a contract unassaible as to its content but concluded under duress, undue

Although Soviet law of *torts* in the majority of cases operates as an expression of Soviet legislative public policy, there are still cases where Soviet judicial public policy should be invoked because the general conflict rule is that in principle the *lex loci delicti* shall apply.

The two guiding rules in this domain as presented by Lunts (1) are the following:

Foreign grounds for the exclusion or restriction of liability may be recognized by Soviet courts only when they are not contrary to the fundamentals of the Soviet system. The matter was illustrated by a reference to the defence based on the English doctrine of common employment. According to this doctrine, an employer is not liable for injuries sustained by his employees if such injuries are caused solely by the negligence of a fellow servant. Although this common law defence was abolished in Great Britain by the Personal Injury Act of 1948 (2) and has "practically disappeared" in the U.S.A. (owing to its abolition by the various Workmen's compensation acts on the one hand and to its unpopularity with the courts on the other), the problem has not yet lost its relevance. There are still many categories of workers and cases in the U.S.A. where the only remedy for

influence, or fraud will not be enforced in this country even if under its proper law the contract is valid." (Wolff, 1950, p. 181).

The relative Soviet substantive provision laid down in Section 58 of the RSFSR Civil Code. 1964, runs as follows:

"A transaction entered into under the influence of fraud, violence, threats,dishonest collusion of an agent of one party with the other party, and also a transaction which a citizen was compelled to enter into under the impact of (a number) of pressing difficulties on conditions extremely unfavourable to himself, will be declared invalid at the instance of the victim or of a State, co-operative or public organization.

If the transaction is declared invalid on one of the above grounds, then everything received by the other party under the transaction must be returned to the victim, or if it is impossible to return it specifically, its value in money must be repaid. Property received by the victum under the transaction from the other party and also everything due to him in return for his performance is forfeited to the State. If it is impossible to transfer such property to the State specifically, its value in money is forfeited.

The victim is also entitled to be reimbursed by the other party his expenses and any loss of or damage to his property. " (Translation by Kiralfy).

It must be observed that the clause concerned with forfeiture to the State will seldom be applied to contracts with international elements. In any case it will not be applied to contracts of international commerce and to other transactions where both parties are foreigners. Similar interpretation was given by Soviet lawyers to the corresponding Section 32 and 33 of the old Civil Code of the RSFSR. Mutual restitution was considered in such cases as the only possible solution.

(1) Lunts, 1949, pp. 121; 275; Lunts, II (1963), p. 237.
(2) See also: Jolowicz, Lewis, pp. 334 et seq.

injuries is that at common law with its fellow servant rule (1). Thus, according to Lunts, no Soviet or foreign employer could invoke this common employment defence in a Soviet court although the tortious act in issue had been committed in a foreign country and although in principle the law of the country admitting the defence should be applied.

Claims for damages unknown to Soviet law, though admissible under the *lex loci delicti* cannot be enforced in a Soviet court. A Soviet judge would therefore reject an action for compensation of mental suffering or "dommage moral" in general as admitted e.g. in England. To this group of damages belong e.g. those for pain and suffering, described in an English textbook on torts: "Compensation must be given for both past and future pain and suffering and both its severity and duration must be taken into account... This head of damages for the mental suffering caused by the knowledge that his life has been shortened or that his capacity for enjoying life has been curtailed through physical handicaps" (2).

In conclusion, a word should be said about the question of when a foreign rule on *limitation of action* would be considered as contrary to Soviet public policy. There is no doubt that if a foreign law, which according to Soviet private international law governs a certain obligation, provides too long a period of limitation as compared with the period laid down by Soviet law (3), the foreign legal provision will not be applied. According to Lunts, a limitation period of 30 years, for instance, will not be taken into consideration (4). This would apply to Article 2004 of The Netherlands Civil Code, which provides: "All actions in law both *in rem* and *in personam*, are barred through limitation after a period of thirty years, and no person invoking expiration of the period of limitation can be forced to prove any title nor can defence based on his *mala fides* be brought against him".

There is even more reason to consider that a Soviet court would reject the claim of a Swiss creditor made indefeasible by means of "poursuite par voie de saisie" as provided by the Swiss law. In the wording of Article 149 of the "Loi fédéral sur la

(1) Cf. Prosser, pp. 551-558.

(2) Jolowicz, Lewis, p. 777.

(3) According to Article 16 of the Soviet civil law fundamentals, the general period for bringing an action is 3 years.

(4) Lunts, II (1963), p. 155. For similar public policy restrictions in some Western countries cf. Rabel, III, pp. 515-516. As to the question of which law shall apply after the rejection of a repugnant foreign provision, Soviet lawyers do not propose a concrete solution. See, however, above "Soviet legal writers in their own system" (Effects of the rejection of a foreign law).

poursuite pour dette et la faillite" of the 11th of April 1889" le créancier saisissant qui n'a pas été payé intégralement reçoit un acte de défaut de biens pour le montant impayé. Cet acte vaut comme reconnaissance de dette.... La dette est imprescriptible à l'égard du débiteur; ses héritiers peuvent invoquer la préscription, si le créancier n'a pas fait valoir ses droits dans l'année de l'addition d'hérédité" (1).

2. PROPERTY RIGHTS

The basic Soviet conflict rule relating to property rights together with the general directive as to the judicial exception from this rule were originally considered in Circular letter no. 42 of the RSFSR People's Commissariat for Foreign Affairs of the 12th of April 1922. The letter provides inter alia as follows.
".... The regime of property rights established by the decrees of the Russian Soviet government regulates relations in the territory of the R.S.F.S.R. But legal relations pertaining to property which is located outside of the territory of the R.S.F.S.R. and not connected with it, cannot be judged outside of the confines of the R.S.F.S.R. under the Russian laws, and they are subject to the effect of the local legislation, regardless of the nationality of the persons involved in such legal relations, even if they are Russian citizens.

Thus, if a given legal institution is, in general, recognized under the local laws, then the fact of non-recognition of this institution by our legislation need not in itself be an obstacle in the way of the protection of a given right by our diplomatic representatives and consulates as a matter of general protection of legitimate interests of the Russian citizens.

This is a general rule. However, the limits within which the protection of such rights may be extended shall also be determined by the general bases of the concept of law of the Soviet State. No protection may be extended, therefore, to claims and acts which, though legitimate, under the law of the country of a person's residence, are contrary to the opinions extablished in the R.S.F.S.R. as to the limits of what is permissible. This is subject to appraisal in each individual case" (2).

The above Letter should be seen not only as an authoritative interpretation of the old implicit rule that the *lex rei citae* governs property rights, as far as they are not contrary to Soviet public

(1) To be read in connection with the other relative provisions of the said law, and in particular those of Articles 88 and 117.

(2) Transl.: Gsovski, pp. 300-301.

policy, but also as a supplementary directive in this domain under the operation of the Fundamentals of Civil Legislation of 1961, which recognized, implicitly again, the same conflict rule with the same reservation (1).

Pursuant to the Soviet public policy reservation, a Soviet authority may deny recognition to some property rights which, although legally acquired under a foreign *lex rei sitae*, are detrimental to the economic interests of the USSR. To this category belong in the first place ownership rights to stolen goods acquired by a *bona fide* purchaser and the rights of the finder of lost goods. Swiss and German law provide us with some examples of this kind.

In Section 934 of the Swiss Civil Code we read: "Le possesseur auquel une chose mobilière a été volée ou qui l'a perdue, ou qui s'en trouve dessaisi de quelque autre manière sans sa volonté, peut la revendiquer pendant cinq ans.
Lorsque la chose a été acquise dans des enchères publiques, dans un marché ou d'un marchand d'objects de même espèce, elle ne peut plus être revendiquée ni contre le premier acquéreur, ni contre un autre acquéreur de bonne foi, si ce n'est à la condition de lui rembourser le prix qu'il a payé..."

Under this provision the *bona fide* possessor of a stolen or lost chattel can acquire either the ownership of it or the right to recover the price he has paid for it; ownership if he has possessed it undisturbed for a period of 5 years, and the right of compensation at any time if the chattel was acquired in the open market or from a merchant dealing in the same goods. Article 973 of the German Civil Code also grants ownership to the finder of a lost chattel provided that he has warned the police, and that for one year the true owner has remained unknown.

Let us now imagine a case where an employee at the Soviet Embassy in Switzerland managed to sell a car belonging to the Embassy illegally to a Swiss car dealer. If a subsequent buyer brought the car to the USSR, it would be seized by Soviet authorities without any compensation. The right of the buyer, acquired under the *lex rei sitae*, to keep the car until he recovers the price he paid, although in principle recognized by Soviet private international law, would be disregarded, because its recognition in this particular case would be contrary to Soviet

(1) See Articles 126 paragraph 2 and 127 paragraph 3 of the Fundamentals and their interpretation in: Lunts, II (1963), pp. 82 and 285; on the effect of the lex rei sitae under the Soviet system see Lunts I (1959), p. 169; and Lunts, II (1963), pp. 75-85. As to the general expression of the public policy reservation we refer to Article 128 of the Fundamentals mentioned in the preliminary remarks to this chapter.

public policy.

Recognition by Soviet authorities of this right with respect to items belonging to the State, would constitute an intolerable infringement of the basic legal principle laid down in Article 28, paragraph 4, of the Fundamentals of Civil Legislation, according to which: "State property, and also the property of kolkhozes, other co-operative and mass organizations unlawfully alienated by any means whatsever, may be recovered by the organizations concerned from any holder" (1).

For the same reason a property right acquired under Article 973 of the German Civil Code to a chattel belonging to the Soviet State or to one of the organizations mentioned above would never be recognized in the USSR.

Furthermore, there is no doubt that Soviet public policy would not allow foreign maritime liens to affect a sea-going vessel pertaining to the USSR or even to a friendly communist State. Thus, the Soviet authorities would refuse to recognize the legal effect of the American legal provision proclaiming that:
"Any person furnishing repairs, supplies, towage, use of dry dock or marine railway, or other necessaries, to any vessel, whether foreign or domestic, upon the order of the owner of such vessel, or of a person authorized by the owner, shall have a maritime lien on vessel, which may be enforced by suit in rem, and it shall not be necessary to allege or prove that credit was given to the vessel" (2).

The recognition of the legal effect of such liens on Soviet vessels would be contrary to the imperative rule of Article 176 of the Merchant Shipping Code of the USSR that State vessels are immune from any enforcement measures for the satisfaction of creditor's claims.

Peculiar examples of foreign property rights giving rise to objection because they are unknown in Soviet law, or incompatible with the purpose of civil rights in a communist society were recently suggested by Rubanov. In his textbook "Succesion in Private International Law", mentioned elsewhere, Rubanov included among these rights the French "droit d'usefruit" and the English "life interest" in favour of the surviving spouse as well as the rights based on the "statutory trusts" of English law in favour of the succeeding issue under the age of 21. The

(1) Cf. also Lunts, II (1963), p. 81.

(2) United States Code, 1964 edition, vol.X, Washington 1965, Title 46, paragraph 971. About the persons presumed to have authority from the owner to procure repairs, supplies, towage, etc. see paragraph 972. For some comments on the above provision see e.g. Rabel, IV, p. 116.

pertinent French provision is laid down in Article 767 of the *Code Civil*, which reads:

"Le conjuint survivant non divorcé qui ne succède pas à la pleine propriété et contre lequel n'existe pas de jugement de séparation de corps passé en force de chose jugée a, sur la succession du prédécédé, un droit d'usufruit qui est:

D'un quart, si le defunt laisse un ou plusieurs enfants issus du mariage;

D'une part d'enfant légitime le moins prénant, sans qu'elle puisse excéder le quart si le défunt a des enfants nés. d'un précédent mariage:

De moitié, si le défunt laisse des enfants naturels ou descendants légitime d'enfants naturels, des frères et soeurs ou des ascendants;

De la totalité dans tous les autres cas, quels que soient le nombre et la qualité des héritiers......

Jusqu'au partage définitif, les héritiers peuvent exiger, moyennant sûretés suffisants (L. no. 63-699 du 13 juillet 1963) et guarantie du maintien de l'équivalence initiale, que l'usufruit de l'époux survivant soit converti en une rente viagère équivalente. S'ils sont en désaccord, conversion sera facultative pour les tribunaux".

Proceeding from the assumption that the main purpose of this kind of property rights is the systematic extraction of unearned profits, which are intolerable from the point of view of communist social conceptions, Rubanov concludes that "the application of the bourgeois law of succession which could lead to the effectuation in the USSR of the above-described rights would be contrary to Soviet public policy" (1). In such case there is no alternative for the heirs but to redeem the capital value of the "usufruit", thus permitting a distribution of the Soviet estate free from any property rights unknown and repugnant to Soviet law. (Of course the distribution itself, including the capacity of the heirs and the shares to which they are entitled, remains subject in the USSR to the general conflict rule in operation stipulating that succession is governed by the law of the last permanent residence of the deceased. We should also recall here the number of imperative exceptions from this general rule indicated in the chapter "Soviet legislative public policy".)

The same reasoning is also of relevance with respect to English law, which provides for a life interest in half the residue for the surviving spouse when the intestate has no issue, and statutory trusts in favour of minor children and some other beneficiaries (2).

(1) Rubanov, p. 174.

(2) For details on English law see: Bromley, pp. 489-493.

Marriage. With respect to marriages of foreigners concluded abroad, Section 137 of the RSFSR Family Code contains the following rather flexible conflict rule.

"Marriages of aliens contracted outside the confines of the USSR under the laws of the countries concerned shall be considered duly legalized in the territory of the USSR within the meaning of Part One, Chapter I, of the present Code" (1).

According to Pergament, whose interpretation is accepted by other Soviet lawyers, this rule means that a marriage should be recognized in the USSR if it is valid either according to the *lex patriae* of the spouses or according to the *lex loci celebrationis* (2). Thus, if the *lex patriae* contains intolerable impediments from the point of view of Soviet social conceptions, while the *lex loci celebrationis* does not know such impediments, the marriage concluded under the latter law will be recognized; if somehow the marriage is concluded despite the fact that the *lex loci celebrations* prohibits it for reasons repugnant to Soviet public policy, while the *lex patriae* admits the marriage, the *lex patriae* will be decisive.

We may take it for granted that all impediments to marriage based on racial or religious grounds are considered contrary to Soviet public policy (3). Racial impediments which would have no effect on Soviet territory can be found in the laws of the USA and South Africa. For instance Article 94 of the Civil Code of Louisiana provides:

"Marriage between white persons and persons of color is prohibited and the celebration of all such marriages is forbidden and such celebration carries with it no effect and it is null and void."

More extensive provisions are contained in the South African Prohibition of Mixed Marriages Act of 1949:

"As from the date of commencement of this Act a marriage between a European and a non-European may not be solemnized, and any such marriage solemnized in contravention of the provisions of this section shall be void and of no effect....

If any male person who is domiciled in the Union enters into a marriage outside the Union which cannot be solemnized in the Union in terms of subsection 1, then such marriage shall be void and of no effect in the Union".

(1) Transl.: Gsovski, II, p. 289. Paragraph 4 of Section 32 of the Principles of Family Legislation is similarly worded.

(2) Pergament, p. 178; Orlova, pp. 153-154; Lunts, II (1963), p. 314.

(3) Pergament, p. 178; Lunts, II (1963), p. 306; Orlova, 1966, p. 217.

It should be noted that Soviet judicial public policy regarding the foreign racial impediments to marriage was operative even at the time when the Soviet legislative public policy amounted to an absolute intolerance with regard to foreigners. This was the case, for instance, in the period between 1947 and 1953, when Section 6[1]) of the RSFSR Family Code was in force with its explicit prohibition of marriages between foreigners (coloured or white) and Soviet citizens. In this, at first sight, surprising manifestation of Soviet public policy we find only a confirmation of the thesis of Nussbaum, already considered, that "no moral or ethical structure is involved in the public policy concept". (1)

Typical examples of marriage prohibitions based on religious grounds which are considered as contrary to Soviet public policy are provided by the Civil Code of Greece, where we read:
"Le mariage entre un chrétien et une personne d' une autre réligion est prohibé (Article 1353).
"Le mariage des membres du clergé de tout rang et des religieux de l' église orthodoxe orientale est prohibé" (Article 1364).

If a Greek monk marries in England, or if a Greek orthodox girl marries a Jewish man in England, where no religious or racial impediments are recognized (2), both marriages will also be valid in the USSR, and objections based on these Greek prohibitions will be disregarded as contrary to Soviet public policy. The same applies to the corresponding religious impediments of canon law.

In addition, it should be mentioned that foreign decisions nullifying marriages on the grounds just described will not be recognized in the USSR, although in principle nullity decrees for reasons not repugnant to Soviet public policy will be accorded their expected legal effect in the USSR (3).

The legal consequences of foreign invalidations of marriages, however, are considered on their own merits. If they happen to be contrary to Soviet public policy, they will be of no effect in the territory of the USSR. This is well illustrated by an example from English family law suggested by Orlova. Before 1959 the children of void marriages were considered as illegitimate at Common Law. Although the Legitimacy Act of 1959 changed the situation with respect to putative marriages the problem of illegitimacy, with its legal consequences repugnant to the Soviet system, still remains.

Section 2 of the Legitimacy Act of 1959 provides:
"The child of a void marriage, whether born before or after the

(1) See, however, Soviet criticism on the German system in the General part of this paper.

(2) See Dicey, Morris, p. 75.

(3) See Orlova, 1960, pp. 156-157.

commencement of this Act, shall be treated as the legitimate child of his parents if at the time of the act of intercourse resulting in the birth (or at the time of the celebration of the marriage if later) both or either of the parties reasonably believed that the marriage was valid" (1).

Thus, whenever the parties to an invalid marriage were aware of the invalidity of their act, their children will be treated as illegitimate children. The position of these illegitimate children is especially detrimentally affected on intestate succession, as they cannot succeed even to the estate of their mother if she has surviving legitimate issue (e.g. child or grandchild) (2). "Such legal results", writers Orlova, "contradicting one of the basic principles of Soviet family law viz. that of the most effective protection of the children's interests, cannot be recognized in the Soviet Union" (3).

Divorce. The guiding principle relating to divorces decreed by foreign authorities is laid down in Section 141 of the RSFSR Family Code and the corresponding sections of the family codes of the other Union Republics:
"Documents issued to aliens certifying a divorce obtained under the law of the country concerned shall have equal validity with excerpts from the record registering the dissolution of a marriage" (4). The exceptions which could be made to this principle on account of public policy, would be concerned, according to Soviet lawyers, solely with the legal consequences of the foreign divorces. These exceptions are so rigidly determined by legal writings that theoretically one can doubt whether to place them under the heading of legislative public policy or under that of judicial public policy. Pending the emergence of a clear attitude in Soviet practice, we can assume that the two categories do not altogether exclude each other. When Soviet lawyers maintain that the legal consequences of a divorce, domestic or foreign, are to be governed in the USSR exclusively by Soviet law (5), having in mind the claims based on Soviet law, we are confronted with a clear manifestation of a legislative public policy. If, however, the claims brought forward in a Soviet court concern the realization

(1) Quoted from: Bromley, p. 298.

(2) Ibid., pp. 493-494.

(3) Orlova, 1960, p. 157.

(4) Transl.: Gsovski, II, p. 290. Section 33 paragraph 4 of the Principles of Family Legislation of June 1968 is to the same effect.

(5) Cf. Lunts, 1949, p. 304; Lunts, II (1963), p. 322; Pereterskii, Krylov 1959, p. 166; Orlova, 1960, p. 166-167.

of rights or the discharge of duties provided in a foreign divorce decree, then there will be a judicial apprecation of these rights or duties and their moral grounds. In such a case Soviet judges or administrative authorities may have recourse to their judicial public policy. Our discussion is limited to this last aspect of the problem. Thus, a copy of a foreign divorce decree, which is treated as if it were an excerpt from a Soviet official record, may contain some clauses or sanctions whose recognition would contravene the fundamentals of the Soviet social system. Such repugnant elements will certainly be denied recognition and wherever necessary they will be replaced by solutions based on Soviet law.

Among the legal consequences of foreign divorces repugnant to Soviet conceptions, the restrictions on remarriage contained in some Western European laws are noteworthy (1). Examples are the consequences provided in Article 89 of the Civil Code of The Netherlands with respect to persons guilty of adultery: "He who by a decision of the court has been found guilty of adultery is forever barred from entering into marriage with his accomplice in that adultery" (2). The same can be said of Article 150 of the Swiss Civil Code affecting the rights to remarry of the spouse found guilty of the divorce: "En prononçant le divorce, le juge fixe un délai d'un an au moins, de deux ans au plus, pendant lequel la partie coupable ne pourra se remarrier; en cas de divorce prononcé pour cause d'adultère, le délai peut être étendue à trois ans".

Before the change of Section 15 of the RSFSR Family Code in Februari 1968, foreign divorce decrees were also denied recognition in the USSR in so far as they contained provisions to the effect that the right to alimony after the dissolution of the marriage depended on the guilt or innocence of the parties (3). Such consequences inconsistent with Soviet public policy could be found for instance in Article 58 of the German Marriage law of 1946, which provides:
"Der allein oder überwiegend schuldige Mann hat der geschiedenen Frau den nach den Lebensverhältnissen der Ehegatten angemes-

(1) Lunts, 1949, p. 303; Lunts II (1963), p. 322; Orlova, 1960, p. 167.
The restrictions on remarriage are also repugnant to the public policy of some Western countries. English courts, for instance will not give effect to foreign laws imposing disabilities and incapacities on divorced persons, such laws being considered as penal (See Dicey, Morris, p. 75).

(2) Similar provision is contained also in the German "Ehegesetz" of 1946, paragraph 6. For a more recent introduction of such an impediment in the USA (1966), see Section 161 of the Louisiana Civil Code.

(3) Cf. Lunts, II (1963), p. 322; Orleva, 1966, p. 234.

senen Unterhalt zu gewähren, soweit die Einkünfte aus dem Vermögen der Frau und die Erträgnisse einer Erwerbstätigkeit nicht ausreichen; Die allein oder überwiegend schuldige Frau hat dem geschiedenen Mann angemessenen Unterhalt zu gewähren, soweit er ausserstande ist, sich selbst zu unterhalten".

Let us take as an example two former spouses, who, after having been divorced in a German court were domiciled in the USSR. If the party whose adultery was the ground for divorce happens to be destitute, she (or he) could (before February 1968) succesfully bring an action in a Soviet court for support from the innocent but wealthy party. The defence based on the German divorce decree and Article 58 of the German Family Law would be rejected as contrary to Soviet public policy. At present, however, the unworthy behaviour of a spouse during the marriage may lead to a denial of any material support by the Soviet court (1).

On the other hand, compensation for "dommage moral" will never be granted by a Soviet court as being unknown to Soviet legislation. Thus Soviet public policy could not tolerate claims based e.g. on Article 151 of the Swiss Civil Code, reading as follows:

"Si les faits qui ont déterminé le divorce ont porté une grave atteinte aux intérêts personnels de l'époux innocent, le juge peut lui alluer en outre une somme d'argent à titre de réparation morale.....".

This last example has brought us to the end of our survey, which must be viewed only as a modest attempt to give a general idea of Soviet judical public policy and not as an exhaustive analysis of all possible cases in this domain.

1. See also p.123 of this paper.

SUMMARY AND FINAL REMARKS

Summary. If we review the main points of the trends of thought and legal findings ontlined in this study, we arrive at the following picture.

Soviet private international law has been assessed quite differently by different legal writers. While Soviet lawyers, following a policy of idealization of their own legal reality, maintain that Soviet private international law is the only truly international law free from superfluous public policy impediments, some Western lawyers, such as Makarov, Pisar and Grzybowsky, have come to the conclusion that Soviet law is dominated by public policy considerations which make the pretended international orientation of Soviet private international law seem very doubtful.

The theoretical basis of this study is the dualistic public policy thesis propounded by Frankenstein, Louis-Lucas, Goldschmidt and others, according to which public policy can manifest itself either positively or negatively, i.e. either as a complex of imperative rules claiming an absolute application or as a device for the non-application of a foreign law normally competent. An attempt has been made to introduce the terms "legislative public policy" and "judicial public policy" in place of the existing, and in the opinion of the author, ambiguous terms, of "positive and negative public policy", "absolute and relative public policy", "règles d'ordre public et exceptions d'ordre public", etc.
Using the new terminology, the author proposes the following general desription of this concept.

Public policy is a complex of ideological imperatives which determine the general limits of application of forgein laws in conflict-of-law cases. These imperatives express the political, economic and moral principles deemed essential for the existence of society by the dominating political forces at a particular time and place. In this perspective public policy manifests itself either as legislative public policy or as judicial public policy, depending on the authorities to which it is addressed and by which it is effectuated. Thus, legislative public policy is a complex of ideological imperatives directly binding on the legislature and incorporated in the law as written or unwritten rules. It is of the exclusive concern of the law-making authorities and does not leave any room whatsoever for a choice of law, whether by courts or by individuals. Judicial public policy, on the other hand, is the same complex of ideological imperatives addressed to the authorities for the administration of justice, by virtue of which a foreign legal provision normally applicable must be discarded if its application would be detrimental to the fundamental values of the forum State.

Soviet legislative public policy as it has materialized in the various branches of law can be summarized as follows:
The Soviet substantive rules relating to *civil law capacity* are absolutely binding on all persons residing on Soviet territory, irrespective of whether they are aliens or citizens. The mandatory character of these legal provisions makes any interference of the *lex patriae*, considered by many private international law systems as decisive in this matter, impossible. The *lex patriae* is applied by Soviet authorities only to determine the capacity of Soviet citizens living abroad. Such a combination of territorial and national principles guarantees the supremacy of Soviet law with regard to all persons permanently or even temporarily connected with Soviet society.

Soviet legislative public policy relating to *foreign commerce* is implemented through the general system of State monopoly in this domain and by the rules considered as emanating from this system. As examples of the particular imperative rules we may mention import-export regulation, the whole system of organization and authorization underlying commercial transactions, formality regulations relating to contracting, the claims of immunity from jurisdiction for Soviet commercial representatives abroad, and many other more specific rules relating to foreign exchange and currency regulations, merchant shipping restrictions, etc.

By virtue of Articles 122 and 123 of Soviet Civil Law Fundamentals, according to which aliens living in the USSR cannot enjoy more extensive civil rights than Soviet citizens, all restrictions imposed on the *property rights* of Soviet citizens are equally binding on aliens. These imperative requirements have also brought about the acceptance of the *lex rei sitae* as a basic conflict rule in Soviet property law. Thus, property rights are governed by the combined effect of the *lex situs* and the principle that the Soviet national régime also applies to foreigners.
However, the conflict rule of the *lex rei sitae* is intended in this context mainly to accentuate and reinforce the internationally binding force of Soviet municipal law. In addition, it is used as a legal ground for the claim that Soviet citizens abroad should enjoy all property rights admissible under the *lex rei sitae* even when they have no such rights at home.

Although according to Soviet private international law *torts* are governed in principle by *lex loci delicti commissi*, many Soviet substantial legal provisions are considered as a matter of public policy and also apply in cases with foreign elements. Thus, Soviet lawyers consider it contrary to the fundamentals of the Soviet system to impose payment of damages for an act done abroad which is not unlawful according to Soviet law. On the other hand, if an act done abroad is lawful according to the *lex loci delicti* but unlawful according to Soviet law, Soviet courts must apply their own law.

In cases of tortious acts committed abroad where only Soviet physical or juridical persons are involved the *lex loci delicti* is superseded entirely by Soviet law. A special rule of legislative public policy is contained in the Soviet Merchant Shipping Code, where it is provided that "a shipwner's liability shall be unlimited in respect of claims by workers for damages for loss of limb or life".

In matters of *succession*, Soviet legislative public policy purports to defend the economic foundations of the USSR. Together with the corresponding rules relating to ownership, succession rules are directed against any intrusion of foreign laws in cases relating to basic means of production, including land, machinery and all kinds of structures situated in the USSR. They also purport to defend the economic monopolies of the Soviet State, e.g. by preventing the accumulation of private capital in Soviet territory. One of the basic rules in this respect is contained in Article 127, paragraph 3 of the Fundamentals of Civil Legislation which reads: "Inheritance of structures located in the USSR shall in any case be determined by Soviet law. The same law shall determine the capacity of a person to make or revoke a will, and also the form of the latter, where a structure located in the USSR is bequeathed".

As far as land is concerned, it should be borne in mind that in the USSR it is State property and is considered as *res extra commercium*. It cannot therefore be the object of succession, either according to municipal law or for the purpose of private international law. This absolute withdrawal from the international legal community is considered as a matter of public policy *par excellence*.

In the domain of *family law* Soviet legislative public policy almost has an absolute reign. In the USSR, as in many Western countries, the formal requirement of secular marriage is a matter of public policy. The same can be said of the material conditions of marriage in the USSR. Soviet public policy also claims to dominate marriages contracted by Soviet citizens abroad. Although the legislature, courts and writing are inclined to recognize the formal validity of such marriages contracted in accordane with the *lex loci celebrationis*, Soviet lawyers unanimously insist on the extraterritorial binding force of Soviet law with respect to the material conditions of marriages of Soviet citizens.

The solutions of the conflict-of-law problems concerned with *divorce* are also based on a general legislative public policy. The courts therefore feel themselves absolutely bound in cases of divorce to apply Soviet substantive law to the exclusion of any foreign legal provisions. The same can be said with respect to the *mutual relations of parents and children*. The rule that Soviet municipal law is solely competent to govern these relations, claims to apply not only to persons residing in the USSR but also to the parent-child relations of Soviet citizens residing abroad.

Soviet judicial public policy, effectuated by the judge, civil status officer, notary public, etc. and by virtue of which a foreign law or foreign acquired rights are denied application or recognition if they contradict the political, economic and moral conceptions of the USSR, has been presented here in the light of several comparative examples. It has been indicated that Soviet judicial public policy plays a role far less significant than is the case with its counterparts in Western countries, owing to the fact that the application of foreign laws on Soviet territory is rather restricted by the imperative application of the *lex fori* by virtue of legislative public policy.

The principal examples relate to the following matters: the restrictions of foreigners' legal *capacity to contract* or to undertake obligations in general are recognized in the USSR only on grounds known also to Soviet law. Thus foreign restrictions based on difference of race, nationality, religion or sex are considered as contrary to the fundamentals of the Soviet system, and have no legal effect in the USSR.

According to Soviet law of *torts*, foreign grounds for the exclusion or restriction of liability may be recognized by Soviet courts only when they are not contrary to the fundamentals of the Soviet system. The matter is illustrated by a reference to the defence based on the doctrine of common employment. According to Soviet lawyers, no Soviet or foreign employer could invoke the common employment defence in a Soviet court although the tortious act at issue had been committed in a foreign country and although in principle the law of the country admitting the defence should be applied.

If a foreign law which according to Soviet private international law governs a certain obligation provides too long a *period of limitation* as compared with the period established by Soviet law, the corresponding foreign legal provision will not be applied.

Ownership rights to stolen goods acquired by a *bona fide* purchaser and the rights of the finder of lost goods recognized by some European countries are considered as contrary to Soviet public policy if the goods, lost or stolen, belong to the Soviet State. A Soviet court will not recognize maritime liens granted abroad if they affect a sea-going vessel pertaining to the USSR. Particular examples of foreign porperty rights open to objection because they are unknown to Soviet law or incompatible with the purpose of civil rights in a communist society, as suggested in Soviet literature, are the French "droit d'usufruit", the English "life interest" in favour of the surviving spouse and the rights based on the "statutory trusts" of English law in favour of the succeeding issue under the age of 21.

In the field of *family law* it is taken for granted that all foreign impediments to marriage based on racial or religious grounds are considered as contrary to Soviet public policy and as such they will not be recognized.

The legal consequences of foreign invalidations of marriages may also be contrary to Soviet public policy. The resulting illegitimacy provided by Sect. 2 of the English Act of 1959 is an illustration.

Lastly, foreign divorce decrees: they are recognized unless they contain clauses or sanctions which would be repugnant to Soviet conceptions. For instance, restrictions on remarriage, provisions making the right to alimony or the right to bring up the children after dissolution of a marriage dependent on the guilt or innocence of the parties, "dommage moral" caused by a divorce, are all matters in point.

Final remarks. From this survey it has become clear that a crucial problem in the legal relations between the Soviet Union and other countries is concerned with the scope of the extraordinarily great number of imperative rules contained in Soviet law. Looking at the matter more broadly, the problem is to find an appropriate answer to the question of whether and to what extent a forum should be bound to recognize and effectuate the public policy of foreign countries as manifested in their imperative rules.

If we take as a starting point the teaching of Von Savigny, whose influence is felt even in most recent writings and court practices, the answer to our question should be in the negative. According to Von Savigny, the laws of public policy, i.e. the laws of a strictly positive, imperative character which rest on moral grounds or on public interests (relating e.g. to politics, police or political economy) are placed outside the community of law between the nations and therefore cannot be applied outside their proper

territory. (1)
Bartin in his turn reaffirmed this principle in a more resolute manner: a legal right created by virtue of the public policy of a given country can never be recognized by other countries. (2) Similar significance is also attributed to the views that public policy has a "caractère essentiellement et exclusivement national" (3), or that it is only "eine häusliche Angelegenheit" (4).

In the course of history, however, some important exceptions to this rigid principle have been suggested. In the first place, it should be mentioned that far-reaching consideration has been given to foreign public policy in cases of *renvoi*. At present it is almost generally admitted that when the forum has to apply the private international law of a foreign country it should also take into account the rules on public policy as incorporated in that law. (5) Apart from this exception, Niboyet and Batiffol have also recognized the so-called "effet reflèxe de l'ordre public" though with a more limited practical significance than originally suggested by Pillet. In their opinion a legal right or a situation created in a foreign country pursuant to its public policy should be recognized only in a third country which has the same public policy attitude with respect to the legal problem at issue. (6)

In contrast to this attitude, which in principle does not recognize foreign public policies, Pillet elevated the application of foreign "lois de garantie sociale ou d'ordre public" to a rule which must be given a universal respect. According to Pillet every legal relation established in violation of the "règles d'ordre public" of the competent law must be considered everywhere as illegal and of no effect. As to the legal relations established in conformity with the "règles d'ordre public" of the competent law, they must be considered, according to Pillet, as valid unless they are

(1) Savigny, § 349; Idem 1869, § 349.
(2) Bartin, § 95.
(3) Maury, 1954, p. 25.
(4) Raape, pp. 97-98.
(5) See e.g. Wolff, 1950, p. 184; Maury, 1954. p. 25; Raape, p. 98, note 96.
Wolff illustrated this matter with the following characteristic example. "In 1930 an Austrian of Christian faith domiciled in Italy married an Austrian Jewess before the English registrar. He brought a suit for nullity of the marriage in an English court. Under English private international law the validity of the marriage falls to be decided by the law of the domicile, i.e. Italian law. According to Italian private international law the validity depends on the national law of the spouses, i.e. Austrian law. The Austrian Civil Code declares marriages between Christians and non-Christians to be void; but Italian law regarded (at that time) the impedimentum disparitatis cultus as incompatible with Italian ordine publico. The English court would probably accept this disqualification irrespective of whether its own public policy is or is not opposed to the application of the Austrian rule."
(6) Niboyet, III (1944), pp. 572-575. Batiffol, p. 417.

contrary to the public policy of the forum country. Here the notion "competent law" is given a special significance. It is deduced from the social purpose of the laws involved and leads to the application of that law whose observance is of the most vital interest for a particular society. (1)

A new impetus of the development in this direction was undoubtedly given by De Winter who pleaded, as early as 1940, for a strict observance and application of the laws of all countries involved in a contractual dispute as far as imperative provisions with important social-economic function, were concerned. This idea found more elaborate expression in the subsequent publications of this scholar. But further, according to De Winter, there should be some reasonable limits to the application of the pertinent foreign provisions. Firstly, they may not run contrary to the public policy of the forum; secondly, they should not be given such an abnormally extensive competence that they would be intolerable from the point of view of a well organized international community. (2)

A similar attitude has been taken by Neumayer (3), Wengler (4) and Francescakis (5), although the solution proposed by the last mentioned scholar is one of a rather limited effect. Francescakis considers that the foreign "lois d'application immédiate" are to be applied only if the forum State is willing to co-operate in the achievement of the purpose which the foreign State concerned has pursued when issuing such laws.

Against this colourful doctrinal background, it would be a worthwhile task for a researcher to investigate how far the Western courts should have to go in the recognition and application of Soviet laws where the demarcation line between private and public law has vanished and where public policy is so widely dominant.

In the meantime, let us hope for a new development in the legislative policy of the USSR, whereby the Soviet administrators of international justice will not have to waver between a policy of peaceful co-operation and their duty to comply with their own municipal law, and when their Western confrères will not need discriminate between the imperative rules of normal and abnormal competence as manifested in Soviet private international law.

(1) Pillet, 1903, p. 423-425.

(2) De Winter, 1940, p. 261; Idem 1964, pp. 356-359; Idem, 1966, p. 939.
For similar opinions in Netherlands legal literature see e.g. Struycken, p. 530; Lemaire, p. 177.

(3) Neumayer, p. 77.

(4) Wengler, pp. 523-525.

(5) Francescakis, 1966 (Comments), p. 263.

SAMENVATTING

Het Sovjet internationaal privaatrecht wordt door Russische en buitenlandse schrijvers verschillend beoordeeld.
Terwijl de Sovjet juristen, die neigen naar idealisering van eigen rechtssysteem, beweren, dat het Sovjet internationaal privaatrecht het enige ware internationale recht is, vrij van buitensporige beletselen van openbare orde, zijn de Westerse juristen, zoals Makarov, Pizar, Grzybowsky e.a. daarentegen van oordeel, dat het Sovjet recht wordt beheerst door overwegingen van openbare orde, die het internationale karakter van het Sovjet internationaal privaatrecht twijfelachtig maken.

De theoretische basis van deze studie is de dualistische stelling geopperd door Frankenstein, Louis-Lucas, Goldschmidt e.a., volgens welke openbare orde zich kan manifesteren in positieve dan wel in negatieve zin, dat wil zeggen òf als een komplex van imperatieve rechtsregels die absolute toepassing eisen òf als middel om de vreemde wet die normaal toepasselijk zou zijn, buiten werking te stellen. Een poging is gedaan om de begrippen *legislatieve openbare orde* en *justitiële openbare orde* te introduceren in de plaats van de bestaande, en naar de mening van de auteur dubbelzinnige termen zoals "positieve" en "negatieve" openbare orde, "absolute" en "relatieve" openbare orde, "regels" en "excepties" van openbare orde, etc.
Uitgaande van de nieuwe terminologie stelt de auteur de volgende omschrijving voor van het begrip openbare orde.
Openbare orde is een komplex van ideologische imperatieven die de algemene grenzen van toepasselijkheid van vreemd recht bepalen op het gebied van het internationaal privaatrecht. Deze imperatieven geven uitdrukking aan politieke, economische en morele beginselen, die door de heersende politieke krachten als fundamenteel voor het bestaan van een gezonde maatschappij worden beschouwd.
In dit perspektief manifesteert openbare orde zich als legislatieve openbare orde of als justitiële openbare orde, afhankelijk van de autoriteit tot welke zij zich richt en door welke zij wordt toegepast.
Legislatieve openbare orde is een komplex van ideologische imperatieven die de wetgever rechtstreeks binden en in de wet worden geincorporeerd als geschreven of ongeschreven rechtsregels. De legislatieve openbare orde richt zich uitsluitend tot de wetgevende autoriteiten en sluit elke mogelijkheid tot rechtskeuze door rechterlijke instanties of individuele personen uit.

Justitiële openbare orde daarentegen, is het zelfde komplex van ideologische imperatieven, gericht tot de rechtsprekende autoriteiten, krachtens welke een buitenlandse rechtsbepaling die normaal toepasselijk zou zijn, verworpen moet worden indien toepassing daarvan schadelijk wordt geacht voor bepaalde fundamentele waarden van de forum staat.
Hieronder volgt een korte samenvatting van de soviet *legislatieve openbare orde*, zoals deze in de verschillende rechtsgebieden wordt aangetroffen.
De materiële rechtsbepalingen betreffende de civielrechtelijke bekwaamheid in de Soviet Unie zijn absoluut bindend ten aanzien van alle personen die zich op Sovjet grondgebied bevinden, onverschillig of zij burgers dan wel vreemdelingen zijn. Het gebiedende karakter van deze bepalingen maakt elke inmenging van de *lex patriae*, die door vele andere systemen internationaal privaatrechtelijk beslissend wordt verklaard, onmogelijk. De *Lex patriae* wordt door de Sovjet autoriteiten alleen toegepast op gevallen die betrekking hebben op de bekwaamheid van zich in het buitenland bevindende Sovjet burgers. Een dergelijke kombinatie van territoriale en nationale beginselen garandeert de supptematie van het Sovjet recht met betrekking tot diegenen, die permanent of tijdelijk verbonden zijn met de Sovjet maatschappij. Op het gebied van de internationale handel wordt de Sovjet legislatieve openbare orde gereflecteerd in het systeem van staatsmonopolie en alle daaruit voortvloeiende rechtsregels. Van de imperatieve bepalingen kunnen wij onder meer vermelden de import-export bepalingen, regelingen ten aanzien van organisatie en competentie in de buitenlandse handel, rechtsnormen met betrekking tot de vorm van handelsovereenkomsten, regels inzake de immuniteit van de Sovjet handelsvertegenwoordigers in het buitenland en andere meer specifieke bepalingen, zoals deviezenbepalingen, restricties op het gebied van de scheepvaart, etc.

Krachtens de artikelen 122 en 123 van de Civielrechtelijke Beginselen van de U.S.S.R. en de Sovjet Republieken, volgens welke buitenlanders woonachtig op Sovjet grondgebied niet méér civiele rechten kunnen genieten dan Sovjet burgers, zijn alle beperkingen op eigendomsrechten van Sovjet burgers ook bindend voor buitenlanders. Deze imperatieve bepalingen hebben geleid tot aanvaarding van de *lex rei sitae* als fundamentele verwijzingsregel in het Sovjet eigendomsrecht, met dien verstande, dat eigendomsrechten beheerst worden door het gecombineerde effect van de *lex rei sitae* en het beginsel dat het Sovjet nationale systeem ook voor vreemdelingen in de Sovjet Unie van kracht is. De verwijzingsregel die de *lex rei sitae* inhoudt, heeft hier slechts ten

doel de internationaal bindende kracht van Sovjet materieel recht te accentueren. Dezelfde regel functionneert eveneens als rechtsgrond ter rechtvaardiging van eigendomsrechten voor Sovjet burgers in het buitenland, ook wanneer deze rechten in de Sovjet Unie zelf niet kunnen worden uitgeoefend.
Ondanks het feit, dat volgens Sovjet internationaal privaatrecht de onrechtmatige daad in beginsel volgens de *lex loci delicti commissi* wordt berecht, worden vele Sovjet materiële rechtsbepalingen op dit gebied beschouwd als regels van openbare orde en als zodanig worden zij ook op internationale gevallen toegepast. Sovjet juristen beschouwen het bijvoorbeeld als strijdig met de fundamenten van het Sovjet systeem om schadevergoeding toe te kennen voor handelingen verricht in het buitenland, die volgens het Sovjet recht niet onrechtmatig zijn. Aan de andere kant dienen Sovjet rechters Sovjet recht toe te passen met betrekking tot handelingen in het buitenland verricht, die volgens Sovjet recht onrechtmatig zijn maar niet volgens de *lex loci delicti commissi*. Wanneer bij een onrechtmatige daad gepleegd in het buitenland alleen Sovjet burgers of rechtspersonen zijn betrokken wordt de *lex loci delicti commissi* volledig verdrongen door Sovjet recht. Een speciale bepaling van openbare orde vinden wij in het Wetboek van Koopvaardij. Daar wordt bepaald, dat de aansprakelijkheid van de eigenaar van het schip onbeperkt is met betrekking tot schade als gevolg van verlies van ledematen of van de dood van werknemers.

Op het gebied van erfrecht heeft de Sovjet legislatieve openbare orde als primaire functie de verdediging van de economische grondslagen van de U.S.S.R. Evenals de overeenkomstige rechtsregels inzake eigendom zijn de betreffende bepalingen gericht tegen iedere inmenging van buitenlands recht ten aanzien van de basis productiemiddelen, zoals land, machines en alle soorten van gebouwen, zich bevindend op Sovjet grondgebied. Dezelfde bepalingen dienen ter handhaving van de economische monopolies van de Sovjet Staat onder andere door verhindering van accumulatie van particulier kapitaal in de U.S.S.R. Een van de grondbeginselen in dit opzicht is neergelegd in artikel 127 alinea 3 van de Civielrechtelijke Beginselen van de U.S.S.R. en de Sovjet Republieken, waar wij lezen:
"De erfopvolging ten aanzien van gebouwen gelegen in de U.S.S.R. wordt in elk geval volgens het Sovjet recht beslist. Dit recht bepaalt eveneens de rechtsbekwaamheid tot uiterste wilsbeschikking en de vorm daarvan, indien het gebouw dat wordt vermaakt zich bevindt in de U.S.S.R."

Aangezien de grond in de Sovjet Unie staatseigendom is en wordt beschouwd als *res extra commercium* kan er in dit opzicht geen sprake zijn van erfopvolging, noch in materiëel rechtelijke zin noch in internationaal privaatrechtelijke zin. Deze onttrekking aan het internationale rechtsverkeer maakt deel uit van de openbare orde.

De Sovjet legislatieve openbare orde speelt een dominerende rol op het gebied van het familierecht. Zoals in vele Westerse landen is ook in de U.S.S.R. de eis van huwelijksvoltrekking door de ambtenaar van de burgerlijke stand een vereiste van openbare orde.
Hetzelfde geldt voor de materiële voorwaarden tot het sluiten van een huwelijk in de U.S.S.R. De Sovjet openbare orde trekt eveneens binnen haar machtssfeer de huwelijken die door Sovjet burgers in het buitenland worden gesloten. Hoewel wetgever, justitie en doctrine in the U.S.S.R. geneigd zijn de formele geldigheid van dergelijke huwelijken te erkennen, maken zij eensgezind aanspraak op extraterritoriale werking van hun recht met betrekking tot de materiële voorwaarden voor huwelijken tussen Sovjet-burgers.

De oplossing van internationale rechtsconflicten inzake echtscheiding wordt in de Sovjet Unie eveneens beheerst door overwegingen van openbare orde. De rechters voelen zich derhalve verplicht in echtscheidingszaken alleen het eigen recht toe te passen en elke vreemde rechtsbepaling te verwerpen. Hetzelfde is van toepassing op de verhouding tussen ouders en minderjarige kinderen. De regel, dat Sovjet intern recht deze verhoudingen beheerst betreft niet alleen personen die in de USSR wonen, maar ook Sovjet burgers en hun minderjarige kinderen die zich in het buitenland bevinden.

Sovjet *justitiële openbare orde*, die wordt gehanteerd door de rechters, de ambtenaren van de burgelijke stand, de notarissen, etc., en krachtens welke aan vreemde wetten of rechten verworven in het buitenland toepassing of erkenning wordt ontzegd indien zij strijdig zijn met de politieke, economische of morele opvattingen van de U.S.S.R., wordt in deze studie aan de hand van vergelijkende voorbeelden bezien. De rol die de Sovjet justitiële openbare orde speelt is aanzienlijk kleiner dan die welke de overeenkomstige openbare orde in Westerse landen speelt. Dit wordt gezien als gevolg van het feit, dat toepassing van vreemde wetten in de U.S.S.R. zeer sterk wordt beperkt door de imperatieve toepassing van de *lex fori* krachtens de legislatieve openbare orde.
De belangrijkste voorbeelden betreffen de volgende materie. De buitenlandse beperkingen op de bekwaamheid om verbintenissen aan te gaan worden in de U.S.S.R. alleen erkend indien deze beperkingen zijn opgelegd op gronden, die ook de Sovjet wetgeving

kent. Dus beperkingen gebaseerd op verschil van ras, nationaliteit, religie of geslacht worden beschouwd als in strijd met de fundamenten van het Sovjet systeem en kunnen derhalve geen rechtsgevolgen hebben in de U.S.S.R.

Volgens het Sovjet recht kunnen buitenlandse gronden voor uitsluiting of beperking van de aansprakelijkheid voor onrechtmatige daad alleen worden erkend, wanneer deze niet in strijd zijn met de fundamenten van het Sovjet systeem. Het probleem wordt onder meer geïllustreerd met een verwijzing naar het verweer gebaseerd op de zogenaamde doctrine van "common employment". Volgens Sovjet juristen zou geen Russische of buitenlandse werkgever zich voor de Sovjet rechter op dit verweer kunnen beroepen, ondanks het feit dat de onrechtmatige daad zou zijn gepleegd in een land waar dit verweer is toegestaan en in beginsel de wet van dat land zou moeten worden toegepast.

Indien een buitenlandse wet, die volgens Sovjet internationaal privaatrecht een bepaalde verbintenis beheerst, in een verjaringstermijn voorziet die te lang is in vergelijking met de verjaring in het Sovjet recht, zal de desbetreffende bepaling van de buitenlandse wet door de Sovjet rechter niet worden toegepast.

Eigendomsrechten op gestolen goederen verkregen door een *bona fide* koper en de rechten van de vinder op verloren objecten, zoals erkend door sommige Europese landen, worden beschouwd als in strijd met de Sovjet openbare orde indien de gestolen of verloren voorwerpen eigendom zijn van de Sovjet Staat. De rechter in de Sovjet Unie zal ook nimmer een in het buitenland gevestigde scheepshypotheek op schepen van de U.S.S.R. erkennen. Als specifieke voorbeelden van in het buitenland verkregen eigendomsrechten die in de U.S.S.R. ontoelaatbaar zijn omdat zij daar onbekend dan wel onverenigbaar zijn met het doel van de civiele rechten in de communistische maatschappij, worden genoemd het Franse "droit d'usufruit", het Engelse "life interest" ten gunste van de overlevende echtgenoot en de rechten gebaseerd op de "statutory trusts" van het Engelse recht ten gunste van de ervende kinderen beneden de leeftijd van 21 jaar.

Ook de rechtsgevolgen van het nietig verklaren van huwelijken kunnen in strijd met de Sovjet openbare orde worden verklaard. De onwettigheid van de kinderen uit zulke huwelijken, zoals voorzien in artikel 2 van de Engelse "Legitimacy Act" van 1959, is ter illustratie genomen.

Het laatste onderwerp van ons onderzoek vormen de in het buitenland uitgesproken echtscheidingen. Deze worden erkend, tenzij zij clausules of sancties bevatten die aanstootgevend zouden zijn voor de heersende opvattingen in de U.S.S.R. Dit zou het geval kunnen zijn met beletselen om te hertrouwen, met bepalingen die de alimentatierechten of de ouderlijke macht na ontbinding van het huwelijk afhankelijk stellen van de schuld of onschuld van een van de echtgenoten, of met schadevergoedingseisen voor morele schade veroorzaakt door de echtscheiding, enzovoort.

BIBLIOGRAPHY

Altanov	- Altanov Ivan, Mezhdunarodno chastnopravnata sistema na NRB (Private international law system of the PRB). Sofiia 1955.
Averin	- Averin D.D., Polozhenie inostrantsev v sovetskom grazhdanskom protsesse (The position of foreigners in Soviet civil procedure). Moskva 1966.
Avsov, Egorev, Keilin	- Avsov Iu.A., Egorev V.V., Keilin A.D., Morskoe pravo (Maritime law). Moskva 1932.
Bar, von	- Bar L.von, Theorie und Praxis des internationalen Privatrechts. 2. umgearb. Aufl. des Internationalen Privat- und Strafrechts. I. Hannover 1889.
Bartin	- Bartin E., Principes de droit international privé, selon la loi et la jurisprudence françaises. I. Paris 1930.
Batiffol, 1938	- Batiffol Henri, Les conflicts de lois en matière de contrats. Paris 1938.
Batiffol, 1967	- Batiffol Henri, Droit international privé, 4me éd. Paris 1967.
Bloembergen	- Bloembergen Samuel, Personal property: downward trends. In: Problems of Communism, March/April, 1965, pp. 42-47.
Boguslavskii	- Boguslavskii M.M., Immunitet inostrannogo gosudarstva i ego sobstvennosti (Foreign state immunity and its elements). In: Voprosy (1956).
Boguslavskii, Rubanov, 1959	- Boguslavskii M.M., Rubanov A.A., The legal status of foreigners in the USSR. (Translation from the Russian.) Moskva 1959.

Boguslavskii, Rubanov, 1962	- Boguslavskii M.M., Rubanov A.A., Pravovoe polozhenie inostrantsev v SSSR; Izd. 2e, pererab. i dop. (The legal status of foreigners in the USSR; 2nd rev. and enl. ed.). Moskva 1962.
Brakel, van	- Brakel S. van, grondslagen en beginselen van Nederlands internationaal privaatrecht. Zwolle 1953.
Brocher	- Brocher Charles, Cours de droit international privé suivant les principes consacrés par le droit positif français. I. Paris etc 1882.
Bromley	- Bromley P.M., Family law. 3rd ed. London 1966.
Bystricky	- Bystricky R., En marge du conflit de qualification. In: Bulletin de droit tchécoslovaque, 1956, pp. 7-38; 196-199.
Cheburakhin	- Cheburakhin G.T., O grazhdanskoi pravosposobnosti inostrantsev. (On the civil law capacity of aliens.) In: Sovetskoe Gosudarstvo i Pravo, 1961: 1.
Cheshire	- Cheshire G.C., Private international law. 7th ed. London 1965.
Deelen	- Deelen J.E.J.Th., Rechtskeuze in het Nederlands internationaal contractenrecht. Een jurisprudentie-onderzoek. Amsterdam 1965.
Despagnet	- Despagnet Frantz, L'ordre public en droit international privé. In: Clunet, 1889.
Dicey, Morris	- Dicey and Morris on the conflict of laws. 8th ed. under the general editorship of J.H.C. Morris. London 1967.

Dobrin - Dobrin S., The Soviet Maritime Code. In: The Journal of Comparative Legislation and International Law, vol. XVI, part I, February 1934, p. 252.

Dölle - Dölle Hans, Der Ordre public im internationalen Privatrecht. In: Deutsche Landesreferate zum III. Internationalen Kongress für Rechtsvergleichung in London 1950, Berlin usw. 1950.

Drucker - Drucker A., Soviet views on private international law. In: The International and Comparative Law Quarterly 1955, pp. 384-389.

Feldbrugge - Feldbrugge F.J.M., A precarious legality. In: Problems of Communism, July/August, 1964.

Fensterwald - Fensterwald B.Jr., Sovereign immunity and Soviet State trading. In: Harvard Law Review, vol. 63, 1949/50, pp. 614-642.

Fleishits - Fleishits E.A., Mezhdunarodnoe znachenie Osnov grazhdanskogo zakonodatel'stva Soiuza SSR i soiuznykh respublik.(International significance of the Fundamentals of civil legislation of the USSR and the Union Republics.) In: Soviet Yearbook of International law, 1963, Moskva 1965.

Fomin - Fomin F.T., Zapiski starogo chekista (The memoirs of an old "chekist"). Moskva 1964.

Francescakis, 1958 - Francescakis Ph., La théorie du renvoi et les conflits de systémes en droit international privé. Paris 1958.

Francescakis, 1966 - Francescakis Ph., Quelques précisions sur les "lois d'application immédiate" et leurs rapports avec les règles de conflits de lois. In: Revue critique de droit international privé, LV(1966), pp. 1-18.

Francescakis 1966 (comments) - Francescakis Ph., Comments on the case "Royal Dutch". In: Revue critique de droit international privé, LV (1966), pp. 238-264.

Frankenstein, 1926 - Frankenstein Ernst, Internationales Privatrecht. (Grenzrecht). I. Berlin-Grünewald 1926.

Frankenstein, 1930 - Frankenstein Ernst, Tendences nouvelles de droit international privé. Recueil des Cours, XXXIII (1930), pp. 245-350.

Garnefsky - Garnefsky A., Soviet private international law relating to carriage by sea. In: The Modern Law Review, 1964: 4.

Genkin - Genkin D. M., Pravovoe polozhenie sovetskikh eksportnykh i importnykh ob"edinenii za granitsei (The legal status of Soviet export and import organizations abroad). In: Problemy (1960).

Goikhbarg - Goikhbarg A. G., Mezhdunarodnoe pravo (International Law). Moskva 1928.

Goldschmidt - Goldschmidt Werner, Système et philosophie du droit international privé. In: Revue critique de droit international privé, XLV (1956), pp. 223-244.

Gorodetskaia, Voprosy opeki - Gorodetskaia I. K., Voprosy opeki i popechitel'stva v mezhdunarodnom chastnom prave (Questions of guardianship and curatorship in private international law). In: Soviet Yearbook of International law 1960, Moskva 1961.

Gorodetskaia, Voprosy usinovleniia - Gorodetskaia I.K., Voprosy usinovleniia v mezhdunarodnom chastnom prave (Questions of adoption in private international law). In: Problemy (1960).

Grabar - Grabar V.E., Materialy k Istorii Literatury mezhdunarodnogo prava (Materials on the history of the international law literature). Moskva 1958.

Graulich - Graulich Paul, Règles de conflit et règles d'application immédiate. In: Mélanges en l'honneur de Jean Dabin, II, Paris 1964.

Graveson - Graveson R.H., The conflict of laws. 5th ed. London 1965.

Grzybowski - Grzybowski Kazimierz, Soviet private international law. Leyden 1965. Law in Eastern Europe, no. 10.

Gsovski - Gsovski Vladimir, Soviet civil law. Private rights and their background under the Soviet regime. Comparative survey and translation (from the Russ.) of: The Civil Code; Code of domestic relations; Judiciary Act; Code of Civil procedure; laws on nationality; corporations; patents; copyright; collective farms; labor; and other related laws. Foreword by Hessel E.Yntema. 2 vol. Vol. I. Comparative Survey.; Vol. II. Translation. Ann Arbor 1948, 49.

Hazard, 1962 - Hazard John N. and Isaac Shapiro, The Soviet legal system, Post-Stalin docu-Mentations and historical commentary. Parker School Studies in foreign and comparative law. New York 1962.

Hazard, 1963 Hazard John N., Socialisme soviétique et droit international privé. In: Mélange en l'honneur de Jean Dabin, I, Paris 1963, pp. 127-139.

Hijmans - Hijmans I. Henri, Algemene problemen van internationaal privaatrecht. Zwolle 1937.

Ioffe - Ioffe O. S., Soverskoe grazhdanskoe pravo (Soviet civil law). Moskva 1958.

Ioffe, Tolstoi - Ioffe O. S., Tolstoi Iu. K., Novyi grazhdanskii kodeks RSFSR (The new civil code of the RSFSR). Leningrad 1965.

Ionasco, Nestor - Ionasco Trajan and Nestor Ion, The Limits of party autonomy. In: The sources of the law of international trade, ed. by Clive M. Schmitthoff, London 1964.

Jezdić - Jezdić Mihailo, Tentencije u razvitku medunarodnog javnog poretka i njegovo medunarodno regulisanje (Tendencies in the development of public policy and its international regulation). In: Jugoslovenska revija za medunarodno pravo, 1963: 2.

Jolowicz, Lewis - Jolowics J. A. and Ellis Lewis, Winfield on tort, 7th ed. London 1963.

Kahn - Kahn Frans, Die Lehre von Ordre public. In: Abhandlungen zum internationalen Privatrecht, I, München usw. 1928.

Kahn-Freund - Kahn-Freund O., Reflections on public policy in the English conflict of laws. (Followed by discussions). In: Transactions of the Grotius Society, 1953, vol. 39, London 1954, pp. 39-83.

Keilin - Keilin A. D., Sovetskoe Morskoe pravo (Soviet maritime law). Moscow 1954.

Kharchev - Kharchev A., Marriage and family relations in the USSR. Transl. from the Russ. Moscow 1965.

Kiralfy - Kiralfy A., A Soviet approach to private international law. In: The International Law Quarterly, 1951, pp. 120-125.

Knapp - Knapp Charles, La notion de l'ordre public dans les conflits de lois. Mulhouse 1933.

Kollewijn - Kollewijn R.D., Het beginsel der openbare orde in het internationaal privaatrecht. 's-Gravenhage 1917.

Koretskii - Koretskii V.M., Ocherki anglo-amerikanskoj doctriny i praktiki mezhdunarodnogo chastnogo prava (Outlines of the Anglo-American doctrine and practice of private international law). Moskva 1948.

Korobov, Sokolov - Korobov A.A., Sokolov K.A., Imushchestvennye prava inostrantsev v praktike sovetskogo suda i notariata (The property rights of aliens in Soviet court and notarial practice). In: Soviet Yearbook of International Law, 1961, Moskva 1962.

Kosters, Dubbink - Kosters J. en Dubbink C.W., Algemeen deel van het Nederlands internationaal privaatrecht. Haarlem 1962.

Krylov, 1930 - Krylov Ş.B., Mezhdunarodnoe chastnoe pravo (Private international law). Moskva 1930.

Krylov, 1947 - Krylov S.B., Mezhdunarodnoe publichnoe pravo (Public international law). Moskva 1947.

Ladyzhenskii, 1948 - Ladyzhenskii A.M., K voprosu o juridicheskoi prirode norm tak nazyvaemogo mezhdunarodnogo chastnogo prava (On the question of the legal nature of the norms of so called private international law). In: Vestnik Moskovskogo Universiteta, 1948: 5.

Ladyzhenskii, 1961 - Ladyzhenskii A., Obsuzhdaem proekty Osnov (Let us discuss the drafts of the Fundamentals). In: Sovetskaia Iustitsiia, 1961: 4.

Lagarde - Lagarde Paul, Recherches sur l' ordre public en droit international privé. Paris 1959.

The law of inheritance - The law of inheritance in Eastern Europe and People' s Republic of China. A symposium by Z. Szirmai, A. Garnefsky, J. Nemec a.o., Leyden 1961. Law in Eastern Europe, no. 5.

Lemaire - Lemaire W. L. G., Book review on: J. E. J. Th. Deelen, De blinddoek van Von Savigny, Rede uitgesproken bij de openbare aanvaarding van het ambt van gewoon hoogleraar in de faculteit der rechtsgeleerdheid van de Katholieke Hogeschool te Tilburg, 15 december 1966, Amsterdam. In: Netherlands International Law Review, XIV (1967), 2, pp. 174-177.

Lerebours-Pigeonnière - Lerebours-Pigeonnière Paule, La déclaration universelle des droits de l' homme et le droit international privé francais. In: Le droit privé français au milieu de XXe siècle; Etudes offertes à Georges Ripert, Paris 1950.

Levitin - Levitin A.B., Voprosy publichnogo poriadka v mezhdunarodnom chastnom prave (Public order questions in private international law). In: Problemy (1960).

Lipson - Lipson Leon, The fight against parasites. In: Problems of Communism, March/April, 1965, pp. 72-92.

Lisovskii - Lisovskii V. I., Mezhdunarodnoe pravo (International law). Moskva 1955.

Literatura - Literatura po sovetskomu pravu; Bibliograficheskii ukazatel' (Literature on Soviet law; Bibliogr. index, ed. by the Inst. of State and Law of the USSR Academy of Sciences). Moskva 1960.

Louis-Lucas - Louis-Lucas Pierre, Remarques sur l'ordre public. In: Revue de droit international privé et de droit pénal international, XXVIII (1933), 3, pp. 393-443.

Lunts, 1947 - Lunts L.A., Problema Kvalifikatsii v Mezhdunarodnom chastnom prave (The problem of classification in private international law.) In: Sovetskoe Gosurdarstvo i pravo, 1947: 9, pp. 18-28.

Lunts, 1949 - Lunts L.A., Mezhdunarodnoe chastnoe pravo (Private international law). Moskva 1949.

Lunts, 1955 - Lunts L.A., Nekotorye voprosy mezhdunarodnogo chastnogo prava (Some problems of private international law.) In: Uchenye Zapiski Vsesoiuznogo Inst. Iurid. Nauk, 1955: 3.

Lunts, I (1959) - Lunts L.A., Mezhdunarodnoe chastnoe pravo, obshchaia chast'; Kurs mezhdunarodnogo prava, I (Private international law, general part; A course of private international law, I.) Moskva 1959.

Lunts, 1961, 64 - Lunts L.A.--L.A. Lunz, Internationales Privatrecht. 2 Bde. Uebers. aus dem Russ. Verantw. für die Fachred. der deutschen Ausg.: Horst Wiemann u.a. (Ost-)Berlin 1961, 64.

Lunts, 1961 - Lunts L.A., Vneshnetorgovaia kupliaprodazha; Normy sovetskogo kollizionnogo prava, otnosiashchiesia k kontraktam po eksportu i importu tovarov (International sale; The norms of Soviet conflict of laws concerning contracts of export and import of goods). In: Soviet Yearbook of International Law, 1960, Moskva 1961.

Lunts, 1962 (in: Novoe) - Lunts L.A., Voprosy pravovogo polozheniia inostrantsev i primeneniia inostrannykh zakonodatel'stva v Osnovakh grazdanskogo zakonodatel'stva i Osnovakh grashdanskogo sudoproizvodstva Soiuznykh respublik (Problems of the legal status of foreigners and the application of foreign laws in the Fundamentals of civil law and the Fundamentals of civil procedure of the USSR and the Union Republics). In: Novoe (1962).

Lunts, 1962 (in: S.G. i Pr.) - Lunts L.A., Voprosy primeneniia inostrannych zakonov v Osnovakh grazhdanskogo zakonodatel'stva SSSR i soiuznych respublik (Problems of the application of foreign laws in the Fundamentals of civil legislation of the USSR and the Union Republics). In: Sovetskoe Gosudarstvo i Pravo, 1962: 6, pp. 100-107.

Lunts, II (1963) - Lunts L.A., Mezhdunarodnoe chastnoe pravo, Osobennaia chast'; Kurs mezhdunarodnogo chastnogo prava, II (Private international law, Special part; Course of private international law, II). Moskva 1963.

Lunts, 1963 (in: Ocherki) - Lunts L.A., Kollizionnye voprosy nasledovaniia v sovetskom prave (Conflict of law problems relating to succession in Soviet law). In: Ocherki (1963).

Lunts, 1964 - Lunts L.A., Les règles de conflit dans les "Principes de droit civil" de l'Union soviétique et des Républiques fédérées. In: Revue critique de droit international privé, LIII (1964), 4, pp. 629-646.

Lunts, 1965 - Lunts L.A., Conflict of laws in international sale: Theories and practice of socialist countries. By L.A. Lunz. In: Recueil des Cours, 1965, vol. I.

Lunts, III, (1966) - Lunts L.A., Mezhdunarodnyi grazhdanskii protses; Kurs mezhdunarodnogo chastnogo prava, III (International Civil Procedure. Course of private international law, III). Moskva 1966.

Makarov, 1931 - Makarov A.N., Conception de droit international privé d'après la doctrine et la pratique Russe. In: Recueil des Cours, XXXVIII (1931).

Makarov, 1933 - Makarov A.N., Précis de droit international privé d'après la législation et la doctrine Russe. Paris 1933.

Makovskii - Makovskii A.L., O roli dogovora pri morskikh perevozkakh gruzov na sovetskikh sudakh (On the role of a contract in the carriage of goods by sea on Soviet vessels). In: "Pravovedenie", 1959: 4.

Mancini - Mancini P.S., De l'utilité de rendre obligatoires pour tous les Etats, sous la forme d'un ou de plusieurs traités internationaux un certain nombre de règles générales du droit international privé, pour assurer la décision uniforme des conflits entre les différentes législations civiles et criminelles. In: Journal de droit international privé, I (1874).

Maury, 1952 - Maury Jacques, L'éviction de la loi normalement compétent: l'ordre public international et la fraude à la loi. Universidad de Valladolid 1952.

Maury, 1954 - Maury Jacques, L'ordre public en droit international privé français et allemand. In: Revue critique de droit international privé, XLIII (1954), pp. 7-27.

Mikhailov - Mikhailov M.P., Ugolovnaia otvetstvennost' za spekuliatsiiu valiutoi (Criminal responsibility for speculation in currency). Moskva 1964.

Nauch.-prakt. komm. GK, 1966 - Nauchno-prakticheskii kommentarii k GK RSFSR (Scientific and practical commentary to the RSFSR Civil Code, ed. by E.A.Fleishits). Moskva 1966.

Nauch.-prakt. komm. gr. sudopr., 1962 - Nauchno-prakticheskii kommentarii k Osnovam grazhdanskogo sudoproizvodstva Soiuza SSR i soiuznykh respublik (Scientific and practical commentary to the Fundamentals of civil procedure of the USSR and the Union Republics, ed. by P. I. Bardin). Moskva 1962.

Nauch. -prakt. komm. gr. zak., 1962 - Nauchno-prakticheskii kommentarii k Osnovam grazhdanskogo zakonodatel'stva SSSR i soiuznykh respublik (Scientific and practical commentary to the Fundamentals of civil legislation of the USSR and the Union Republics, ed. by S. N. Bratus and S. A. Fleishits). Moskva 1962.

Neumayer - Neumayer Karl H., Autonomie de la volonté et dispositions impératives en droit international privé des obligations. In: Revue critique de droit international privé, XLVI (1957) pp. 579-604; XLVII (1958) pp. 53-78.

Niboyet, 1928 - Niboyet J. P., Manuel de droit international privé. 2e éd. du Manuel de A. Pillet et J. P. Niboyet d'après la meme méthode. Paris 1928.

Niboyet, 1938-1948 - Niboyet J. P., Traité de droit international privé français. 5 vol. Paris 1938-1948.

Niemeyer - Niemeyer Theodor, Vorschläge und Materialien zur Kodifikation des internationalen Privatrechts. Leipzig 1895.

Novoe - Novoe v grazhdanskom i grazhdansko-protsessual'nom zakonodatel'stve Soiuza SSR i soiuznych respublik (The novelty in civil and civil-procedural legislation of the USSR and the Union Republics). Trudy nauchoi sessii Vsesoiuznogo instituta iuridicheskikh nauk. Moskva 1962.

Nussbaum, 1939 - Nussbaum Arthur, Money in the law. Chicago, Ill. 1939.

Nussbaum, 1940 - Nussbaum Arthur, Public policy and the political crisis of the conflict of laws. In: Yale Law Journal, 1940: 6, pp. 1027-1058.

Nussbaum, 1943 - Nussbaum Arthur, Principles of private international law. New York etc. 1943.

Ocherki - Ocherki mezhdunarodnogo chastnogo prava (Outlines of private international law, ed. by L. A. Lunts). Moskva 1963.

Orlova, 1960 - Orlova N. V., Voprosy braka i razvoda v mezhdunarodnom chastnom prave (Questions of marriage and divorce in private international law). Moskva 1960.

Orlova, 1966 - Orlova N. V., Brak i sem'ia v mezhdunarodnom chastnom prave. (Marriage and family in private international law). Moskva 1966.

Osnovy teorii gos. i pr. - Osnovy teorii gosudarstva i prava (Principles of the theory of State and law, ed. by N. G. Aleksandrov). Moskva 1960.

Paulsen, Sovern - Paulsen Monrad G. and M. J. Sovern, Public policy in the conflict of laws. In: Columbia Law Review, LVI (1956) pp. 968-1116.

Pereterskii, 1924 - Pereterskii I. S., Ocherki mezhdunarodnogo chastnogo prava RSFSR (Outlines of private international law of the RSFSR). Moskva 1924.

Pereterskii, 1946 - Pereterskii I. S., Sistema mazhdunarodnogo chastnogo pravo. (System of private international law.) In: Sovetskoe gosudarstvo i pravo, 1946: 8/9.

Pereterskii, Krylov 1940 - Pereterskii I. S., Krylov S. B., Mezhdunarodnoe chastnoe prave. (Private international law). Moskva 1940.

Pereterskii, Krylov, 1959 - Pereterskii I. S., Krylov S. B., mezhdunarodnoe chastnoe pravo (Private international law). Moskva 1959.

Pereterskii, Krylov, 1962 - Pereterskii I. S., S. B. Krylov -- Lehrbuch des internationalen Privatrechts. Von I. S Pereterski und S. B. Krylow. Uebers. aus dem Russ. Verantw. für die

Fachred. der deutschen Ausg.: Horst Wiemann u.a. (Ost)-Berlin 1962.

Pergament - Pergament A.J., Nehororye kollizionnye voprosy semeinogo prava v SSSR (Some conflict of law questions in Soviet family law). In: Voprosy (1956).

Pergament, 1963 (in: Ocherki) - Pergament A.I., Voprosy razreshenija del o vzyskanii alimentov v mezhdunarodnom chastnom prave (Problems of settling disputes for payment of alimony in private international law). In: Ocherki (1963).

Pillet, 1903 - Pillet Antoine, Principes de droit international privé. Paris etc. 1903.

Pillet, 1923 - Pillet Antoine, Traité pratique de droit international privé, I. Paris 1923.

Pillet, 1929 - Pillet Antoine, De l'ordre public en droit international privé. In: Mélange Antoine Pillet. Paris 1929.

Pisar - Pisar Samuel, Soviet conflict of laws in international commercial transactions. In: Harvard Law Review, LXX (1957).

Problemy - Problemy Mezhdunarodnogo chastnogo prava (Problems of private international law, edited by L.A. Lunts). Moskva 1960.

Prosser - Prosser William L., Handbook of the law of torts. 3rd ed. St. Paul, Minn. 1964.

Raape - Internationales Privatrecht. 5. neubearb. Aufl. Berlin usw. 1961.

Rabel - Rabel Ernst, The conflict of laws. A comparative study, 2nd (1st ed.). 4 vol. I and II vol. (2nd ed.) prepared by Ulrich Drobnig. III vol. (2nd ed.), prepared by

Herbert Bernstein. Ann Arbor, Mich. 1958-1964.

Raevich - Raevich S.I., Mezhdunarodnoe chastnoe pravo (Private international law). Moskva 1934.

Ramzaitsev, 1957 - Ramzaitsev D.F., Vneshnetorgovyi arbitrazh v SSSR, 2e pererab. izd. (Foreign trade arbitration in the USSR). Moskva 1957.

Ramzaitsev, 1964 - Ramzaitsev D.F., The law applied by arbitration tribunals. In: The sources of the law of international trade, ed. by Clive M. Schmitthoff, London 1964, pp. 139-153.

Reczei - Reczei Lásztó, Internationales Privatrecht. Budapest 1960.

Reese - Reese Willis, The ever changing rules of choice of law. In: De conflictu legum; Bundel opstellen aangeboden aan Kollewijn (en) Offerhaus, Leiden 1962. Ned. Tijdschrift voor Internationaal Recht, IX (special issue).

Ripert, Boulanger - Ripert Georges, Boulanger Jean, Traité de droit civil, d'après le traité de Planiol. I. Paris 1956.

Rubanov - Rubanov A.A., Nasledonvanie v mezhdunarodnom chastnom prave (Succession in private international law). Moskva 1966.

Ruden - Ruden Bernard, Soviet housing and the new Civil Code. In: The International and Comparative Law Quarterly, XV (1966), 1, pp. 231-262.

Savigny, von 1849 - Savigny Friedrich Carl von, System des heutigen römischen Rechts. VIII. Berlin 1849.

Savigny, von 1869 - Savigny Friedrich Carl von, A treatise on the conflict of laws and the limits of their operation in respect of place and time. Transl. with notes by William Guthrie. Edinburgh 1869.

Schmitthoff - Schmitthoff Clive M., The law of international trade, its growth, formulation and operation. In: The sources of the law of international trade, London 1964.

Serebrovskii - Serebrovskii V.I., Ocherki Sovetskogo nasledstvennogo prava (Outlines of Soviet inheritance law). Moskva 1953.

Setser - Setser V.G., The immunity of the State and government economic activities. In: Law and Contemporary Problems, 1959, no. 2, pp. 291-316.

Shmigel'skii Iasinovskii - Shmigel'skii G.L., Iasinovskii V.A., Osnovy sovetskogo Morskogo prava (Principles of Soviet Maritime law). Moskva 1959.

Smirnov - Smirnov A.N., Mezhdunarodnye valiutnye i kreditnye otnosheniia SSSR (International exchange and credit relations of the USSR). Moskva 1960.

Stalev - Stalev Zhivko, Angelov A., Niakoi vaprosi na teoriiata na mezhdunzrodnoto chastno pravo (Some questions on the theory of private international law). Sofiia 1959.

Stoupnitzky - Stoupnitzky A., Etude sur le droit international privé soviétique. In: Revue de droit international privé, XXII (1927).

Struycken - Struycken A.V.M., Comments on the Case "Van Nievelt, Coudrian et Co's Stoomvaartmij N.V. c. N.V. Hollandsche Assurantie Sociëteit et autres". In: Revue critique de droit international privé, 1967, pp. 522-530.

Sverdlov - Sverdlov G., Family law. In: Fundamentals of Soviet law, ed. by P.S. Romashkin, translated from the Russian by Iuri Sdobnikov, Moscow (c. 1960).

Szászy, Budapest, 1964 - Szászy István, Private international law in the European People's Democracies. Budapest 1964.

Szászy, The Hague, 1964 - Szászy István, Private international law in socialist countries. In: Recueil des - Cours, The Hague, 1964, I.

Szirmai - Szirmai Z., The law of inheritance in the Soviet Union. In: The law of inheritance in Eastern Europe and in the People's Republic of China, Leyden 1961. Law in Eastern Europe, no. 5.

Tumanov - Tumanov V.A., O nekotorykh teoriiakh v sovremennoi burzhuaznoi doktrine mezhdunarodnogo chastnogo prava (On some theories in the contemporary bourgeois doctrine of private international law). In: Voprosy (1956).

Valery - Valery Jules, Examen critique de Remarques sur l'ordre public de M. Pierre Lucas. In: Revue de droit international et de législation comparé, 1934: 2, pp. 194-218.

Verdam - Verdam P.J., Volksdemocratische denkbeelden en het internationaal privaatrecht. In: Netherlands International Law Review, XIV (1967), 3, pp. 229-244.

Vilkov - Vilkov G.E., Mezhdunarodnoe chastnoe pravo v izbrannykh dokumentakh (Private international law in selected documents, compiled by G.E. Vilkov). Moskva 1961.

Vitta - Vitta Eduardo, L'ordre public en matière de divorce et de nulleté de mariage dans la jurisprudence italienne. In: Revue critique de droit international privé, LIV (1965), 2, pp. 267-278.

Vondracek - Vondracek Th. J., Wijziging in het Sowjet echtscheidingsrecht. In: Themis, 1967: 2, pp. 237-248.

Voprosy - Voprosy mezhdunarodnogo chastnogo prava (Problems of private international law, edited by L. A. Lunts). Moskva 1956.

Weiss - Weiss André, Manuel de droit international privé. Paris 1925.

Wengler - Wengler Wilhelm, Les conflits de lois et le principe d'égalité. In: Revue critique de droit international privé, LII (1963), pp. 203-231, 504-527.

Winter de, 1940 - Winter L. I. de, De grenzen van de contractsvrijheid in het internationaal privaatrecht. In: Weekblad voor Privaatrecht, Notarisambt en Registratie, LXXI (1940). (Publ. under the name L. I. Barmat).

Winter de, 1947 - Winter L. I. de, De sociale functies der rechtsnormen als grondslag voor de oplossing van internationaal privaatrechtelijke wetsconflicten. In: Rechtsmagazijn Themis, 1947, pp. 101-165. (Publ. under the name L. I. Barmat de Winter.

Winter de, 1952 - Winter L. I. de, Het nieuwe internationaal privaatrecht. In: Weekblad voor Privaatrecht, Notarisambt en registratie, LXXXIII (1952), no. 4238-4239.

Winter de, 1964 - Winter L. I. de, Dwingend recht bij internationale overeenkomsten. In: Netherlands International Law Review, XI(1964), pp. 329-365.

Winter de, 1966 - Winter L. I. de, Het Alnati-arrest. In: Nederlands Juristenblad, 1966, no. 37, pp. 933-941.

Wolff, 1950 - Wolff Martin, Private International Law, 2nd ed. Oxford 1950.

Wolff, 1954 - Wolff Martin, Das internationale Privatrecht Deutschlands. 3. Aufl. Berlin usw., 1954.

Zvekov - Zvekov V.P., Obiazatel'stva iz prichineniia vreda v mezhdunarodnom chastnom prave (Obligations resulting from damages in private international law). In: Ocherki (1963).

LIST OF LAWS AND LEGAL DIGESTS

Das Allgemeine BürgerlicheGesetzbuch. [Österreich] 9. Aufl. Hrsg. von Hans Kapfer. Wien 1966.

Burgelijk Wetboek. [Nederland.] Verzameld en bewerkt door G. J. L. Seesing onder toezicht van J. M. Polak, 17e dr. Zwolle, 1963.

Bürgerliches Gesetzbuch und zugehörige Gesetze. [Deutschland.] München usw. 1964.

Civil Code of Louisiana. Revision of 1870, with amendments to 1947. Edited by Joseph Dainow. Louisiana State Law Institute, 1947.

The Civil Code of the R. S. F. S. R., 1922. Translated (from the Russian) by Vl. Gsovski. In: Gsovski, II (1949).

The Civil Code and the Code of Civil Procedure of the R. S. F. S. R., 1964. Translated by A. K. R. Kiralfy. Leiden 1966. Law in Eastern Europe no. 11.

Code Civil. Petits Codes Dalloz. Paris 1966-67.

Le Code Civil de la République de Russie (1964). Trad. (du russe) par René Dekkers. Centre national pour l' étude des états de l' est, en coll. avec le Centre d'étude des pays de l' est. (Inst. de sociologie). Bruxelles 1964.

Code Civil Hellénique. Trad. de l'Institut Hellénique de droit international et étranger. Athènes 1956.

Code Civil Suisse et Code Fédéral des Obligations. Lausanne 1957.

Code of Civil Procedure of the R. S. F. S. R., 1923. Translated (from the Russian) by Vl. Gsovski. In: Gsovski, II (1949).

Code of laws on marriage, family and guardianship of the R. S. F. S. R., 1962. Translated (from the Russian) by Vl. Gsovski. In: Gsovski, II (1949).

Les Codes et les lois spéciales les plus usuelles en vigueur en Belgique. Par Jean Servais et E. Mechelynck. 31 éd. par Jean Blondiaux et Jean Masquelin. I. Matières civiles et commerciales. Bruxelles 1965.

Codice Civile (della Republica Italiana). In: I cinque codici, a cura di Rosario Nicolo, Giovanni Leone; Nuova ed. aggiornata, Milano 1964.

Constitution (Fundamental law) of the Union of Soviet Socialist Republics. (Official translation). Moscow 1956.

Decree of C. E. C. and C. P. C. of March 1931. On the procedure for admission of foreign firms to carry out commercial transactions in the territory of the U. S S. R. In: Sobraniė Zakonov SSSR, 1931, no. 24. Moskva 1932.

Dekrety Sovietskoi Vlasti (Decrees of the Soviet Government). III. Moscow 1964.

Fundamentals of civil legislation of the U. S. S. R. and the Union Republics; Approved by the Supreme Soviet of the U. S. S. R., December 8, 1961. (Translated from the Russian by Yuri Sdobnikov). In: Soviet civil legislation and procedure; Official text and commentaries. Moscow 1963.

General Conditions of delivery of goods between foreign trade organisations of member-countries of the Council for mutual economic aid. (Translated from the Russian) by Harold J. Berman. In: The International and Comparative Law Quarterly. Vol. 7 (1958).

Gornoe Polozhenie Soiuza SSR, 9-IX-1927 (The Mining Statute of the USSR, 9-IX-1927). In: Sobranie zakovov i rasporiazhenii, 1927. Moskva 1928.

Grazhdanskii Kodeks R. S. F. S. R.; Grazhdanskii Protsessual' nyi Kodeks RSFSR (Civil Code of the RSFSR; Code of Civil Procedure of the RSFSR. Published by: Iurid. Kommissiia Soveta Ministrov RSFSR). Moskva 1965.

Internationales Ehe- und Kindschaftsrecht. Begründet von Alexander Bergmann. Frankfurt am Main 1967.

Juris classeur. Droit comparé. Paris 1967.

Kodeks Zakoniv pro simiu, opiku, shliub i akti gromadianskogo stanu. Ukraiins' koi RSR (Code of laws on family, guardianship, marriage and civil status acts of the Ukrainian SSR). Kyiiv 1958.

Kodeks Zakonov o brake, sem'e i opeke Belorusskoi SSR (Code of laws on marriage, family and guardianship of the Belorussian SSR). Minsk 1958.

Kodeks Zakonov o brake, sem'e i opeke (RSFSR Code of laws on marriage, family and guardianship). Moskva 1934.

Kodeks zakonov o brake, sem'e i opeke RSFSR (RSFSR Code of laws on marriage, family and guardianship) Moskva 1949.

Kodeks Zakonov of brake, sem'e i opeke RSFSR (Code of laws on marriage, family and guardianship of the RSFSR). Moskva 1961.

Kodeks Zakonov ob aktakh grazhdanskogo sostoianiia, brachnom, semeinom, opekunskom prave, 1918 (Code of laws on civil status acts, marriage, family and guardianship, 1918). In: Dekrety Sovetskoi Vlasti, III, Moskva 1964.

Konstitutsiia (Osnovnoi zakon) Soiuza Sovetskikh Sotsialisticheskikh Respublik (Constitution - fundamental law - of the USSR). Moskva 1965.

Law on the criminal responsibility for crimes against the State, of December 1958. Translated from the Russian by F.J.M. Feldbrugge. Leiden 1959. In: Law of Eastern Europe, no. 3.

Loi uniforme relative au droit international privé. In: Tractatenblad van het Koninkrijk der Nederlanden, 1951., no. 125.

Martindale-Hubbel Law Directory. 99th Annual édition 1967. (Louisiana Law Digest). Summit, New Jersey 1967.

The Merchant Shipping Code of the USSR (1929). Transl. and notes by Z.Szirmai and J.D.Korevaar. Leiden 1960. Law in Eastern Europe, no. 4.

Mezhdunarodnoe Chastnoe Pravo v izbrannykh dokumentakh (Private international law in selected documents). Compiler: G.E.Vilkov. Moskva 1961.

Nederlandse Wetboeken. Uitgegeven door J.A.Fruin, bewerkt door N.J.Bink. 's-Gravenhage 1952.

Osnovy grazhdanskogo sudoproizvodstvo Soiuza SSR i Soiuznykh respublik (Fundamentals of civil procedure of the USSR and the Union Republics). In: Sovetskoe Gosudarstvo i Pravo, 1962: 1.

Osnovy grazhdanskogo zakonodatel'stva Soiuza SSR i Soiuznych respublik (Fundamentals of civil legislation of the USSR and the Union Republics). In: Sovetskoe Gosudarstvo i Pravo, 1962: 1.

Osnovy zaronodatel' stva Soiuza SSR i Soiuznych respublik o brake i sem'e (Principles of legislation of the USSR and the Union Republics concerning marriage and family). In: Izvestiia, 28-6-1968.

The Principles of Civil Legislation and Principles of Civil Procedure of the USSR and the Union Republics and the decree putting these into effect. Transl. by A.R.Kiralfy. Ed. by Z.Szirmai. In: Law in Eastern Europe, no. 7, Leiden 1963, pp. 263-320.

Principles of legislation of the USSR and the Union Republics concerning marriage and family. A draft. Transl. from the Russian by Z. Szirmai. In: Themis, 1968: 3 et seq.

Recueil des lois usuelles suisses, publ. pàr W. A. Liebeskind, J. Thorens, A. Widmer. Genève c. 1961.

Sbornik postanovlenii Plenuma Verkhovnogo Suda SSSR, 1924-1963 (Collections of resolutions of the Plenum of the Supreme Court of the USSR, 1924-1963). Moskva 1964.

Sbornik reshenii Morskoi Arbitrazhnoi Komissii pri Vsesoiuznoi Torgovoi Palate za 1936g., vyp. III (Collection of decisions of the Maritime Arbitration Commission at the All-Union Chamber of Commerce for 1936, III, comp. and ed. by P. P. Vinogradov and S. T. Denin, publ. by All-Union Chamber of Commerce). Moskva i t.d. 1937.

South African Prohibition of Mixed Marriages Act of 1949. In: International Law Quarterly, III (1950).

Soviet Civil Legislation and Procedure. Official texts and commentaries. Transl. from the Russian by Yuri Sdobnikov. Moskva 1963.

Soviet criminal law and procedure. The RSFSR Codes. Introd. and analysis: Harold J. Berman. Transl. by Harold J. Berman and James W. Spindler. Cambridge, Mass. 1966.

Ugolovnyi Kodeks RSFSR. Ofitsial'nyi tekst s izmeneniiami na 1 dek. 1963g. (Criminal Code of RSFSR; Official text with changes, status juris, Dec. 1, 1963). Published by: Iuridicheskaia Komissiia Soveta Ministrov RSFSR, Moskva 1964.

Ukaz Prezidiuma Verkhovnogo Soveta SSSR "O nekotorom izmeninii poriadka rassmotreniia v sudakh del o rastorzhenii braka" (Decree of the Presidium of the Supreme Soviet of the SSSR on some changes in the procedure of dealing in court with cases of dissolution of marriage, December 10, 1965). In: Vedomosti Verkhovnogo Soveta Soiuza SSR, no. 49, text 725.

Ukaz Prezidiuma Verkhovnogo Soveta SSSR "Ob ugolovnoj otvetstvennosti inostrantsev i lits bez grazhdanstva za zlostnoe narushenie pravil predvizhenija na territorii SSSR" (Decree of the Presidium of the Supreme Soviet of the USSR on the criminal responsibility for a persistent infringement of the rules relating to travel in the territory of the USSR). In: Vedomosti Verkhovnogo Soveta SSSR, 1966, no. 30, p. 581.

United States Code, 1964 edition, vol. X. Washington 1965.

The U.S.S.R. Law on the criminal responsibility for crimes against the State. Transl. (from the Russ.) by F.J. Feldbrugge. In: Law in Eastern Europe, no. 3, 1959.

Vozdushnyi kodeks soiuza SSR (Air Navigation code of the USSR, of 23rd December 1961, in force since 1-I-1962). In: Vedomosti Verkhovnogo Soveta 1961, no. 52.

Wet van 13 october 1950 (Staatsblad no. K 452), houdende regelen nopens de huurprijzen van onroerend goed en de bescherming van de huurders (huurwet). In: Burgerlijk Wetboek, Zwolle 1963.

LIST OF CASES

Alekseev v. Alekseeva N. Biulleten' Verkhovnogo Suda RSFSR, 1967: 8, pp. 4-5.

Amalia P.v.Raisa Sh. Lunts, III (1966), pp. 104-105.

Antipina V.D.v.Emel'ianov S.A. Biulleten' Verkhovnogo Suda SSSR, 1961: 1, pp. 7-9.

Banco National de Cuba v. Sabbatino. American Journal of International Law, vol. 58 (1964), pp. 796 et seq.

Belgian husband's authority, Re. Boguslavskii, Rubanov, 1959, p. 37.

Breach of charter of the steamship "Phoenix", Re. Collection of Decisions of the Maritime Arbitration Commission for 1936, III. Moscow etc. 1937.

C.v.L. Orlova, 1966, p. 217.

Contractual discharge of payment of alimony. Sovetskaia Iustitsiia, 1962: 7, p. 30.

The de facto marriage of Zaustinskaia E.M. and Durov G.G., Re. Biulleten' Verkhovnogo Suda SSSR, 1961: 3, pp. 24-26.

Fedotkin's pension claims, Re. Sovetskaia Sustitsiia, 1961: 16, p. 31.

Frolov N.F.v.Frovola N.F. Biulleten' Verkhovnogo Suda SSSR, 1967: 2, pp. 36-37.

Graf Iren case. Korobov, Sokolov, pp. 365-366.

Jordan Investment Ltd. v. Soviet All-Union Foreign Trade Corporation "Soiuzneftexport". Transl. from the Russian by Martin Domke. American Journal of International Law, 1959, pp. 800-806.

Korotkova and others v. A.A.Tatarkina. Sovetskaia Iustitsiia, 1961: 12, p. 28.

Kozhinov's kolkhoz household, Re. Sovetskaia Iustitsiia, 1964: 18, p. 30.

Krasii Ia. v. Krasii V.Averin, p. 179.

Lebed' A.I.case. Cheburakhin, p. 111.

Lizardi v. Chaize and others. Dalloz: Jurisprudence général, Paris 1861, I, pp. 193-195.

Luther A.M.v.Sagor & Co., 1921, 1921, K.B.3, 532.

Marvyn Matthews Case. Daily Telegraph, June 22, 1964, p. 1.

Postanovlenie Plenuma Verkhovnogo Suda SSSR ot 16 sent. 1949g., no. 12/8/u, s izmeneniiami, vnesennymi postanovleniem Plenuma ot 5 sent. 1952g. (Ruling of the plenum of the Supreme Court of the USSR of September 16, 1949, no. 12/8/u with the changes introduced by the Ruling of the Plenum of the 5th of September 1952). Sbornik postanovlenii Plenuma Verkhovnogo Suda SSSR, 1924-1963, Moskva 1964, pp. 43 et seq.

Postanovlenie no. 13 Plenuma Verkhovnogo Suda SSSR, 29 dekabria 1965 (Ruling no. 13 of the Plenum of the Supreme court of the USSR, Dec. 29th, 1965). Biulleten' Verkhovnogo Suda SSSR, 1966: 1, p. 16.

Postanovlenie no. 6 Plenuma Verkhovnogo Suda SSSR, 1 iulia 1966. (Ruling no. 6 of the Plenum of the Supreme Court of the USSR, July 1, 1966). Biulleten' Verkhovnogo Suda SSSR, 1966: 4, pp. 20-23.

Radi Edgar case. Cheburakhin, p. 111.

Rakitianskii and others, Re. Biulleten' Verkhovnogo Suda SSSR, 1966: 1, pp. 33-37.

Rudnev v. Krasnogorsk Construction Works. Sovetskaia Iustitsiia, 1961: 4, p. 28. Transl. in Engl.: John Hazard and Isaac Shapiro, The Soviet Legal System, New York 1962, part III, pp. 94-95.

Ruling of the Presidium of the RSFSR Supreme Court of August 13/14, 1934. Transl.: Gsovski, I (1948), pp. 288-289.

Shenker v. Raznoimport. Lunts, 1949, pp. 236-237.

Slavikova v. Zhukovskii- Iatsenko. Averin, pp. 160-161.

Soviet - Belgian divorce case. Orlova, 1960, pp. 161-162.

Soviet - Canadian divorce case. Orlova, 1960, pp. 161-162.

Soviet citizen's marriage in China. Lunts, III (1966), pp. 104-105.

Soviet - Hungarian divorce case. Cheburakhin, p. 110.

Tatarkina's Kolkhoz household, Re. Sovetskaia Iustitsiia, 1961: 12, p. 28.

Tatiana F. case. Gorodetskaia, Voprosy opeki, pp. 148-149.

Tsezarin case. Mikhailov, pp. 31-32.

U.S.A. v. Pink, Superintendant of Insurance, Febr. 2, 1942. American Journal of International Law, XXXVI (1946), pp. 309 et seq.

Weber v. Promsyrioimport. Nederlandsche Jurisprudentie 1942, no. 757.

Zakharii Zhdanov case. Fomin, pp. 200 et seq.

Zimovets autocar, Re. Biulleten' Verkhovnogo Suda RSFSR, 1967: 5, p. 13.

GPSR Compliance

The European Union's (EU) General Product Safety Regulation (GPSR) is a set of rules that requires consumer products to be safe and our obligations to ensure this.

If you have any concerns about our products, you can contact us on ProductSafety@springernature.com

In case Publisher is established outside the EU, the EU authorized representative is:

Springer Nature Customer Service Center GmbH
Europaplatz 3
69115 Heidelberg, Germany

Batch number: 10824476

Printed by Printforce, the Netherlands